Prisoners of Freedom

CALIFORNIA SERIES IN PUBLIC ANTHROPOLOGY

The California Series in Public Anthropology emphasizes the anthropologist's role as an engaged intellectual. It continues anthropology's commitment to being an ethnographic witness, to describing, in human terms, how life is lived beyond the borders of many readers' experiences. But it also adds a commitment, through ethnography, to reframing the terms of public debate — transforming received, accepted understandings of social issues with new insights, new framings.

Series Editor: Robert Borofsky (Hawaii Pacific University)

Contributing Editors: Philippe Bourgois (UC San Francisco),
Paul Farmer (Partners in Health), Rayna Rapp (New York University),
and Nancy Scheper-Hughes (UC Berkeley)

University of California Press Editor: Naomi Schneider

1. *Twice Dead: Organ Transplants and the Reinvention of Death,*
   by Margaret Lock
2. *Birthing the Nation: Strategies of Palestinian Women in Israel,* by Rhoda Ann
   Kanaaneh (with a foreword by Hanan Ashrawi)
3. *Annihilating Difference: The Anthropology of Genocide,* edited by Alexander
   Laban Hinton (with a foreword by Kenneth Roth)
4. *Pathologies of Power: Health, Human Rights, and the New War on the Poor,*
   by Paul Farmer (with a foreword by Amartya Sen)
5. *Buddha Is Hiding: Refugees, Citizenship, the New America,* by Aihwa Ong
6. *Chechnya: Life in a War-Torn Society,* by Valery Tishkov (with a foreword
   by Mikhail S. Gorbachev)
7. *Total Confinement: Madness and Reason in the Maximum Security Prison,*
   by Lorna A. Rhodes
8. *Paradise in Ashes: A Guatemalan Journey of Courage, Terror, and Hope,*
   by Beatriz Manz (with a foreword by Aryeh Neier)
9. *Laughter Out of Place: Race, Class, Violence, and Sexuality in a Rio
   Shantytown,* by Donna M. Goldstein
10. *Shadows of War: Violence, Power, and International Profiteering in the
    Twenty-First Century,* by Carolyn Nordstrom
11. *Why Did They Kill? Cambodia in the Shadow of Genocide,* by Alexander
    Laban Hinton (with a foreword by Robert Jay Lifton)
12. *Yanomani: The Fierce Controversy and What We Can Learn from It,*
    by Robert Borofsky
13. *Why America's Top Pundits Are Wrong: Anthropologists Talk Back,*
    edited by Catherine Besteman and Hugh Gusterson
14. *Prisoners of Freedom: Human Rights and the African Poor,* by Harri Englund

Prisoners of Freedom

Human Rights and the African Poor

Harri Englund

UNIVERSITY OF CALIFORNIA PRESS
Berkeley / Los Angeles / London

University of California Press, one of the most distinguished university presses in the United States, enriches lives around the world by advancing scholarship in the humanities, social sciences, and natural sciences. Its activities are supported by the UC Press Foundation and by philanthropic contributions from individuals and institutions. For more information, visit www.ucpress.edu.

University of California Press
Berkeley and Los Angeles, California

University of California Press, Ltd.
London, England

Library of Congress Cataloging-in-Publication Data

Englund, Harri.
    Prisoners of freedom : human rights and the African poor / Harri Englund.
        p.   cm. — (California series in public anthropology : 14)
    Includes bibliographical references and index.
        ISBN-13 978-0-520-24924-0 (pbk. : alk. paper), ISBN-10 0-520-24924-0 (pbk. : alk. paper)
        1. Human rights — Malawi.   2. Poverty — Malawi.   3. Ethnology — Malawi.   4. Democracy — Malawi.   I. Title. II. Series.
JC599.M3E54   2006
323.096897 — dc22   2005032837

Manufactured in the United States of America

15   14   13   12   11   10   09   08   07
10   9   8   7   6   5   4   3   2

This book is printed on New Leaf EcoBook 50, a 100% recycled fiber of which 50% is de-inked post-consumer waste, processed chlorine-free. EcoBook 50 is acid-free and meets the minimum requirements of ANSI/ASTM D5634–01 (*Permanence of Paper*).

For Guðrún

Contents

Acknowledgments

Polemba bukuli ndidafuna kuwunikira mbiri ya ufulu wa demokalase ku Malawi kuti timvetsetse bwino zotsatira za zimene zidachitika kumeneko m'zaka za 1993 ndi 1994. Ambirife tikudziwa kuti malamulo oyendetsa dziko adasintha pa nthawi imeneyi, koma zikuoneka ngati anthu wamba achiMalawi akuvutikabe ngakhale zinthu zidasintha motero. Choncho ndidaganiza kuti ndifufuze tanthauzo la ufulu limakhala pati pamene anthu ambiri alibe chakudya chokwanira, ntchito imawasowa ndipo maphunziro a ana awo adalowa pansi. Cholinga changa sichinali kudandaulanso za zimene atsogoleri a ndale adapanga poyambira 1994 mpakana 2004. Mabuku owunikira zimenezo adasindikizidwa kale. Ndidafuna kukwanitsa cholinga china: kufufuza mbali imene adatenga mabungwe oyang'anira ufulu wachibadwidwe ku Malawi. Apa ndidafuna kuzindikira ngati ntchito imene mabungwewa amagwira ndi yothandiza ndithu pa nkhani ya ufulu wa anthu wamba. Ngakhale mabungwe amene si aboma amasiyana, ndidaona kuti ambiri adatanganidwa ndi maufulu amene analibe tanthauzo lenileni kwa anthu wamba. Kodi chifukwa chiyani maufulu amenewa adachititsa chidwi kwa mabungwewa? Yankho lili m'bukuli, koma ndinene mwachidule kuti anyamata ambiri omwe adalowa mabungwe oyang'anira ufulu wachibadwidwe adanyadira poganiza kuti iwo okha adazindikira tanthauzo la demokalase. Choncho adaiwala kuti nawonso anthu wamba ali ndi nzeru zawo. Polemba bukuli ndidafuna kukumbutsa awerengi anga kuti ngati tikufuna kudziwa m'mene zinthu ziliri kwa anthu omwe amavutika ndi umphawi tiyenera kukhala nawo nthawi yaitali kuti atiphunzitse. Tiyenera kulankhula zilankhulo zawo, kufufuza chikhalidwe chawo ngakhale kuzindikira bwinobwino mavuto

ix

omwe ali nawo. Izi zidaiwalika pamene anyamata oyendetsa mabungwe adatanganidwa ndi maufulu awo. Chifukwa chake anthu wamba sadapeze mpata wokhazikitsa mfundo zawo pa nkhani ya demokalase.

Akuluakulu a kale sadalakwe ponena kuti mlendo ndi amene ayenda ndi kalumo kakuthwa. Ngakhale ndinali mlendo wofunsa mafunso osayenera, mabungwe adandilandira ndi manja awiri. Ndithokozenso abale anga onse kwa Chinsapo kudera la Lilongwe ngakhale kumidzi ku Dedza omwe amandithandiza kuzindikira chochitika cha m'dziko. Si-ndidzaiwala zimene amandiphunzitsa.

In addition to the above appreciation of the organizations, villagers, and township dwellers I worked with during my research for this book, I would like to single out two scholars for their inspiration to my project. Fidelis Edge Kanyongolo and Pascal Kishindo, scholars of law and language, respectively, have addressed in their own remarkable work similar quandaries that exercise me here, leaving me hopeful that my work contributes to a momentum in the study of Malawian experiences with democracy and human rights. They are in no way responsible for what I argue here.

Centre for Language Studies at the University of Malawi provided a much-appreciated institutional affiliation during my research. Gregory Kamwendo and Al Mtenje were indefatigable in their efforts to facilitate my work. I am grateful to the Academy of Finland for funding this project and to the Nordic Africa Institute for sustaining my engagement with Malawi for several years before it began.

I thank all who listened to, and commented on, my presentations of this material in Cambridge, Copenhagen, Dakar, Edinburgh, Helsinki, Lilongwe, Oslo, and Port Elizabeth. Robert Borofsky's enthusiasm proved to be a decisive influence during the final stages of writing. Francis Nyamnjoh set an example with his intellectual rigor and commitment. His capacity to see light at the end of the tunnel even when circumstances suggested otherwise was invaluable, as was Michael Neocosmos's. In retrospect, it is difficult to identify an aspect of my argument that met with Richard Werbner's approval, but it does seem clear that his criticisms both strengthened my resolve and improved the final product. James Ferguson and Anthony Simpson offered very instructive readings of my writings. Gudrun Haraldsdottir led the way in turning my unproductive outrage into critical analysis. I hardly dare to contemplate the subtleties and sharp insights that this book would have contained had she penned it. As it stands, and for better or for worse, the book bears the imprint of an agitated mind.

Abbreviations

CARER	Centre for Advice, Research, and Education on Rights
CHRR	Centre for Human Rights and Rehabilitation
CILIC	Civil Liberties Committee
FINCA	Foundation for International Community Assistance
FODEP	Foundation for Democratic Process
HRCC	Human Rights Consultative Committee
HRRC	Human Rights Resource Centre
MASAF	Malawi Social Action Fund
MBC	Malawi Broadcasting Corporation
MCP	Malawi Congress Party
MCTU	Malawi Congress of Trade Unions
NICE	National Initiative for Civic Education
PAC	Public Affairs Committee
PCE	para–civic educator
TVM	Television Malawi
UDF	United Democratic Front
UNDP	United Nations Development Programme

Introduction

Politicians' fervor either to denounce or to claim freedom can have surprisingly similar consequences for public debate. In the People's Republic of China, denunciation has led to attempts to eliminate the concept itself. In 2005, the regime made it impossible for its citizens to use the words "freedom," "democracy," or "human rights" in weblogs or diaries posted on the Internet.[1] A new software package, developed by an enterprise in which Microsoft was reported to hold a 50 percent stake, produced automatic denials of these contentious concepts.

Regimes sometimes choose to exercise control over hearts and minds through earnest approval rather than oppressive denial. Political leaders in the United States have always professed passion for freedom, but few have embraced the concept more fully than George W. Bush. Because of the regime's claim on the word "freedom," it has been eliminated to an extent from the vocabulary of the administration's critics. In 2005, while the Chinese government was enlisting its corporate partner to police the Internet, President Bush opened one of his weekly radio addresses to the nation with these words: "Good morning. Today I can report to you that we are making good progress in advancing the cause of freedom, defeating the forces of terror, and transforming our military so we can meet the emerging threats of the twenty-first century. As I speak, Laura is in the

Middle East to help advance the freedom agenda; and her message is a powerful one — that by working together for liberty, we will create a future of peace and opportunity for women and men worldwide."[2]

Here was another kind of political response to the idea of freedom, one that not only claimed to spread the "freedom agenda" worldwide but also *owned* it. Dissent was hardly more welcome than in the Chinese case. By defining what freedom was, the U.S. regime could suggest that dissent served "the forces of terror," also known as the enemy. Moreover, by tying its idea of freedom to the notion of "emerging threats," the regime could also showcase its military as the backbone of freedom.

Attempts to define freedom have exercised scholars and politicians for a very long time, but regimes, despite major differences among their political institutions, have rarely acknowledged the recurrent insight from political philosophy that freedom is an essentially contested concept.[3] Philosophical debates aside, the exportation of "freedom" across historical periods and geopolitical areas has given the term new meanings, which are often ill understood by those who have a specific agenda to pursue. In many parts of Africa, for example, the idea of political freedom has gathered increasingly variable significance in the course of a history extending from the late-colonial past to the postcolonial present. *Uhuru*, the Kiswahili term for "freedom," has been used across much of Africa in discussions of national liberation. When Kwame Nkrumah wrote *I Speak of Freedom* (1961), the issue he addressed was the freedom of the African people from colonial rule. In a similar vein, Julius Nyerere's books, *Freedom and Unity* (1966) and *Freedom and Socialism* (1968), were attempts to envisage what national independence and international solidarity might mean in Africa. It was only after decades of independence that an ostensibly new generation of African leaders began to countenance the notion that individual freedoms might also be included within the scope of *uhuru*.

This history is thick with tragic ironies — so tragic and so ironic, in fact, that a poet is needed to elucidate them. Writing soon after the triumph of national liberation in many parts of Africa, the Ugandan poet Okot p'Bitek (1931–82) demonstrated the difference that a *perspective* made amid official euphoria. In several poems, he devised the character of a politician to ask some insolent questions after the unjust division of wealth in the postcolony had become all too apparent:

What did you reap
When Uhuru ripened
And was harvested?

Is it my fault
That you sleep
In a hut
With a leaking thatch?
Do you blame me
Because your sickly children
Sleep on the earth
Sharing the filthy floor
With sheep and goats?

(p'Bitek [1967] 1984, 139–141)

The politician's arrogance found its sharpest contrast in a later p'Bitek poem. A prisoner, made listless by the unfolding tragedy of a postcolonial tyranny, languished in its dungeons:

Crippled by the cancer
Of Uhuru
Far worse than
The yaws of
Colonialism,
The walls of hopelessness
Surround me completely

(p'Bitek 1971, 50)

What was from one perspective a harvest that had ripened to yield infinite riches was from another perspective a crippling cancer, a source of despair over the direction history had taken. Not only did freedom mean different things to different people; also its variable meanings could not attract public discussion as long as those in power were able to define it as emancipation from the yoke of colonialism. The prisoner made an attempt to reach beyond the walls of hopelessness:

Wake up
You pressmen of the world
I want to speak to you,
For the candle
Of Uhuru
Has been blown out

(p'Bitek 1971, 90)

The "pressmen of the world" would not wake up to hear the prisoner's plea until some two decades after p'Bitek had written the poem. Only then were the silences of the Cold War era broken to make popular protests in Africa more audible. The extent to which the nationalist rhetoric of liberation was replaced by new notions of freedom varied from country to country, but maintaining state monopolies on the definition of freedom was an increasingly arduous task at the dawn of the twenty-first century. More contentious definitions appeared feasible, if only because national subjects came to be seen as citizens whose individual rights could no longer be sacrificed to some degenerate version of nation building.

New freedoms entail new prisoners. In pursuing this improbable, if not heretic, observation, this book moves from the dungeons of post-colonial tyrannies to the offices of non-governmental organizations and the villages and townships of ostensibly free citizens. The new prisoners are no longer confined within the walls of hopelessness, and their rhetoric of freedom is enthusiastically parroted by politicians and expatriate experts alike. Dissent, officially more welcome than ever before, must take a prescribed form before it is recognized. It is not the idea of freedom that is at fault. Renewed critical reflection is required when "freedom" once again threatens to obscure differences in perspective, differences that are so well captured by p'Bitek's poetry. What appears as freedom from one perspective can be mere trivia from another, but a crucial issue is whether those who occupy the public sphere are prisoners of their particular perspectives. The obligation to rethink the promise of freedom is constant and riddled with moral, political, and intellectual quandaries.

Expectations of Democracy

Efforts to rethink freedom are challenged by the way the evocation of the concept can disarm critics. When I have described my findings on the state of democracy in Malawi, I have sometimes been rebuked for not being charitable enough toward Malawians' efforts to institute various freedoms. While few would claim that the transition to liberal democracy has been accomplished in full, many would argue that enough has changed to warrant considerable satisfaction, especially when compared with the autocratic era of Kamuzu Banda, president from independence in 1964 until 1994. During the first decade of liberal democracy, the period explored in this book, death penalties were not effected, the harassment of journalists was rare, and multipartyism thrived. Things could have been worse, and they certainly were during the first three decades of independence.

A wave of democratization was said to have swept Malawi and other countries emerging from autocracy since the 1980s (Huntington 1991), bringing in its wake a process that could surely be reversed but whose consolidation seemed to concern citizens and foreign observers alike (Diamond et al. 1997). President Bakili Muluzi, who led Malawi from 1994 until 2004, often expressed the issue in these terms: "When I am speaking here, people in the United States have been under democracy for over two hundred years. We just started to build democracy, to build the house of democracy."[4] The evidence in this book suggests a parallel between the nationalist project in Africa, often seen as the "first wave of liberation," and the transitions to democracy underway since the late 1980s. Just as the expectations of progress in independent Africa disarmed citizens and observers who might have objected to abuses by nationalist leaders, so too do the expectations of democracy encourage a kid-glove approach to the wrongs that remain. One would hope that analyses informed by expectations would be discarded rather more swiftly than during the nationalist project. Instead of building our understanding on expectations for the future, on a telos, the need is to consider *how* and *why* things are as they are.[5]

This book focuses on one of the most obvious features of the new era, the unprecedented public interest in human rights. The liberal expectations that democracy would beget competitive market economies and better services were enhanced by universalist evocations of human rights. As this book shows for Malawi, human rights, which are ostensibly universal, came to be defined in very particular ways. While hardly conspiratorial in a strict sense, foreign donors and creditors steered official rhetoric with their expectations. Countries such as Malawi, with neither notable resources nor strategic significance in the post–Cold War era, found their best chance of attracting development aid and foreign investment by projecting an image of movement toward democratic consolidation (Abrahamsen 2000). In Senegal, one of the pioneers of transition in Africa, the new institutional image virtually replaced the traditional export commodity of groundnuts as an item for foreign exchange (Bayart 2000, 226; see also Englund 2002c). The direction thus confirmed, the regimes that were *not yet there* could count on considerable international charity as long as they were seen to be *on the move*.

As in many other sub-Saharan countries during the 1990s, the great expectations in Malawi were not matched by improvements in the conditions of life among the majority. In Malawi, as is discussed below, the indicators of human development generally plummeted after the so-called democratic transition, while the ruling elite's self-indulgence appeared to continue unabated. The upshot has been uncertainty over whether countries like Malawi are "on the move" to anywhere in particular. Paul Tiyambe Zeleza has observed that "the current struggles and transitions to democracy have been dazzling and messy, their results contradictory and unpredictable" (1997, 11). It seems plausible to assert, with Achille Mbembe, "the hypothesis that the organizations likely to emerge from current developments will be anything but the result of coherent premeditated plans" (2001, 77).[6]

Virtually as soon as the new rhetoric asserted its universalist aspirations, challenges to it abounded. In Malawi, naïve expectations were crushed by a prolonged but ultimately failed attempt to amend the new constitution to serve the interests of the new regime. With painful memories of Banda's life presidency still fresh, Malawians refused to allow President Muluzi to remain in office beyond the maximum of two consecutive terms (see below). Yet such challenges to the "democratic" regime must themselves be analyzed, if only to ascertain whether they actually pose any challenge at all.[7] The conundrum brings forth uncomfortable questions about the extent to which various interests are entertained in a new democracy, and about whether disputes between ruling politicians and human rights activists circumscribe rather than expand the public sphere. According to Richard Werbner (2004, 62), who writes on the basis of his experience in Botswana, a "thriving public sphere" ensures that arguments and disputes actually enhance liberal democracy instead of undermining it. The Malawian experience suggests, by contrast, that the mere allowance of arguments and disputes to take place in public is less crucial to democracy than what those arguments are *about*. A narrow definition of human rights as freedoms captured the attention of politicians, donors, journalists, and activists alike. Much as this definition provoked argument, its limited relevance to understanding the situation of the impoverished majority made democracy the preoccupation of the privileged few.

Many of these disputes were by no means inconsequential, as the argument about Muluzi's unconstitutional third term attests. Yet high-profile disputes give little insight into the ways in which human rights activists and their foreign donors envisage the role of the impoverished majority in the new democracy. For all the evocations of participation and empowerment in the rhetoric of freedom, the rural and urban poor had few opportunities to participate in defining what freedom, human rights, and democracy might mean in a Malawian context. And when they focused on the national elites, activists often shared a common assumption with academic critiques. While critical analyses focusing on elites can be illuminating, exposing those who most conspicuously wield political and economic power (see Bond 2000; Good 2002), they may also end up obscuring other social and political dynamics involved. Such analyses often seem to reinforce the expectation that if the self-serving agendas of national elites could be better controlled, transitions to genuine democracy would ensue. The evidence in this book, by contrast, draws attention to the processes by which human rights activists themselves become particular kinds of subjects, keen to define human rights as freedoms. My intent is not to exculpate national elites but to include a broader cross section of agents and agencies — some national, others foreign — as prisoners of a very specific idea of human rights and freedom.

Elites and Elitism

The exclusive focus on national elites can be challenged on at least three counts. First, especially since the onset of multipartyism, elites must be conceived of in the plural, with the new prospects for competition making earlier reciprocity and mutual interests among elites somewhat obsolete (Bayart 1993). The implications for democratization are, therefore, rather more complex than what a categorical condemnation of national elites allows for. In particular, little will be achieved if analysis is guided by, in Werbner's words, "a bias, notoriously well established among social scientists, against elites, as if they were the curse of liberal democracy" (2004, 61). Pluralism fosters a politics of recognition, bringing to the fore the long-suppressed diversity of many sub-Saharan nations (Berman et al. 2004; Englund and Nyamnjoh 2004). Counterelites emerge to challenge those who pursue particularist interests under the guise of national leadership. Because these processes can yield both liberals and warlords, social democrats as well as conservative patriarchs, the actual consequences for democratization cannot be determined without empirical investigation. Moreover, the same discourse may contain resources for both oppression and contestation (Foucault 1972). Much as the widespread imagery of political leaders as "fathers" and their subjects as "children" can facilitate exploitation and abuse, the same moral ideas may also direct attention to the rights of dependents (Schatzberg 2002). Honor, after all, has long been a key concern in African polities (Iliffe 2005).

Second, the focus on national elites obscures the appeal of entrenched inequalities among the nonelite. This oversight is especially unfortunate when the analytical purview is extended to non-governmental organizations (NGOs). A conspicuous feature of new democracies worldwide, NGOs have attracted considerable donor support as agencies that are believed to provide independent voices. Although the executive directors of some NGOs belong to the educated and affluent elite, much of the organizations' work among so-called beneficiaries, often spoken of as "the grassroots," is conducted by modestly educated and poorly paid officers and volunteers. The evidence in this book shows that these NGO and project personnel maintain the same distinctions toward "ordinary" subjects as the elites. Despite their cherished ability to criticize power, activists, including those claiming to promote the causes of freedom, democracy, and human rights, are quite as much embedded in entrenched inequalities as anyone else and often fail to resist the seductions of status distinctions. Thus, a focus on national elites would miss an important dimension of democratization as it is being introduced to the populace. Taking activists' rhetoric for granted, the focus would fail to notice how their practice of activism actually contributes to maintaining inequalities.

Third, the case of NGOs and various human rights projects not only demonstrates the importance of considering agents other than elites; it also indicates how democratization is embedded in transnational political processes. The focus on national elites is likely to assume specific spatial relations in which power is located in national urban centers (for a critique, see Guyer 1994). Both the masses and NGOs are placed "below" the state, with critics attaching great hopes to a "civil society" that would challenge and resist the elites "from below." Yet the fact is that most NGOs and human rights projects depend on complex transnational links for their material and political survival. As such, they may challenge or, as is more often the case in Malawi, tacitly support the state not "from below" but as agencies with capacities that are equal, if not superior, to those of the state (Lewis 2002; Migdal 2001). A concept of transnational governance is central to the argument of this book, pointing to the need to understand how African activists and their foreign donors together deprive freedom, democracy, and human rights of substantive meaning (Ferguson and Gupta 2002; Jenkins 2001).

The shift of focus from national elites to a broader range of agents and agencies should not be seen as a denial of *elitism* as a central aspect of democratization in countries like Malawi. On the contrary, the salience of elitism as a cultural disposition appears more clearly precisely when the focus is thus expanded. It is a cultural disposition partly shared by both African activists and foreign donors, a habit of thought and practice that conceals entrenched inequalities in a rhetoric of popular participation. While some aspects of that rhetoric may appear new — such as the appreciation of "community" as the locus of democracy and development — the ways in which it is put into practice frequently suggest historical parallels with both the colonial rule and postindependence autocracy. More precisely, elitism maintains the status quo not by promoting self-professed elites but by associating democracy and development with particular indices and institutions, many of which bear little relevance to the impoverished majority. Those who become, often with support from foreign donors, the vanguards of democracy are the progressive ones, the enlightened few leading the way out of darkness. In contrast to some definitions of democracy, the starting point is not the actual concerns and aspirations of the people, their particular situations in life and experiences of abuse, but freedom, democracy, and human rights as universal and abstract values. It is the task of this book to show how this preoccupation with abstraction both fosters elitism and undermines substantive democratization.

Elitism has played a crucial role in making individual freedom seem a natural definition of human rights. As such, activists and volunteers working for human rights organizations and projects have themselves been made into particular kinds of subjects, capable of guiding others to find the path to freedom. In this book, I follow activists and volunteers to the various contexts of their lives and work to show how this making of self-consciously free subjects takes place. Nikolas Rose has stressed the inculcation of "codes of civility, reason and orderliness" in such processes (1999, 69). In one sense, civility as the key marker of a free subject stands in sharp contrast to an earlier era when "colonial subjects were seldom thought even potentially competent to take up the burdens of freedom" (Rose 1999, 107). In another sense, aspects of both late colonialism and postcolonial autocracy live on in the way civility is exclusive, defined against the assumed ignorance of the masses. Concepts of human rights, personal manners, styles of clothing, and the language of everyday life are all implicated in producing these distinctions. The making of individual subjects, in a democracy no less than under colonialism, depends on objectifying others (Vaughan 1991).

At the core of this book's argument is the contention that freedom is a means of governance, a project in which subjects' capacity for action is recognized (Rose 1999). The contention goes beyond those theories that define democracy as the production of leadership for modern bureaucratic societies. Max Weber (1970) and Joseph Schumpeter (1976) are notable proponents of these theories, and as Rita Abrahamsen has recently discussed (2000, 68–71), their views entail a sharp division between the politically active and the politically passive. In Malawi after the democratic transition, this division was made in the very rhetoric of participation. Appeals to "community participation" urged the poor to supply their labor for various development projects at the local level (see chapter 4). Both politicians and non-governmental watchdogs emphatically defined such participation as nonpolitical. Politics, as such, quickly became, or rather remained, a semiprofessional occupation pursued by a particular class. What was expected to make the system democratic was the intermittent opportunity of the populace to endorse or reject representatives of this class through elections (for a critique, see Ake 2000). Governance, however, is a much broader complex of ideas, relations, and practices than politics in this narrow sense (see chapter 1). Configuring the ways in which power is exercised in society, governance hinges as much on the interventions by human rights activists and their foreign donors as on the maneuvers of the political class.

Elitism is inseparable from the actual political and economic conditions it helps to maintain. Consider, for example, how empowerment, a key concept in the current rhetoric, has become vacuous (Cooke and Kothari 2001; Hickey and Mohan 2005). It has assumed an individualistic content to match the particular definition of human rights it is now associated with. Regardless of whether the subject of empowerment is an individual human being or an individual community, empowerment through relationships with others is rendered unthinkable (see Englund 2004b). Individuals and communities are expected to be self-sufficient and free subjects, rights-bearing even when those rights yield few material entitlements.[8] In Malawi, the definition of human rights as freedoms was understandable — and disarming — after three decades of ruthless dictatorship, but its severely confined notion of rights quickly diminished the significance of the democratic transition. Squabbling over political and civil freedoms, the ruling elite and its non-governmental watchdogs effectively silenced public debates on social and economic rights. An impression of robust democratic processes was thereby created, not least for the benefit of foreign donors, but structural inequalities were hidden behind the notion that "poverty alleviation" was basically a technical issue. Empowerment, in effect, became *disempowerment* by using the notions of freedom, democracy, and human rights to confine the scope of what could be discussed.

My claim to reveal disempowerment in the notion of empowerment — and unfreedom in the notion of freedom — recalls a central tenet in critical social science, one that deserves critical reflection of its own. It informs critics' efforts at "removing the veil of ideology" (Donham 1990, 3), their attempts to lay bare power and its disguises (Gledhill 1994). Some element of revelation, reaching beyond that which is immediately apparent in dominant rhetoric, is inevitable in any social scientific pursuit. Yet three caveats should restrain social scientists' belief in their own acuity. First, they are not the only ones seeing through official rhetoric. One aim of this book is to show how little legitimacy the dominant definition of human rights has acquired among the Malawian populace, with popular frustrations finding outlets in other discourses (see chapter 7). Second, the extent to which elitism informs public life varies according to the political history of particular places and regions.[9] Malawi's first two postcolonial regimes subscribed to strong presidentialism and staged frequent spectacles of power. I will on several occasions throughout this book indicate how human rights activists and volunteers, compensating for their personal frustrations over education and employment, engaged in practices and discourses that virtually mimicked the elitism of the political class. Third, a critique of actually existing liberal democracies does not necessarily constitute a wholesale rejection of political liberalism (Kelly 2005). My critique of entrenched inequalities in Malawi carries more than a hint of liberal egalitarianism, even if I acknowledge the unlikelihood of absolute equality.

How Democracy Disempowers

The above remarks and the analysis in the main text do not seek to trivialize political and civil freedoms; nor are they based on a hierarchy of rights that, for example, the "founding fathers" of newly independent African states deployed to justify repression (see Shivji 1989). The best minds in political philosophy have long since discarded a hierarchy of rights in favor of an appreciation of how various rights and freedoms constitute one another. Amartya Sen (1999, 36), for example, has argued that freedom has both a constitutive and an instrumental role in development. Freedom is, in other words, both the primary end and the principal means of development. Sen's argument takes issue with those who have doubted the importance of political freedoms in ensuring economic development. The instrumental role of freedom reveals how "freedom of one type may greatly help in advancing freedom of other types" (Sen 1999, 37).

Moreover, Sen warns against rhetorical assertions of democracy's contribution to development. "The achievement of social justice," he writes, "depends not only on institutional forms (including democratic rules and regulations), but also on effective practice" (Sen 1999, 159).

The evidence in this book, however, advises caution with Sen's admiration for freedom. Normative approaches often become entangled in the very rhetoric that needs to be scrutinized. At the very least, this book demonstrates the perils of isolating political freedoms as the essence of democracy. Yet the task of this book is not to tell a familiar tale of failure, a story of crushed expectations of democracy. Such a narrative would do little more than provide illustrations for Afropessimists.[10] The task is to reach beyond optimism and pessimism through an empirical investigation of what actually takes place on the ground. The initial task is not even to produce a critique, because the question of *how* things are as they are needs to be addressed before attempting a response to the critical issue of *why*. The task is not to expose freedom as a sham, nor to deny its potential to spark dissent (Rose 1999, 10). It bears repeating that democracy and its associated contemporary connotations are contested concepts, open to multiple definitions, all suggesting particular social, economic, and political arrangements (Abrahamsen 2000, 67). The intent of this book is less to promulgate my own definition of democracy than to find out whether a debate about the multiple definitions of democracy is allowed to take place.

A narrative that does not begin with expectations can better capture the dynamics of disempowerment. It discloses, for example, the extent to which undemocratic dispositions are compatible with the interests of people who would seem to belong to distinct socioeconomic classes. Freedom, democracy, and human rights are, in this perspective, rhetorical constructs that contribute to status distinctions among Malawians no less than to the largely unquestioned influence that foreign agencies continue to wield in African countries. Yet the agents involved are sufficiently distinct to eliminate the possibility of a conspiracy. Although the processes described here certainly serve particular interests and power relations, they result from a complex of historical and cultural factors, not from a deliberate effort to keep the majority shackled to poverty and deprivation.

For my empirical investigation of these dynamics and processes, I have chosen those domains in which Malawians most directly came to grapple with the new rhetoric and practice. The first domain is translation, quite appropriately so in a country where the majority depend on a national language for effective communication. With complementary evidence from

Zambia, I show how the narrow definition of human rights as political and civil freedoms emerged through a profoundly undemocratic process of translation (chapter 2). The second domain of empirical investigation is civic education, a well-resourced intervention that both Malawian activists and foreign donors deemed necessary in a new democracy. By examining how Malawians were recruited to act as civic educators and how the crowds they encountered in villages and townships responded to their messages, I show the extent to which a nationwide civic education project effectively disempowered the masses (chapters 3 and 4). The third domain is legal aid, a rare instance of human rights NGOs actually attempting to organize tangible benefits for poor Malawians. My detailed analysis of legal aid shows how its providers treated claimants as individuals rather than as people whose grievances, such as exploitative labor relations, derived from similar structural problems (chapters 5 and 6). In order to analyze popular concerns beyond these domains of human rights activism, I describe, in chapter 7, the eruption of a moral panic in Malawi's capital. Rather than representing a permanent state of disorder, the moral panic serves as a standpoint for a contextualized ethnography of everyday civil virtues. These virtues, pursued under unfavorable conditions, indicate what "freedom" might mean among the poor and how it challenges the dominant notion of human rights as individual freedoms.

Land of the Less Privileged

Although the first two postcolonial regimes in Malawi used different terminology for their impoverished subjects, the approaches were arguably the same. Banda's regime discouraged the use of "poor" as the label for Malawians; "needy" was the term of choice. Muluzi's regime had no qualms about calling Malawians poor, and it adopted "poverty alleviation" as its principal tool of soliciting foreign aid. Yet the suggestion that the majority languished in poverty because of entrenched inequalities, for reasons that were profoundly political, was as unpalatable to the democratic regime as it had been to the autocratic one. Poverty was, in the official rhetoric, essentially a technical problem, a result of dysfunctions in local and global markets. As some academics and aid workers found out, to call impoverished Malawians "marginalized" was to invite official reproach. The state-controlled media, for example, often referred to the poor as "the less privileged." Everyone was privileged, but some were more privileged than others.

Bakili Muluzi, president of Malawi from 1994 until
2004, poses with one of his subjects and the First Lady
(photo courtesy of *The Nation,* Malawi).

Poverty and inequality define the history of Malawi from the onset of
colonial rule. As a British protectorate called Nyasaland, established in
1891, the country did not attract major investments in industry and infra-
structure. Land alienation to Europeans had taken place in the area that
is present-day southern Malawi already before the establishment of
British administration, and a handful of settlers and companies had acquired vast estates (Vail 1983). Central Malawi participated in commercial
agriculture only after the end of World War I, while northern Malawi

received educational advantage through the Livingstonia Mission and began the large-scale export of male labor before the other two regions did (see McCracken 1977). The origins of settler agriculture in Nyasaland can be traced to the expansion of mining capital based in South Africa and the Rhodesias (present-day Zimbabwe and Zambia), a further indication of Malawi's rather subservient role in the colonial economy of southern and central Africa (Mandala 1990, 118). Coffee, cotton, sisal, tea, and, above all, tobacco constituted the main crops of commercial agriculture.

Independence in 1964 followed widespread popular discontent with the Federation of Nyasaland and the Rhodesias, further stirred by Kamuzu Banda, who returned to Nyasaland in 1957 after some forty years abroad (Chiume 1975; Rotberg 1965; Short 1974). Large agricultural estates remained the backbone of the country's economy, now firmly situated in the patronage networks of the one-party state (Kydd and Christiansen 1982; Mhone 1992; Sindima 2002). The vast majority of the population remained smallholders, most of whom cultivated maize as their staple crop without commercial incentives, and the export of male labor to mines and plantations elsewhere in the region continued on a large scale until the 1970s (Chirwa 1996; Christiansen and Kydd 1983). The mode of postcolonial rule stifled any attempt at more equitable development, constantly constricted by unquestioned loyalty to the head of state, known as the life president since 1971. The so-called Cabinet Crisis had demonstrated already in 1964 Banda's intolerance of dissent, and his regime became increasingly brutal during its thirty-year reign (Baker 2001; Mapanje 2002; Williams 1978). Dissidents were "meat for crocodiles" or detainees for several years without trial, and compulsory membership in the Malawi Congress Party (MCP) extended even to infants (Africa Watch 1990). Political assassinations were an inevitable feature of this kind of dictatorship (van Donge 1998).

The chanting of *ndatopa Malawi Kongresi* (I am tired of the Malawi Congress Party) in 1993–94 expressed widespread desire for a new Malawi, even in areas that belonged to Banda's power base in the Central Region (see Englund 1996). The movement for change had been greatly emboldened by Malawi's Catholic bishops' Lenten Letter of 1992, the first high-profile criticism of the regime within Malawi for decades, and by aid donors' demand for enhanced human rights (Lwanda 1996; Schoffeleers 1999; van Donge 1995). A referendum, in which the supporters of the multiparty system of government triumphed, was held in 1993, followed by the first genuinely competitive elections in 1994. Yet as John Lwanda (1996) has shown in detail, while the transition was sparked by profound popular grievances, its conduct and agenda bore little resemblance to a popular revolt. Pressure groups were quick to emerge, led by wealthy businessmen, former officials of the MCP, and people who were, such as Muluzi himself, a combination of the two. The United Democratic Front (UDF), after its transformation into the new ruling party, gave a particularly clear example of business interests replacing the urge to democratize the economy, with intellectuals and many religious leaders feeling increasingly marginalized.

Muluzi's regime established a form of patronage in which development *(chitukuko)* often took the form of handouts, personalized as gifts from the compassionate president and made conditional on votes for the UDF.[11] New economic policies favored private entrepreneurship, but their focus on microcredits, trade, and consumption proved fatal to Muluzi's oft-repeated preoccupation with poverty alleviation. The few domestic manufacturers that existed in the early 1990s found it difficult to compete with cheap imports, and the manufacturing sector declined to about 12 percent of the economy in 1999 (Chinsinga 2002, 27). Trading was increasingly conducted with imported or smuggled commodities, and the government continued to promote unprocessed tobacco as the main export commodity, albeit in a more liberalized environment (see van Donge 2002). Smallholder agriculture remained neglected, further weakened by the removal of subsidies in the name of liberalization, making essential inputs too expensive for many rural Malawians. Amid all these economic hardships, however, political and civil freedoms *(maufulu)* were a major legitimizing achievement for the new regime, always available as a rhetorical ploy to divert attention from its dismal record in alleviating poverty.

Popular grievances hardly steered Malawi's path beyond the transition, with dependence on foreign donors and creditors remaining as profound as ever. During the first five years of independence, British aid accounted for almost a third of Malawi's total expenditure (Sindima 2002, 72). Other important donors and creditors have included Germany, the European Union, the World Bank, the United States, Canada, Japan, Taiwan, the Netherlands, Norway, and Denmark. In 2001, dependence on foreign aid amounted to thirty-eight U.S. dollars per capita (Dorward and Kydd 2004, 344). Donors' insistence on particular definitions of democracy and human rights during the democratic transition was congenial to neoliberal reform in the economy. Although neoliberal reform also became the norm in many other countries, the Banda regime had already demonstrated Malawi's commitment to a market economy and thereby its allegiance to the West during the Cold War. Malawi was the first in the region to adopt, in 1981, the Structural Adjustment Programme under the auspices of the International Monetary Fund (IMF) and the World Bank (Banda et al. 1998; Chinsinga 2002).

The National Human Development Report in 2001, prepared by the United Nations Development Programme (UNDP 2001), laid bare some of the consequences of that adoption. Malawi's poverty incidence by head count had been about 60 percent of the population in 1992, but it rose to 65 percent by the end of the decade. Out of the 65 percent, nearly 30 percent were "ultrapoor"; that is, their basic food requirements were chronically unmet. Furthermore, the 1998 housing survey had revealed that nearly 60 percent of households experienced periodic food shortages. The life expectancy at birth had lowered from forty-eight years in 1990 to about forty years in 1999. Chronic malnutrition provided fertile ground for diseases such as tuberculosis and HIV/AIDS to wreak havoc. Moreover, inequalities were shown to be particularly striking by Malawi's 2001 ranking as the third worst country in the whole world in terms of income inequality (UNDP 2001, 20).

Writing before the democratic transition, Leroy Vail and Landeg White noted that "both the colonial rulers and the post-colonial ruler have assumed that paternalism — the landowner dealing with his peasants, the chief with his subjects, the master with his servants, the President with his people — constitutes the form of government best suited both to the economy and the general temperament of Malawians" (1989, 181). This paternalism reached unprecedented depths of cynicism under Muluzi's democratic regime. Multipartyism quickly became an ever-changing mosaic of alliances and intrigues, often pursued by party leaders with woeful disregard of their electorate's opinions (Englund 2001c, 2002c). Nobody, not even a chief or Muluzi's own ailing mother, could be spared in this pursuit of particular political and business interests.[12] In 2002–3, following Muluzi's reelection in 1999, there were attempts to amend the 1995 constitution, which stipulated that the state president could stay in office for only two consecutive five-year terms. While Muluzi was careful not to express his interests in public, he systematically sacked those cabinet ministers who harbored presidential ambitions. Chiefs, in turn, were paraded in the state-controlled media as staunch supporters of the constitutional amendment. Muluzi's sycophants first attempted to remove all limits on the presidential terms in office. Once defeated in the National Assembly, the bill nearly returned to propose the limit of three consecutive terms. Sensing widespread dismay among parliamentarians and the general public, Muluzi's sycophants ultimately never presented the bill to the National Assembly.[13]

While the members of Parliament had variable motives to oppose the constitutional amendment,[14] the real heroes of this difficult phase in Malawi's democratization were several non-governmental and church-based organizations. Despite the ban that Muluzi had imposed on all demonstrations on the issue, they organized public prayers against the constitutional amendment, lobbied parliamentarians, chiefs, and donors, and issued numerous press releases. Their interventions were consistently fearless, indisputable proof of the extent to which political and civil freedoms needed constant vigilance in democratic Malawi. In contrast to the malleability of Malawi's party politics, human rights NGOs beamed admirable righteousness.[15]

As much as these organizations gave the impression of a united civil society confronting self-interested politicians, little is known about how they conducted themselves outside such high-profile interventions. In trying to provide such insight, this book carries forward the critical impetus of two previous studies from Malawi. The first is by Wiseman Chirwa (2000a), who argues that so-called civil society organizations have largely failed to shift the focus of public debates from narrowly conceived politics to wider issues of socioeconomic inequalities. The second is by Peter VonDoepp (2002), who shows through empirical research among the local-level clergy that they are often too preoccupied with their own material survival to be the civil society activists that contemporary rhetoric suggests they are. The need is for more research on NGOs and projects in real-life situations and for a perspective that sees democracy and human rights as requiring more than the establishment and protection of political and civil freedoms.[16] Poverty is not simply a threat to democracy in Malawi; it is the surest sign of democracy's limited success. A concept of democracy that does not extend beyond political and civil freedoms provides few tools to address inequalities underlying poverty. The contribution of human rights NGOs and projects to entrenched inequalities reveals that genuine democratization did not commence in Malawi during the first decade of liberal democracy.

Controlling NGOs

Any critique of human rights NGOs risks being unduly useful to ruling politicians, in Malawi as in many other countries. Precisely because these organizations do act as watchdogs of political and civil rights, they are often at odds with the political elite. Some of this elite may manipulate popular suspicions in an effort to discredit the NGOs. A high-ranking Malawian civil servant and former politician, for example, commented that "some people have started NGOs while married with one wife, but end up having five wives after getting money from donors."[17] A leading columnist announced that "non-governmental organizations are funded to participate in the affairs of a country. . . . In most cases it is the ideals of the country from which the funds come that they promote."[18] As is discussed in chapter 4, somewhat similar suspicions are conveyed in Malawian popular culture. While research results may always be manipulated, enough has already been said about the political elite's complicity in disempowerment to warrant a critical look at human rights activists. Donor involvement and elitism are issues too complex to be left for partisan critics only.

NGOs, particularly those that seek to promote human rights, sometimes face far more serious challenges than the caustic remarks mentioned above. In 2001, Malawi's National Assembly passed the Non-Governmental Organizations (NGO) Bill. The stated intentions were all upright: the promotion of a strong civil society, the definition of the rights and obligations of NGOs, and the provision of information on registered organizations. What was controversial was the establishment of the NGO Board, a statutory body designed to coexist with the already established Council for Non-Governmental Organizations of Malawi (CONGOMA).Whereas CONGOMA was the initiative of the NGOs themselves, the NGO Board was to be closely supervised by the government. A government minister was accorded the duty to appoint seven members to the board, while three members, secretaries from government ministries, would be there ex officio. All NGOs wishing to operate in Malawi were expected to register with this board, and a "line ministry" would be asked for its assent before the registration would come into force. The bill provided for criminal offenses when an NGO failed to comply with the law.

The NGO Board was widely seen as an instrument by the government to control NGOs (Tenthani 2002). The composition of the first board seemed to confirm these fears, because its seven appointed members were all from charitable and "developmental" NGOs, with human rights NGOs conspicuously absent. After the government had issued an ultimatum that all NGOs must be registered by the end of 2003, the Human Rights Consultative Committee (HRCC), an aggregation of about forty human rights NGOs in Malawi, protested through the media.[19] Among other things, it argued that the new law contradicted the freedom of association enshrined in the Constitution. It also urged NGOs not to register with the board. Many human rights NGOs appeared to consider registration with CONGOMA sufficient, but their reasons for not registering with the board did not always stem from the noble cause of civil disobedience. The executive director of the Civil Liberties Committee (CILIC) is quoted to have said that NGOs wanted some form of registration in order to retain the benefits of their duty-free status.[20]

The government did not respond to the NGOs' disobedience immediately, and its image of democratic governance partly depended on avoiding the outright suppression of human rights NGOs. Ambiguity and contestation were therefore likely to prevail, but this book demonstrates for human rights NGOs what has already become a commonplace observation in the study of faith-based and "developmental" NGOs — their contribution to undemocratic governance.[21] This conclusion is not intended to erase considerable diversity among and within NGOs (Hilhorst 2004). The HRCC's intervention in Malawi was predicated on a tacit distinction between "critical" and "acquiescent" NGOs. This book also shows the impact of status distinctions among NGO and project personnel. Yet perhaps the greatest challenge is to understand how, indeed, the apparently critical and independent NGOs and projects end up maintaining the status quo in society. Although this may appear to be the uniform result, different kinds of NGOs arrive there through different routes.

The historical and cultural features identified in this introduction — elitism, the preoccupation with individual freedoms, transnational governance — loom large in my analysis of particular human rights NGOs and projects in the main text. It is precisely initiatives like the NGO Board that keep contentious activists preoccupied with issues that most directly affect themselves, while the plight of the impoverished majority receives little systematic and imaginative attention. Confined to political and civil freedoms, democracy and human rights are taken for granted as objects of thought, not as intrinsically contestable concepts, by both the government and non-governmental watchdogs. The capacity to imagine democratic alternatives, informed by an understanding of conflicting interests and perspectives, is curtailed (Abrahamsen 2000; Ake 2000; Englund 2004b). NGOs, in effect, exercise a form of self-control, potentially far more insidious than any law that the government can formulate. Their discourse is elitist, even though many of the self-proclaimed experts of freedom, democracy, and human rights do not belong to the elite.

The Uses of Ethnography

Although this study builds on a whole range of sources, independent fieldwork has provided the bulk of its findings. The method has been ethnographic, involving sustained observation, participation in the observed practices and events, and extensive conversations with research subjects. In this regard, ethnography is about method rather than subject matter. As a number of anthropologists have argued for at least the past two decades, ethnographic fieldwork retains its salience in a world of widespread spatial mobility and transnational links, its proper definition no longer being a descriptive study of "a people" or "an ethnic group" (see Fog Olwig and Hastrup 1997; Gupta and Ferguson 1997). At the same time, aspects of the ethnographic method have appealed, since the 1980s, to practitioners in development work, from ostensibly radical development professionals (Chambers 1983) to the planning and evaluation procedures of the World Bank (Kumar 1993). Anthropologists may be gratified that this shift has occurred in response to perceived difficulties to grasp poor people's experiences and knowledge through large-scale surveys. Yet the actual application of the ethnographic method has often been rather different from the one to which this book subscribes. The crux of the difference is the interest in knowledge production, with the interests of development practitioners dictated by their desire to produce rapid research results for practical interventions. Indeed, Robert Chambers has warned, somewhat sarcastically, against adopting anthropologists' "full, respectable, professional, approach" (1983, 59). I discuss in chapter 3 the corollary of this impatience with long-term fieldwork — the notion that the object of both research and development is an identifiable and coherent "community."

While this book certainly seeks to engage with practical and political concerns, its approach is also based on the conviction that the complexity of the subject matter is ill-served by attempts to force the ethnographic method into a form of rapid research. The involvement of several agents and agencies in shaping the scope of freedom, democracy, and human rights in Malawi presents an opportunity to demonstrate how versatile the ethnographic method, in its anthropological application, can be. Even more, this complexity *demands* ethnographic work, because a perusal of published documents and media reports, even when complemented with formal interviews, is unlikely to disclose the actual extent of complexity. Fieldwork, the method whereby the researcher follows the research subjects to the natural contexts of their practices, is indispensable.

Fieldwork is also a response to a widely perceived crisis in African studies, expressed by Mbembe (2001, 7–9), among others. Africa has always been the ultimate "other" for Western social thought and history, no less so at present when the expectations of democracy occasion instant judgments and endless lamentations about Africa's failures to develop. Mbembe bemoans the lack of fieldwork and "linguistic inadequacy" that give rise to these proclamations (2001, 9). Scholars' knowledge of local languages in Africa appears to be waning, their monolingual reliance on English or French curtailing the scope of their understanding. As this book shows for Malawi and Zambia, the situation on the ground demands a higher degree of linguistic competence. Many of the findings presented here have, in fact, been possible because of my long-term interest in Chichewa (also known as Chinyanja), the national language of Malawi and one of the main lingua francas in south-central Africa. Although my fieldwork for this study properly began in 2000, it effectively built on the cultural and linguistic knowledge that I had begun to acquire in the region since 1991.

Linguistic competence enhances the potential of the ethnographic method to reach beyond appearances and rhetorics. The self-images of human rights activists, conveyed in their own publications and generously described to interviewers, emphasize their devotion to the good cause. As I noted above in the discussion of democratization in Malawi, many activists have certainly displayed such devotion in their fearless advocacy of political and civil rights. Yet without ethnographic fieldwork this devotion would be all there is, and the prevailing exploitation and deprivation in society would appear all the more puzzling. By following activists to their closed workshops and to their encounters with the beneficiaries of their work, and by subjecting their written and spoken discourses in the vernacular to a careful analysis, a richer understanding is possible. The result is a kind of knowledge that is rarely available in the studies of African democratization.

I was, at first, intrigued to study translation as an aspect of democratization in Malawi. It is not obvious how new concepts and ideas associated with human rights and liberal democracy are to be translated into African languages. Moreover, I realized during my previous fieldwork projects that the Chichewa translation of human rights as "birth freedoms" (*ufulu wachibadwidwe*) presents an extremely narrow understanding of rights. Popular doubts about the desirability of "freedoms" (*maufulu*) abounded. Arrogant youths confronting their elders, young women dressing (or undressing) themselves as if, as one mother put it, "they had no parents" *(ngati alibe makolo),* crime and insecurity, the rich getting richer while the poor realized that they could not eat the new freedoms — all these were frequently cited as consequences of the new era (see Englund 2000, 2001a). I felt the need to study how this particular translation of rights as freedoms contributed to popular discontent and whether the process of translation had itself been democratic. Beyond translation, the need was to investigate those contexts in which Malawians came to grapple with the new discourse, whether as its publicists or as its recipients. Civic education was one such context, but I was also interested in finding out whether the increased freedom to claim rights enabled disgruntled Malawians to improve their conditions. Legal aid provided insights into this issue.

During fieldwork, I divided my time between these different contexts and questions. I established the first contacts and did my first systematic reviews of translated documents in 2000. For most of the period from early 2001 until the end of 2003, I lived in Malawi, working with several organizations operating in the field of human rights. My focus on the particular NGOs and projects described in the subsequent chapters stemmed both from their prominence in this field and from my having used Lilongwe, Malawi's capital, as my base. The NGO whose legal-aid services I studied operated only in Lilongwe, whereas the civic education project had its headquarters there but a nationwide network of local offices. While studying civic education, I accompanied officers and volunteers on several occasions to the field in rural and urban areas in various districts.[22] I also participated in several closed workshops with civic education officers and volunteers. I spent, in all, several months at a center for legal aid recording and observing cases as they were discussed by clients, lawyers, and paralegal officers. A period of fieldwork in Zambia in 2002 enabled me to put some of the emerging findings in a comparative perspective. I also followed discussions on freedom, democracy, and human rights in the Malawian and Zambian media, collected all the material I could find on these topics in Chichewa, and visited the sites of my previous fieldwork projects in an effort to, among other things, keep abreast of popular experiences with democracy and human rights. Throughout the fieldwork, I worked alone, without assistants, and all the transcriptions and translations in this book are my own.

I felt almost always warmly welcome while conducting my fieldwork. Activists and others whom I met generally appreciated my project and anticipated that it would assist in developing the Chichewa discourse on human rights. Chapters 3 and 8 describe two exceptions to the warm welcome. One occurred when a regional officer of a civic education project suspected that I had political motives. The other involved a hostile reaction by the same project's expatriate manager to the early results of my study. Although I cannot expect my findings to please some of the organizations and projects that I studied, I realize that this disapproval can be expressed as doubts over the integrity of my scholarship. No scholar will let such doubts go unchallenged.

One issue worth reflection is objectivity, whether a bias has made me ask certain questions rather than others and thus produced a skewed picture of the subject matter. I would not deny the existence of biases in scholarly work, including those that are "political" in the broadest sense of the term. Expectations of democracy aside, it is obvious that a study like this is at least partly inspired by an interest in scholarship as a form of political action. Yet before seeking solutions to perceived problems, it is essential to know *how* those problems exist. Perhaps something of the elusive objectivity is retained if I note that, initially, I also took much of the prevalent rhetoric for granted. Dismayed at the failure of multiparty politics to address Malawi's social and economic ills, I turned to NGOs for reassurance, only to discover the problems described in this book. It is for others to make another research-based intervention that refutes my argument.

Another contentious issue is representativeness, even though the NGOs and projects studied in this book were prominent representatives of their field in Malawi. Doubts may arise over the extent to which the examples I give are representative of their activities. This was a major concern for the expatriate manager mentioned above: did I have a representative sample of the project's activities in different districts? This study is, however, about neither individual activists nor particular organizations or projects. It is about cultural dispositions, analyzed in a specific historical context, that appear to hijack the transformative potential of freedom, democracy, and human rights. Cultural dispositions never erase individual differences. Cultural dispositions evince coherence across cases and domains, and ethnographic fieldwork is the method to discover them. Yet fallibility in both method and interpretation is always a possibility. If this book provokes debate rather than dismissal, argument rather than accusation, research rather than reproach, it will have accomplished its task.

CHAPTER I

The Situation of Human Rights

Debating Governance and Freedom

A Malawian human rights activist resisted my interest in the national language of his country by asking a sarcastic question. "Where will you go with it?" *(mupita nacho kuti?),* he asked, using Chichewa for the first time during our conversation, rather than English, Malawi's official language. The activist saw little value in a foreigner's efforts to master a language that was, in his view, confined to a small and predominantly poor population. Whereas English opened out a world of opportunities, Chichewa appeared to close it. It seemed natural for foreigners and educated Malawians to converse in the language of opportunities rather than the language of deprivation.

That many other Malawians, including human rights activists, greeted my interest in Chichewa with mirth rather than sarcasm is beside the point. Virtually all Malawians who considered themselves educated regarded a Chichewa-speaking white man as an exotic curiosity, especially anomalous because he was not in Malawi to spread the gospel. Human rights activists working for non-governmental organizations and projects were accustomed to receiving white visitors who, whether as expatriate aid administrators or fly-by-night consultants, rarely proceeded beyond basic greetings in their study of Chichewa. These visitors' relations with Malawians who did not speak English, the vast majority of the population, were never direct. In this regard, a white person *(mzungu)* speaking Chichewa did have unusually extensive opportunities, if only for unmediated interaction in the local context. Before his sarcastic question, the activist had attempted to convince me that "Malawian culture" was to blame for the apparently slow pace with which Malawians used the new talk about human rights to make claims. Culture told them to "suffer in silence." But if this *mzungu* could actually hear the claims that were made in Chichewa, would he consider them silenced by culture or by activists themselves? If he had no need to be chaperoned by activists, what would he witness in villages and townships?

The notion of human rights depends on universalism in order to have any meaning at all. Much as this statement obliterates sterile debates with cultural relativists, it is only the beginning for other theoretical and political quandaries. For instance, if universals are made through translation (Butler 2000), Chichewa and other indigenous languages have little to offer, according to some Malawian activists. As the language of universalism, English appears as the sole source of a new discourse (see chapters 2 and 3). This approach to translation informs the making of Malawian activists as particular kinds of subjects, distinct from those whom they imagine as the beneficiaries of their efforts. The process may be peculiar to some African postcolonies, but certain aspects of these perspectives have also impeded human rights universalism more generally. Too often have the exhortations of universalism been accompanied by equally vehement assertions of the particular origins of the concept. One recent example is in the confident attempt of Micheline Ishay (2004) to provide *the* history of human rights. Underlying its laudable commitment to universalism is a troubling particularism. One of this history's "most consequential realities," we are told, is that "the influence of the West, including the influence of the Western concept of universal rights, . . . has prevailed" (Ishay 2004, 7). The assertion builds on exclusion as the cornerstone of a certain kind of universalism. Not only does the assertion about origins exclude those scholars of human rights who feel no allegiance to the West; it also fails to explain how a universal notion can be the prerogative of one particular civilization.[1]

This book subscribes to the view that universals emerge through friction, a relational condition for which translation is only one possible metaphor. Anna Lowenhaupt Tsing (2005) has written about "engaged universals," suggesting that universality in the abstract remains a chimera. Sensitivity to context should no longer be mistaken for particularism, whether as a simple opposite of universalism or as an espousal of a particular civilization. Engaged universals never actually take over the world; their universalism is situational. This perspective finds further philosophical justification in the thought of Alain Badiou (2001), who has insisted on considering situations in which human rights are evoked as ineluctably *political*. This chapter must, therefore, also examine the assumption that human rights discourse contributes to governance in its transnational and subjective modalities.

Varieties of Rights and Citizenship

I write in a cultural context in which positive values attached to individual freedoms are so ingrained that some may consider ethnographic insights from another context inconceivable or morally repugnant. As a preliminary step, it is important to note that this book seeks to achieve more than a simple inversion of priorities in discourse on human rights. To promote economic and social rights as if they took precedence over civil and political liberties would be to make the same mistaken assumption that many human rights activists in Malawi made during the first ten years of democratization — the assumption of a hierarchy or generation of rights.[2] Civil and political rights are not realized in full as long as social and economic rights remain rudimentary. Conversely, and against many of the "founding fathers" of independent Africa, socioeconomic development is not a more urgent matter than the establishment of civil and political rights. Rather than deciding which set of rights should come first, we should replace abstract considerations with empirical investigations into the actual situations of rights and wrongs. Issa Shivji's statement, formulated before the recent wave of democratization in Africa, is as cogent at present as when it was written: "[H]uman rights-talk should be historically situated and socially specific. . . . Any debate conducted on the level of moral absolutes or universal humanity is not only fruitless but ideologically subversive of the interests of the African masses" (1989, 69).

While it may be unwarranted to assume a hierarchy of rights, the different scope of different rights challenges the view that human rights are first and foremost individual freedoms. Talal Asad (2003, 130) has drawn attention to a basic grouping of rights in political philosophy. In this dualistic scheme, rights that are intrinsic to the individual irrespective of social relationships contrast with rights that entail and are entailed by obligations toward other people. The distinction is, however, rather inconsequential as it stands, as evidence from Malawi and Zambia will demonstrate (see especially chapter 2). Obligations can be envisaged as individualistically as freedoms, and the critical issue is the extent to which rights discourses enable subjects to claim entitlements. The idea of entitlement presupposes membership in political society, institutional arrangements that ensure historically specific standards of life. These arrangements have conventionally been the responsibilities of the state, but the predicament of many African postcolonies, as is discussed below, demands analysis of the transnational conditions of state formation. For the moment, more needs to be said about citizenship as the basis for rights as entitlements.[3]

As soon as citizenship becomes the focus of struggles over rights, the meaning of "human" in human rights begins to look less certain. The paradox, as Asad (2003, 129) has pointed out, is that while human rights are instrinsic to all persons irrespective of their cultural or political affiliations, the realization and protection of these rights depend on judicial institutions belonging to nation-states and international organizations. Membership as civil status appears, therefore, more crucial than bare humanity; presocial individuals are replaced by political subjects. It is in this sense that Shivji, as quoted above, warned against adopting "universal humanity" (1989, 69) as the rallying cry for human rights discourse in Africa. Yet it is not clear, in turn, whether this warning should itself be taken as universally valid. In his discussion of how ideas of humanity have variously informed struggles over rights, Asad (2003, 141–148) recalls the civil rights movement in the United States. Particularly revealing is the frustration that Malcolm X expressed over a political project that remained confined to the jurisdiction of the American state. The issue for him was to transcend a discourse on civil rights by appealing to human rights. A whole new world of possibilities would open out: "You can take Uncle Sam before a world court. But the only level you can do it is the level of human rights. Civil-rights keeps you under his restrictions, under his jurisdiction" (quoted in Asad 2003, 141–142).

The transnational dimensions of governance in postcolonial Africa may lend relevance to analogous concerns over rights debates that are confined to national jurisdictions. At the same time, the *human* rights that those concerns evoke gain meaning within situational arguments about membership in political society, not through arguments that depend on the concept of abstract humanity.[4] There is every reason to imagine this political society as a transnational or worldwide society (Ferguson 2002). At any rate, whatever the scale of society in which persons can claim membership, it is important to recognize as much variation in the types of citizenship as in the notions of rights. In a classic discussion, T. H. Marshall ([1950] 1977) identified political, civil, and socioeconomic elements in citizenship. His particular concern was the exclusion of the working class in postwar Britain from social rights to the kinds of education, health care, and social security that would have generated a shared sense of equal citizenship.

More recent theorists of citizenship have insisted that exclusion is not only a consequence of material deprivation, but it can also occur from a lack of recognition for cultural citizenship (Kymlicka 1995). One more dimension has thus been added to Marshall's typology of citizenship, with those countries in mind in which the presence of immigrants and other minority groups has come to challenge discriminatory definitions of citizenship. This "multiculturalist" challenge has, however, been ill served by those studies that have deployed a notion of discrete cultures confronting one another within the same society (see, e.g., Parekh 2000; Tully 1995). The contrast to current anthropological explorations of cultural citizenship is sharp. Anthropologists investigate how culturally defined subjects are constructed within the specific political and economic conjunctures of ostensibly liberal societies (see, e.g., Comaroff and Comaroff 2004; Povinelli 2003). These anthropological studies, in other words, take as problematic what some multiculturalists have taken for granted. Far from arising from primordial identities, cultural citizenship may be constrained and molded by the very operations of state-sponsored recognition its proponents demand.

The frequent reference to "liberalism" in some of these critiques also presents an opportunity to specify the contemporary political and economic conditions of many emerging democracies in Africa and beyond. Liberalism encompasses such a complex legacy of thought and practice that it can be a misnomer for what has informed state policies and foreign aid since the Cold War (see Kelly 2005). *Neoliberalism* appears to be a more proper description, acknowledging historical resonances with some aspects of liberalism while revealing a distinctively contemporary predicament. Of particular relevance to a discussion of citizenship is the way in which political subjectivity is envisaged under the neoliberal regime. It is a subjectivity that seems congenial to the assertion of "the uncompromising autonomy of the individual, rights-bearing, physically discrete, monied, market-driven, materially inviolate human subject" (J. L. Comaroff and J. Comaroff 1999, 3). At the same time when multicultural citizenship was contemplated in some European and North American contexts, many emerging democracies in Africa were built on the assumption that citizens are individuals.[5] The assumption supported neoliberal reform in national economies, with privatization, for example, creating the conditions for bringing to fruition the individual's entrepreneurial essence. That human rights came to be defined in a particular way did not surprise critics, as Asad, among others, noted: "The historical convergence between human rights and neoliberalism may not be purely accidental" (2003, 157).

Citizenship was, in other words, largely one-dimensional, a passport to political rights at the expense of socioeconomic justice. Hence, also, the emphasis on developments in the narrowly defined political sphere, especially in the realm of electoral competition, in much academic and policy-oriented discussion on these new democracies (for a critique, see Caldeira and Holston 1999). Yet precisely because the regime is best described as neoliberal, alternatives to it can be sought both in the more radical strands of liberalism and in the actual situations uncovered by ethnography. To be sure, democratic proceduralism, giving special weight to the constitutional distribution of political and civil rights, has been handed down from liberalism's foundational figures, such as Immanuel Kant (Kelly 2005, 29). Alongside, and perhaps increasingly against, one-dimensional citizenship stand the intellectual and political legacies of civil and socioeconomic citizenship and entitlements, as indicated above. Moreover, despite their compatibility with the neoliberal regime, certain interventions can also be reclaimed for potentially transformative projects. The rhetoric of participation has been eagerly repeated by human rights activists in Malawi as elsewhere (chapter 4), but the allocation of responsibility to abstract individuals and resource-poor communities has done little to address neoliberal injustices. As has recently been argued, however, the idea of participation is not intrinsically tied to the neoliberal order it may serve (Hickey and Mohan 2005). Much hinges on what kind of citizenship informs participatory projects — it is possible to envisage other dimensions of citizenship that address the situations of marginalized and subordinate persons.

In a similar vein, civil citizenship, while only superficially promoted by some human rights agencies, is crucial to the realization of political and socioeconomic citizenships. Violence and insecurity have been the flip side of new democracies where civil citizenship has had little impact beyond legislative reforms. The popular experience in Malawi has been strikingly similar to the one in Brazil, where elite citizens have responded to insecurity by criminalizing the poor (Caldeira and Holston 1999, 699). Chapter 7 describes how insecurity and violence in Malawi's impoverished townships led to a moral panic that was criminalized as "mob justice" by both the police and human rights activists. The extent to which this incident was triggered by a lack of civil citizenship, defined as it was through an individualistic notion of freedoms, was rendered unthinkable.

"Rights-based development" (see, e.g., DFID 2000) presents one more example of how current interventions can have contradictory consequences depending on the interests they are made to serve. Critics, such as Mark Duffield (2001, 221–224), have been quick to point out that this development's apparent commitment to social and economic rights can translate into yet another depoliticized humanitarian effort to satisfy social and economic needs. By contrast, the case from Malawi, discussed in chapter 8, shows how the transformative potential of rights-based development was too much for the Malawian and British governments to bear, resulting in the project's closure even before it was officially launched. Intriguing in this case is that it would have offered resources for Malawians to claim their rights as entitlements rather than as individual freedoms. The status quo prevailed, and two alternative forms of citizenship and rights remained alien to the new democracy (Kymlicka 2002, 327). On the one hand, civil virtues and active political participation were deemphasized, if not discouraged altogether. On the other hand, group-differentiated rights, uniting claimants as a collective force, were nipped in the bud by associating them with pathological and dangerous ideas, such as regionalism and tribalism.[6] These reflections suggest that the necessary task of critique is not advanced if it merely attacks concepts and procedures that the neoliberal moment has made fashionable. Throughout this book, the critical focus is on the making and conduct of subjects who put those concepts to specific uses. The focus, in short, is on the *situational* character of human rights and citizenship.

Situating Universal Rights

The situation of human rights, it was claimed above, is invariably political. Much of this book is concerned with showing how various participants in human rights discourse, deliberately or not, *depoliticize* the situation of human rights. Yet as some critics of the post–Cold War wave of democratization have argued, there was no lack of politics in emerging democracies (see Abrahamsen 2000; Caldeira and Holston 1999). Political citizenship, as was mentioned above, became a major preoccupation all over the world. Busying themselves with issues such as regime change and electoral competition, analysts and activists were often slow to assess whether political reforms, including the introduction of human rights discourse, brought legitimacy and efficacy to the ways in which these countries were governed. At the same time, analysts and activists might have been excused for thinking that they were merely being loyal to popular priorities. In Malawi, talk about politics became the nation's favorite pastime, with a handful of political leaders providing entertaining, if sometimes controversial, topics for conversation after many years of great circumspection about political life. President Muluzi often lamented, especially toward the end of his regime, that wherever two or more Malawians met, they started to talk politics.

Muluzi's lament was, of course, a thinly veiled attempt to discourage popular debate on his regime's intrigues. To this extent, talk about politics could be consequential, and a human rights project that studiously avoided such talk contributed to depoliticization in a rather literal sense (chapters 3 and 4). It is, however, precisely these ostensibly nonpolitical agencies that make the actual scope of the political extend far beyond political institutions and politicians themselves. At issue is the constitution of power whose structures and processes are not reducible to the domain of political science. The cultural disposition of elitism is a historically constituted way of legitimizing and exercising power in Malawi. As is discussed further in this chapter, it introduces both subjective and transnational modalities to the study of governance.

A key procedure by which human rights discourse in Malawi and elsewhere has depoliticized the exercise of power is the denial that human rights acquire significance situationally. The procedure is familiar from a wide range of contemporary contexts and is one that, according to the French philosopher Alain Badiou (2001, 9), posits a universal human subject who is split into two modalities. On the one hand, the subject is passive and pathetic, the one who suffers. On the other, the subject is active, the one who identifies suffering and knows how to act. Note the ease with which such a procedure articulates with one historical legacy of elitism in Malawi — the association of knowledge with elites and those who mimic their ways. The education of the poor and the ignorant has long been an aspect of liberal democracy (Asad 2003, 61), pregnant with historical parallels with missionary and colonial projects in many African settings. The situation of human rights is political because the decision over abstract humanity always precedes any actual claim or grievance. This decision holds, in effect, some protagonists in contempt by precluding participation in defining the universal in their situation. Badiou has emphasized the transnational and racial underpinnings of this procedure: "On the side of the victims, the haggard animal exposed on television screens. On the side of the benefactors, conscience and the imperative to intervene. And why does this splitting always assign the same roles to the same sides? Who cannot see that this ethics which rests on the misery of the world hides, behind its victim-Man, the good-Man, the white-Man?" (2001, 12–13).

Malawian activists' admiration for formal education, which involves the uncritical acceptance of English as the language of power and contempt for those whose skills in literacy are limited, is an instance of this split subjectivity in an African postcolony. What Badiou calls "the singularity of situations" (2001, 14) and "the real of situations" (2001, 7) are sacrificed to abstraction. Badiou's (2001, 14–15) analogy comes from the medical domain. Just as a human rights activist conceives of victims as an indistinct crowd, so too does a medical doctor following a bureaucratic procedure forget the singularity of the medical situation and see her patients as "the sick," anonymous statistical entities. Badiou's assault is on the proliferation of a certain ethical discourse that has brought to the medical situation concerns that are radically exterior to it, such as health-care expenses and managerial responsibilities. The result can be a lack of care for bureaucratic and political reasons, for instance when the patient is an illegal immigrant.

Analogies aside, thinking across domains gives little guidance as to how to define a situation. It may be the philosopher's privilege to create an impression that human rights discourse is incorrigibly inimical to the interests of the poor.[7] By contrast, those who actually study "the real of situations" often need to include within it contests over the very idea of human rights. On the one hand, aspects of the discourse as promoted by activists and their foreign benefactors do find their way into popular vocabularies, although the interests they are made to serve can be incompatible. On the other hand, incompatibilities can be even more radical, beginning with the inability of some activists to accept certain grievances and practices as belonging to the domain of human rights (chapters 6 and 7). Neither of these observations undermines Badiou's insight that human rights discourse tends to bury actual contests and incompatibilities under the abstraction of universal subjectivity. The observations, moreover, lend support to a critique of the expectation that rational debate in the public sphere could alone resolve even the sharpest of these contradictions (Calhoun 1992). A fundamental problem is subjects' uneven capacity to be heard in a human rights discourse that delineates the public sphere less as a realm of rational deliberation than as a site of power (Asad 2003, 184). At the same time, and as Badiou's philosophical critique entails, even if some subjects are assigned the status of victims, their engagement with the situation bespeaks a far more active disposition. Notions of resistance and agency have little to offer here, linked as they often are to social scientists' "easy populism" (Brennan 1997, 65) that forgets the real of situations in which different subjects enter the debate on human rights. Rather, engagement compels a reconsideration of what freedom might be once it is recovered from its individualistic connotations in a particular human rights discourse (see below).

Engagement also represents the source of universals in the situation of human rights. The universalism of victimhood and those who claim to know how it is defined gives way to engaged universals (Tsing 2005). It is through contingent collaborations that incompatible interests and dispositions can turn into compatible ones, moments of shared vision and hope. As universals, human rights concepts must satisfy two conditions. The first is the conventional expectation that they travel across the situations in which they are evoked. The second is the more contentious requirement that they come to operate as universals within a situation. Even though the second condition finds relatively little support in the ethnography of human rights discourse in Malawi, this by no means entails pure victimhood or a lack of engagement. If anything, disengagement has been activists' mode of undermining the universalist promise of human rights.[8] By describing how other Malawians actually have engaged with the situation of human rights, this book may be read to suggest possibilities for collaboration and coalitions. However, because the situation of human rights is political, more is needed than improved translation between activists and their impoverished partners in villages and townships. The situation is an instance of governance, not rational debate.

Transnational Governance and Neoliberal Governmentality

The concept of governance would hardly feature in an ethnography of human rights discourse if it did not, somewhat paradoxically, extend our purview beyond the workings of national governments. Such an extension was not envisaged by those who first introduced the notion in policy and academic debates on the post–Cold War world. Good governance was the business of good governments. "Governance" signaled a renewed interest in engineering state institutions to manage the assumed economic and developmental consequences of neoliberal reforms. When the World Bank, for example, defined governance as "the manner in which power is exercised in the management of the economic and social resources for development" (1993, 2), it was clear that at issue was the power of political and bureaucratic agents in a nation-state.

Despite intensifying doubts over such limiting notions of power and governance, as discussed in this chapter, the focus on state institutions has remained an item of faith among influential thinkers. An obvious example is the recent attempt of Francis Fukuyama (2004) to highlight the importance of rebuilding institutions in "failing states," an ideological program that is thought to safeguard the entire world order. Similar assumptions are evident even when authors' sense of complexity surpasses Fukuyama's policy-oriented panacea. The study of Africa's fledgling democracies, for instance, is said to benefit from a subtle notion of "governance quality," a means to differentiate governments according to their success in institutionalizing developmental procedures and values (see, e.g., Alence 2004). The world thus envisaged may well be interconnected, composed of myriad political and economic forces, but it also lends itself to a view of governance as mutually independent governments' prerogative.

The search for a more plausible notion of governance must be mindful of especially two aspects of state-centered and institutional perspectives. The first informs Fukuyama's (2004) caution against an unvarnished belief in the benevolence of the market. His focus on state institutions comes as a refinement of the neoliberal credo that, from at least the 1980s onward, promoted the free market economy as the solution to virtually every conceivable problem in society. The tyranny of the market, so abhorrent to neoliberalism's critics (see, e.g., Bourdieu 1998; Chomsky 1998), troubles some of neoliberalism's apologists too. As a means to enhance good governance, the institutions of liberal democracy are thought to ensure development, if only for the benefit of the market. This is linked to the second preoccupation of institutional neoliberalism. "Failing states" are an anathema to a world order in which the interests of Western economic and political predominance are increasingly gauged in terms of security. Popular discontent breeds protest, which may, in the absence of deliberate institutional reforms toward liberal democracy, jeopardize the security of rich nations. When institutional reforms are thought to ensure participation and partnership in this world order, the commitment of the discourse to the status quo is unmistakable.

In point of fact, Fukuyama joins a long lineage of concerned policy makers and intellectuals who have seen in impoverishment a haunting possibility of insurrection. This concern is at least as old as the notion of international development itself, with the Truman Doctrine of 1947, for example, arguing that the suffering of the poor was "a handicap and a threat to both them and the more prosperous areas" (quoted in Escobar 1995, 3).[9] Interventions by rich nations appear legitimate when the avowed objective is to assist poor nations in democratic state building. Current institutional perspectives, calling for measures to curb the excesses of neoliberalism, assert the natural order of things in which nation-states carry the primary responsibility for their citizens' well-being. Critical responses to this false naturalism had been publicized even before neoliberalism assumed its present predominance. By the 1960s, the roots of "underdevelopment" had been located in the unequal exchange between rich and poor countries (e.g., Amin 1976; Frank 1969). More recent perspectives have emphasized not only nations as "imagined communities" (Anderson 1983) but also the imaginative and symbolic work that makes states seem the ultimate repositories of power and authority (see, e.g., Malkki 1992; Scott 1998; Taussig 1996).

The critical issue here is, on the one hand, that governance, pace Fukuyama and other institutionalists, is by no means the prerogative of governments. Governance takes place in a transnational context of non-governmental organizations and multilateral and financial institutions, perhaps even more so during the neoliberal era, when some state functions have been increasingly delegated to nonstate agencies.[10] Few would dispute the continuing salience of states in the world; the challenge is to account for this salience without merely repeating commonsensical ideas of the state as the most encompassing element in governance (Ferguson and Gupta 2002). On the other hand, if the exercise of state power has always depended no less on symbolic than on bureaucratic procedures — if indeed the symbolic and the bureaucratic are two sides of the same coin — the task is to discern the symbolic and subjective efficacy of governance under neoliberalism. As this book shows for Malawi, diverse agencies, often seen to be antagonistic toward one another, contributed to the undemocratic governance of an African country by entering into a tacit agreement over the scope of human rights. How can this instance of neoliberal governance be demonstrated ethnographically?

"Governmentality," a neologism first introduced by Michel Foucault in a lecture in 1978 (see Foucault 1991), offers one set of ideas for such a project, although, as is discussed below, important caveats must also be observed. Exploring government from a broad philosophical and historical perspective, Foucault extended the notion beyond its modern confines of state institutions. He argued that a shift from a Machiavellian emphasis on territory occurred to produce a population as the target of government, with territory and property as mere variables in "the general form of management" (Foucault 1991, 94). Foucault's innovation was to depict the practices of government in the plural and to locate them even in the most intimate realms of family, let alone in such domains as education, religion, and the law. "Governmentality" thus refers to "the conduct of conduct," the acts and norms of governing from state institutions to a plurality of agencies and authorities, to aspects of personal behavior governed as much by self-regulation as by these authorities (Dean 1999). What appears to make governmentality conducive to ethnographic research is the manner in which it brings faceless institutions and active subjects within the same purview. The problem of subjectivity is at the core of governmentality, arising from people's continuing capacity to think and act when governed by others (see Burchell 1991).

The great interest of governmentality as a notion is the possibility it opens out to examine how people, including those with no formal involvement in the political system, participate in governing both themselves and others. This book shows how a particular translation of human rights came to represent individual freedoms as the natural grounds for making claims. In addition to the political history described in the introduction, the allure of defining human rights as individual freedoms lay in its apparently postcolonial approach to governance. Rights-bearing subjects were free to take up the burdens of governing and developing themselves. Yet precisely because the vast majority of subjects were given little else than abstract notions to work with, the establishment of a human rights regime appeared perpetually unfinished. The assumed reason was the low level of understanding among the poor, calling for more inculcation of the abstract notions. The involvement of activists and donors thus persisted, their status as vanguards asserted over and again.

Discourse on human rights was, therefore, instrumental in governmentality, and its efficacy rested as much on external donor agencies' financial support as on activists' own efforts to mold the behavior of not only authorities but the population at large. At the same time, much as activists and state authorities appeared to be at loggerheads, their approach to governing the populace shared remarkable affinities. Governmentality built on the cultural disposition of elitism, understood here in historical terms. The subsequent chapters will describe how notions of self-esteem, personal hygiene, linguistic habits, and modes of dress shaped self-regulation among youthful activists who themselves hardly belonged to the national elite.

Yet it is precisely because of history that the notion of governmentality cannot be applied without important caveats. The making of self-regulating subjects builds on objectification as much as on subjectification. The status of "the grassroots" as the ignorant recipients of others' wisdom resonated with the coercion and control that colonialism had periodically asserted as its main methods of governance. Historical parallels are also apparent in contest and contradiction, with the narrow definition of human rights only partly successful in erasing the actual variety of making claims. The notion of governmentality may, after all, provide rather limited insights into this variety in the situation of human rights. Ethnographic knowledge, based on fieldwork, complicates the inexorable schemes that Foucauldian theorizing, at least in its unvarnished forms, conjures up.

Beyond Foucault's Prison

A major theoretical advance is involved when an analytical vocabulary permits the description of governance in its subjective and transnational modalities, reaching beyond institutionalist perspectives. At the same time, the notion of governmentality may prove to be too persuasive in its reinvention of functionalism, a totalizing explanatory framework in which everything fits, including contradictions. As soon as neoliberalism's apologists had celebrated new freedoms, critics inspired by the notion of governmentality enthusiastically exposed new operations of power. Tsing is sardonic about the "mirror opposite" that some of these critiques have provided: "Non-governmental organizations, human rights advocacy, and civil society spread as a transnational governmentality, a new imperial power that reaches deeply into human souls. The new subjects of liberalism are even more trapped in power because they imagine it as freedom" (2005, 214).

In spite of obvious empirical problems, such as the diversity of NGOs (Hilhorst 2004), the response to the persuasive fictions of governmentality requires further conceptual work. It is, after all, equally tempting to see agency and resistance in every instance of governmentality. Following such a procedure would obscure the life-worlds of activists themselves, whose embrace of the neoliberal rhetoric did not make them the individuals that the rhetoric promoted. As is described in chapter 3, the elitism that enabled activists to imagine a cleavage between themselves and the grassroots also fostered a sense of obligations and responsibility in their own lives, not as rights-bearing individuals, but as providers of welfare through the resources that involvement in NGOs and projects was expected to provide. Conversely, the room for maneuver among those who found themselves in the category of the grassroots was not simply determined by the new rhetoric. To assume resistance as a reflection of power is to misrecognize claims and concerns that owe little to the organizing assumptions of powerful rhetoric. These considerations, while certainly informed by ethnographic observation, can be developed through a discussion of two themes that the analytic interest in governmentality has tended to overlook. The first is the idea of freedom, whether it has any applicability in contexts in which it appears to have become a key instrument of governmentality. The second concerns the interplay between subject making and objectification, the role of coercion in a mode of governance that appears to assign to the poor the burdens of developing themselves.

Anthropologists have been successful in applying the idea of freedom in their ethnographies of civilizations that can claim no direct link to liberalism (see, e.g., Barrett 2004; Fabian 1998; Riesman 1977). A recurrent insight in these studies has been the recognition that freedom as a potential to transform oneself can be achieved only through social relationships, not in the unproductive state of abstract individuality. It also follows that freedom is precarious and discontinuous, very different from the permanent condition that neoliberal rhetoric promises. Situational analysis is pertinent here, and, as Badiou (2001, 40) has insisted, the deceit of the abstract subject must give way to explorations of how people *become* subjects under specific circumstances. This insistence underlies his impatience with those critics who have misunderstood the political implications of the theoretical antihumanism that has informed the thought of certain French philosophers since the 1960s, including Foucault (Badiou 2001, 5–7). Rather than marking a cynical detachment from all political action, this theoretical position has been necessary precisely for a committed engagement in the real of situations. The apparent emphasis on surveillance and domination, associated with the early work of Foucault (1977), was something he spent many years undoing (Laidlaw 2002, 322). Foucault's deepening interest in the "techniques of the self" was crucial to a sense of freedom that some readings of governmentality have missed (Burchell 1996). The forms of freedom vary according to historical situations, and Foucault's project was less to prescribe the conditions in which freedom is achieved than to investigate how it is exercised (Laidlaw 2002, 323; see also Bell 1996). His position differed from the reduction of freedom to the exercise of choice in singular acts, a procedure that has characterized the use of "agency" as an analytic concept. What has been recognized by social scientists as agency has too often been determined by their tacit assumptions of what lies in agents' true interests (Laidlaw 2002, 315).

Whereas Foucault was able to demolish the prison he may have erected, others continue to reconstruct it as an even more solid confinement. The debate on governmentality overlaps with that on sovereignty, a debate that has the merit of discussing subtle and direct uses of power within the same framework. The maddening capacity of some scholars to argue that black is white (and vice versa) finds an illustration in Giorgio Agamben's (1998) view that democracy and totalitarianism share the same foundations in biopolitics, in the value both attach to human life in its barest, most abstract form. Every decisive event in one political form, such as winning new liberties in emerging democracies, entails the other, such as the preparation of "a new and more dreadful foundation for the very sovereign power from which [people] wanted to liberate themselves" (Agamben 1998, 121). It is certainly possible to identify empirical contexts in which the line between democracy and totalitarianism risks becoming indistinct.[11] Yet a grand theory of sovereign power can also become another instance of depriving freedom and governance of any other content than the one given to them by power itself. The prospect is all the more bleak when the new politics that the theory is said to require remains, in Agamben's words, "largely to be invented" (1998, 11). Objectification and becoming a subject are, more often than not, simultaneous processes that need not be consigned to the sinister shadows of incipient totalitarianism.

According to John Comaroff's critique of the colonial state as a topic of Foucauldian reflections, for example, fault is to be found with the habit of regarding the colonial state as a uniform phenomenon. His charge against governmentality is the way in which the idea can contribute to this reification, to a false concreteness of what he considers to be "historically fluid forms and processes" (Comaroff 2002, 121). Specifically, Foucauldian narratives give short shrift to the limits of self-regulation in the contexts of abuse and unfulfilled promises. The very process of eliciting consent may also produce new vocabularies of riposte and unforeseen practices of subversion. The distinction between rights-bearing citizens and custom-oriented subjects may have been instrumental to colonial rule — and it may have limited subjects' scope for revolt (Mamdani 1996) — but the emerging disputes could also be about citizenship *tout court*. In the contemporary situation of human rights in Malawi, human rights activists are the ones who have the greatest difficulty in seeing beyond the fictions of neoliberal governance. Yet there is no inexorable condition of governmentality awaiting ethnographic description. Rather, inexorability would be all there is without ethnographic description.

Lest another set of abstract notions emerges to push the analysis to ever

more postmodern heights of indeterminate power, the historical continuities alluded to above must be kept in mind. If in colonial Africa, as
Megan Vaughan has argued, "group classification was a far more important construction than individualization" (1991, 11), postcolonial Malawi
offers an example of how the two were connected. The new human rights
discourse individualized claimants by recourse to old fixations with group
membership. "Communities" took the form of individuals when donors
and activists asked them to provide for their own development (chapters
3 and 4). Persons seeking legal aid were made to believe that their grievances were particular, while, in practice, activists treated claimants as
generic representatives of ignorant masses (chapters 5 and 6). The rhetoric appeared distinct enough from the paternalism of the previous regime
to effect a certain amnesia. Community development, after all, had a much
longer history in the governance of African countries than what the
exhortations of participation suggested (Hickey and Mohan 2005, 239–
240). At the same time, the emphasis on individual freedoms ensured that
old images of tribal communities no longer applied. Objectified as "the
grassroots" in human rights advocacy, communities were taught to consider themselves as nationals who shared political citizenship.[12]

As an example of how self-regulation is not far removed from the practices of objectification, consider a recent ethnography of a secondary
school in postcolonial Zambia (Simpson 2003). Teachings and the
school's official association with a certain type of Christianity may not
have been contested onstage when teachers were present, but they became
elements in a complex process of identity formation, with students simultaneously drawing on and reworking the religious, gendered, and racial-
ized discourses that their education presented to them. Much as their
world-views may not have been exactly what their school as an institution
of surveillance might have led their teachers to expect, the students, as an
elite-in-the-making, did learn to regard their position in society in specific
ways. It was a position that relegated their less-educated kin and compatriots to the status of "dirty villagers" (Simpson 2003, 121–122). While
learning to consider themselves as sophisticated gentlemen, the students
came to embrace a long tradition of objectifying others.

Similar "techniques of the self," deriving from missionary education,
can be seen to have produced Malawian human rights activists' image of
themselves as clean, assured, and civilized subjects. The potential for coalitions with the impoverished recipients of their advocacy was evident only
occasionally. When activists in some NGOs appealed to human rights in
their critique of a manipulative regime, many Malawians rejoiced. Yet

contested as they may have seemed, only some human rights were recognized for public debate by activists and authorities alike, while others
were silenced. Popular frustrations loomed large when it became apparent that protests remained confined to particular liberties, far removed
from the everyday concerns of impoverishment and exploitation. The
deafness of activists and authorities became particularly acute when popular concerns and claims were expressed in ways that refused the naturalism of individual freedoms.

Who Were the Prisoners?

Those whose imagination was imprisoned by the idea of individual freedoms did not share the same identity or subjectivity. The view of governance that emerges in this study emphasizes not only its transnational
character but also its sources in an uncanny alliance between agents and
agencies that would seem to have little in common. It is precisely because
their interests were divergent that a conspiracy can be ruled out. Rather,
the diverse interests were locked in a mutually beneficial dispute, although
this dispute excluded the vast majority of Malawians whose interests were
not served by the particular hierarchy of rights on which the dispute was
based. As is argued throughout this book, Malawi's political history
makes this situation of human rights understandable. Human rights
activists, from an acquiescent project of civic education to a vociferous
NGO, were particularly concerned about political and civil liberties,
precisely the kinds of rights that affirmed their own identity as the har-
bingers of a new order. They were supported by an independent press
that, while contracting after the first years of multiparty democracy, was
admirably forthright in exposing ruling politicians' self-serving tactics.[13]
Paradoxically, however, these interventions maintained the discourse
that self-styled democrats were most comfortable with — a discourse on
political and civil liberties. On numerous occasions during the first
decade of multiparty democracy, the ruling UDF retorted that it had
played a leading role in dismantling Banda's autocracy and continued to
protect Malawians' "hard-won freedoms." A common strategy for leading
politicians was to turn the tables by highlighting activists' dependence on
external donors. Cycles of dispute thereby followed, with little scope for
an expansion of the terms of those disputes.[14]

Such was the impact of political history that alternative imaginings
were not readily available to intellectuals and politicians. Malawi's post-

colonial era had been remarkable in the region for its complete exclusion from socialist experiments. Whereas Mozambique, Tanzania, Zambia, and Zimbabwe adopted various aspects of socialist ideologies, Malawians harboring them could operate only in exile during Banda's regime and had little impact on the developments in the country. On the other hand, the facility with which the neighboring countries were able to discard socialist ideologies during the 1990s was matched by former exiles' enthusiasm for individual freedoms. Chapters 5 and 6 describe how an NGO they founded had an agenda that was compatible with neoliberal reforms. The few NGOs that had economic issues in their focus, notably the Economics Association of Malawi and the Malawi Economic Justice Network, were as averse to field-based collaboration and advocacy as human rights NGOs were. Their agenda was to offer professional economists' independent analysis of the national budget and macroeconomic issues, patently valuable service but not designed to mobilize the poor.

Crucial to this situation of human rights were the expatriate representatives of donor agencies, the most obvious embodiments of transnational governance in Malawi. As elsewhere in the postcolonial world, foreign nationals working as expatriates did not normally offer their opinions for public scrutiny. An exception was foreign diplomats, whose views on Malawi's developments were sought by the press and eagerly discussed by many Malawians. Donors preferred to represent themselves as "partners" and often employed Malawians as deputies in their country offices, available to act as the public faces of these agencies. As will become clear in the subsequent chapters, by funding projects and NGOs that focused on political and civil liberties and by ignoring the effects of other kinds of interventions, such as legal aid, donor agencies were complicit in maintaining the status quo. The European Union–funded project on civic education, with its incomparably extensive reach and resources, was an example of a quite deliberate silencing of those interests that might have revealed the threat that a different sense of human rights posed to neoliberalism.

Like human rights activists, expatriate officials may have begun with genuine intentions to transform Malawi's structural inequalities. Just as activists were embedded in particular circumstances that blinded them to the limited relevance of their own interests, so too were most expatriates predisposed to live highly circumscribed lives in Malawi. Working for donor agencies, they typically lived in the affluent parts of urban areas, mixing with other expatriates during their spare time, surrounded by domestic servants, often the only Malawians with whom they were able to establish some measure of familiarity during their stints in the country (see also chapter 5). A relation between a servant and a master, or between a maid and a madam, was a poor substitute for lived experience among the impoverished majority, never compensated by "field trips" in which donors' lack of language skills became especially apparent. It remains rare to find an expatriate who has made an effort to learn the national language of Malawi, let alone its other indigenous languages. The most frequent excuse I have heard is that expatriates see no reason to learn a language that they will never need outside Malawi. This book lays bare some of the consequences of this attitude.

All the prisoners of freedom mentioned above — and the organizations that are in the empirical focus of this book — are primarily secular in orientation. This focus can be seen to introduce a bias to the study, given that Christian organizations played a major role in Malawi's democratization. The majority of Malawians are Christians, and Islam as the second largest faith commands a following of about 12 percent of the population. As mentioned in the introduction, the new era in Malawi is commonly seen to have dawned with the Lenten Letter of the country's Catholic bishops in 1992 (see, e.g., Newell 1995). Churches remained vocal critics of ruling politicians in "democratic" Malawi, and both Presbyterian and Catholic clergy, representing the leading mainstream denominations, issued a continuous flow of critical "pastoral letters" during the decade after the transition (see Englund 2000; Ott 2000; Ross 2004). While individual religious leaders were susceptible to political patronage throughout the Muluzi era, churches as institutions were remarkably consistent as watchdogs of democracy and, if anything, grew more united as the cynicism of the regime became more apparent. The contrast with Zimbabwe, where civil society also found leadership in Christian churches, is illuminating (see Dorman 2002, 2003). Different Christian organizations, even within the Catholic community, came to swear allegiance to different initiatives during the run-up to the constitutional referendum in 2000, making the voice of Christian churches less clear in Zimbabwean public life than it was in Malawi.[15]

A good example of churches' activism in Malawi was the opposition to the UDF's attempts to remove the limits on the number of terms that the state president could stay in office. The introduction pointed out the fearless activism in which several organizations, both secular and religious, participated during 2001–2. With Muluzi banning all public demonstrations on the issue and the UDF appearing at times as formidable as Banda's MCP before the transition,[16] the churches from mainstream to many charismatic denominations offered an unrivaled infra-structure of dissent and courage. Indeed, such is their role as watchdogs of democracy in Malawi that Kenneth Ross sees them holding almost "a monopoly of civil society activism" (2004, 105). His concern is whether this indicates a failure in the development of Malawi's civil society.

Ross's concern may seem unfounded if it is observed that a network of about forty human rights, women's, youth, church, and media organiza-tions constituted Malawi's Human Rights Consultative Committee in 2002. Moreover, the evidence in this book on secular organizations shows that they are by no means inconsequential agents in Malawi's civil society. Perhaps a more crucial concern is whether church activism carries any prospects for a wider set of issues to be addressed in human rights dis-course. Ross (2004, 104) is hopeful, reporting that the silence of the churches on economic issues during the early years of multiparty democ-racy has changed into a greater awareness among the clergy. Yet at the level of public statements — from "pastoral letters" to press releases — there is nothing new in the churches' comments on the exploitation of Malawians. The Catholic bishops' letter in 1992 already lamented the growing gap between the rich and the poor. More significant is the churches' virtual incapability to launch concrete programs and cam-paigns to debate and revise neoliberal economic policies. Interventions on this front have been haphazard and localized, ranging from microcredit schemes, in line with the neoliberal insistence on self-empowerment, to more radical attempts to institute economic and social justice, such as the initiative of expatriate priests in a tobacco-growing area to organize ten-ants into a union (Englund 2000, 588–589). The economic situation of the local clergy themselves has hardly improved over the years, keeping their concerns focused on personal survival and security (see VonDoepp 2002).

Muluzi's blatant abuse of personal and public resources for buying support did direct church leaders' attention to his management of the economy. They were not alone, however, in condemning his handouts, and popular reflections on the issue extended from mere moral consid-erations, as expressed by the clergy, to concrete suggestions of proper policies. Time and again, I was told by both urban and rural poor in Malawi that Muluzi's gifts were much less desirable than economic poli-cies that would have benefited the nation as a whole. People frequently arrived at innovative calculations of how many millions of kwacha Muluzi had spent on gifts and patronage during a given week and the extent to which those millions could have decreased the price of fertilizer in the country. The removal of subsidies on agricultural inputs after the democratic transition had come as a shock to ordinary Malawians, most of whom, whether in town or in village (Englund 2002d), depended on cultivation for their food security. The clergy's preoccupation with civil and political liberties failed to bring the question of livelihoods to the public arena that they had helped to expand since autocratic rule. While Malawians remained as resolutely Christian as ever, mainstream denominations may have seen a certain alienation between the top clergy and the laity, with the spiritual security offered in Pentecostal and charismatic churches attracting new adherents (see Englund 2000, 2001b, 2003, 2004a).

These developments in Malawi's popular Christianity indicate yet another challenge to a human rights discourse that puts an emphasis on individual freedoms. Prisoners of freedom are unlikely to accept discourses on debt, obligation, and entitlement within the realm of the conceivable in this situation of human rights, even when some of these alternatives are voiced in Christian idioms that they otherwise cherish. The situation of human rights delineates a sphere of governance in which public debate has to conform to predetermined standards of what is worth saying. Yet to stop the analysis there is to give the last word to power. How freedom can retain any actual meaning, in the lives of both human rights activists and the impoverished majority, is a puzzle that must not disappear into the fury of critique.

CHAPTER 2

Rights as Freedoms

Translating Human Rights

Contemplating human rights in the abstract is a luxury that only the most isolated occupants of the ivory tower can afford. People generally articulate, claim, and resist human rights in real-life situations. Moral or cultural relativism does not need to underlie the view that the understandings of human rights are particular. Their particularity is evident not only in relativist arguments but also in the ways in which official definitions of human rights can be highly selective. Whereas the Universal Declaration of Human Rights, for example, recognizes civil, political, social, and economic rights alike, various governments have emphasized only some rights at the expense of others. When the ambassador of the United States to the United Nations dismissed the provisions of the Universal Declaration on social and economic rights as "a letter to Santa Claus" (quoted in Chomsky 1999, 21), universalism was sacrificed to political expediency. The study of language use, enhanced by ethnographic witnessing, opens up a possibility of considering *how* human rights might actually be universal (Hastrup 2001a). Studying the translation of human rights discourse presents a particularly good opportunity to reach beyond both politically expedient relativism and unvarnished universalism. Who controls the translation and decides what the appropriate notions are? How does the political history of a country influence the translation that gets adopted there?

Translation in an African context presents a set of salient empirical problems, not least because the vast majority of Africans depend on national and vernacular languages for efficient communication (Bamgbose

47

2000; Mazrui and Mazrui 1998). Human rights discourse, as a relatively recent phenomenon associated with the post–Cold War wave of democratization, has arrived through official languages inherited from colonial rulers. As this chapter shows for Malawi and Zambia, major political and cultural issues are raised by the way in which the discourse is translated, even though these issues have received little official and academic attention.[1] Of fundamental importance is that translation in these countries has taken place as a "top-down" exercise, with no evidence of attempts to consult a broad cross-section of native speakers before launching a translation for human rights. What Steven Archibald and Paul Richards (2002) have called "local cultures of human rights" have been allowed little space to develop and to influence the introduction of a new discourse. Instead, activists, politicians, journalists, and others spearheading the translation have taken their particular interest in democratization as a universal concern. They have, accordingly, translated rights as *freedoms,* with a particular emphasis on political and civil liberties.

More than the choice of lexical items underlies the political and cultural challenges to translating human rights discourse. Contemporary discussions about human rights, whatever the country or society in which they are held, are remarkable for the extent to which they presuppose abstraction, the ability to apply the same notions and principles across a wide variety of actual situations. While research on what might constitute equivalent terms for "human rights" in African languages is scant, it appears plausible to assume that the meaning of such equivalents has often been situational rather than abstract. For example, the Kiswahili word for "right" is *haki,* which, according to Diane Ciekawy, is "glossed as a privilege, claim, or right held by a person in a particular circumstance, or a legitimate decision by a person in position of authority such as the supreme being or a king" (2000, 24). The Luganda expression for "democracy" contains the word *eddembe,* whose connotations include "liberty" and "peace" (Karlström 1996, 485–486). It is combined with *ery'obuntu* to specify "the people" as the custodians of that liberty in a democracy. Yet *obuntu* differs from an inclusive notion of "the people." It is used situationally as an ethical and civic ideal rather than as an abstraction that assumes intrinsic equality among all individuals.

The Kiswahili and Luganda examples are a poor substitute for a systematic survey of African-language equivalents of "human rights." Yet they illustrate a point that has often been made about the introduction of legal language. It replaces relationships with rules; situational considerations, with abstract principles (see, e.g., Conley and O'Barr 1990). The distinction between the jural and the moral in some African languages (Shipton 2003, 62) is subverted in the post–Cold War preoccupation with human rights. The preoccupation has assumed a decisively legalist content. In contrast to the Kiswahili and Luganda understandings of rights as things that are associated with moral authority, itself unevenly distributed in society, the legalist discourse on human rights asserts universal equality before the law. As the supreme arbiter of conflicts and disputes, the law is regarded as being above any actual political and cultural factor influencing those conflicts and disputes (Kanyongolo 1998, 2004). Interestingly, a similar process of abstraction has been observed among those who seek to oppose human rights discourse by appealing to cultures and traditions. Rather than situating culture in shifting everyday practices, "culture talk" often revolves around an abstraction that is claimed to define a people's essential characteristics (Cowan et al. 2001). More often than not, and in postcolonial no less than in colonial Africa, such an abstraction serves elite privileges rather than the democratic expectations of rights talk (Chanock 2000).

As this book shows, human rights discourse — even when asserting all individuals as equals — can be deprived of its democratizing potential and made to serve particular interests in society. The problem, patently, is intrinsic not to particular words themselves but to translation as a cultural and political process, its own situational characteristics obscured by human rights activists' commitment to abstraction and universalism. In Chichewa, which is the sole national language of Malawi and, known as Chinyanja, one of the seven national languages of Zambia, the established translation summons up rights as individual freedoms — a highly consequential, albeit scarcely premeditated, move. *Ufulu wachibadwidwe* hinges on the meanings of *ufulu* as "freedom," "liberty," and "independence," defined by the recent Chichewa/Chinyanja monolingual dictionary as "an opportunity to live freely, happily and without fear" (Centre for Language Studies 2000, 345).[2] The adjectival *wachibadwidwe* uses the verb *kubadwa,* "to be born," to specify such freedom as the individual's birth right.

Pascal Kishindo (2000, 25), a Malawian linguist, has suggested that, despite being offered as a translation of "human rights," *ufulu wachibadwidwe* is actually a new coinage. As such, the way in which Malawians and Zambians arrived at this particular coinage offers insights into the politics of translation, as do its appearances in the Chichewa/Chinyanja versions of international human rights documents and national laws. While pursuing such insights, one must keep in mind that *ufulu,* like most lexical items, has multiple connotations and can be used to advance competing interests. Kishindo (2000) has analyzed the shift in its primary connotations from national independence to personal freedom and liberty. Although *ufulu* continues to be used for independence from colonial rule, the transition to multiparty politics in the early 1990s made freedom from postcolonial dictatorship a more urgent topic in political discourse, with the plural form *maufulu,* "freedoms," gaining wider currency. Its equivalent in Kiswahili, *uhuru,* has had a similar trajectory, evident in its application by some women for transformed gender relations (Talle 1998, 36). Later in this chapter I examine, however, how the emancipatory potential of *ufulu* is qualified by, among other things, another central concept in the Chichewa/Chinyanja discourse on human rights — *udindo,* translating as "responsibility."

The idea of responsibility merits attention, because it has proven a convenient construct for human rights activists, politicians, and journalists to counter the criticisms of their excessive emphasis on individual freedoms. Just as the idea of freedom can be conjured up to advance different political agendas, so too is it necessary to ask *what kind* of responsibility a particular human rights discourse exhorts. Several generations of political philosophers have understood rights and responsibilities to be entwined, and liberal egalitarianism has not been confined to individual freedoms. It has involved a commitment to securing positive rights to economic justice (Kelly 2005, 12–13). That such a commitment can be expressed through the idea of freedom has become apparent on various occasions during the past century, perhaps most famously in the "Four Freedoms" proposed by Franklin D. Roosevelt in his 1941 address to the United States Congress (see, e.g., Ishay 2004, 213). Freedom from want was as important as, among others, freedom of expression. Insofar as a particularly impoverished version of freedom has been promoted by the Chichewa/Chinyanja discourse, it has been more compatible with a neoliberal economic and political order than with the legacies of liberalism per se.

The Predominance of Freedoms

During my fieldwork in Malawi and Zambia, no one would claim authorship for *ufulu wachibadwidwe.* In many cases, my inquiries into the origins of this construct were received with some surprise. Few human rights activists had thought of how its semantic content as individual freedom and liberty might constrain popular understandings of human rights discourse. Many of those whom I consulted on the origins of the construct — activists, politicians, journalists, linguists — stubbornly maintained the equivalence between *maufulu* and "rights" until my questions concerning, for example, the expression of socioeconomic rights created a need for alternative lexical items. Kishindo's (2000) argument that *ufulu wachibadwidwe* is a coinage was not generally known.

That the construct of *ufulu wachibadwidwe* was taken for granted is understandable for mere lexical and idiomatic reasons. Although the construct is new, it draws on the established political connotations of *ufulu*, now situated in the context of a struggle against postcolonial dictatorship. The adjectival *wachibadwidwe*, on the other hand, is an old idiom used to express a trait or a quality that belongs or ought to belong to a person as a defining characteristic. John Gwengwe, one of the renowned novelists writing in Chichewa, described in 1965 how a character's behavior "indicated a distressed person who lacked the peace one is born with" *(kusonyeza munthu wankhawa ndi wosowa mtendere wachibadwidwe)* ([1965] 1998, 46). *Ufulu wachibadwidwe* as "the freedom one is born with," therefore, makes sense idiomatically, but its capacity to act as a medium for expressing a whole range of rights is less convincing. The critical issue is not so much to replace the construct with alternatives as to allow those alternatives to exist in the first place. The story of how human rights became hijacked by particular interests includes the virtual disappearance of alternative translations and coinages.

While probing the background to the dominant position of *ufulu wachibadwidwe*, I have come to appreciate the significance of two factors. On the one hand, Malawi's important role in standardizing Chichewa during the postcolonial period has contributed to the remarkable uniformity with which Chichewa speakers in different countries have adopted this particular construct. On the other hand, the political history of the countries in which Chichewa is spoken, and particularly of Malawi, pushed some aspirations rather than others to the forefront during the transition to multiparty democracy. For those who led the opposition against the one-party rule, it was expedient to maintain the public discourse on these aspirations also after the transition.

Chichewa/Chinyanja rose to prominence as a lingua franca in colonial Malawi and Zambia and continued to flourish after the independence of these countries. In Zambia, it provided a useful medium among migrants, only recently beginning to lose its leading position to Bemba among the officially recognized Zambian languages (Posner 2003).[3] In postcolonial Malawi, the quest for standardizing and developing Chichewa became particularly intense as a part of Kamuzu Banda's project of nation building (Vail and White 1989; Kishindo 1994). After renaming the language as Chichewa at the 1968 convention of the Malawi Congress Party, the regime enhanced its status by establishing the Chichewa Board in 1972 to standardize and develop the language (Kishindo 2001). Its role as a subject and, during the first four years, the medium of instruction in the school system also advanced Chichewa/Chinyanja as a truly national language. In Zambia, the language is a compulsory subject in the national curriculum only in Eastern Province and the city of Lusaka.

Banda's language policy, now seen as an ethnic ploy in the guise of nation building, caused resentment among some Malawians and was discarded after the democratic transition (Kishindo 1998). Its legacy remains considerable, however, in the unrivaled position of Chichewa as a lingua franca, with around 70 percent of Malawians giving it as their primary language in the 1998 population and housing census (National Statistical Office 2002).[4] Accordingly, despite opening itself up to Chitumbuka, Chiyao, Chilomwe, Chisena, and Chitonga after the transition, the Malawi Broadcasting Corporation (MBC) kept Chichewa as the main language, its share being over 70 percent of the daily nineteen hours of broadcast on Radio One.[5] Since the MBC has remained the only nationwide electronic medium in Malawi, its influence in coining and sustaining specific uses of the language has been considerable. Indeed, two journalists at the MBC, who retired in the 1990s, were named on several occasions during my research as the most likely inventors of *ufulu wachibadwidwe*. Broadcasters responsible for Chinyanja in Zambia likewise stressed the influence of the MBC in standardizing this particular construct as the translation for the term "human rights."

While the dismantling of the Chichewa Board was one outcome of the democratic transition, it did not significantly threaten the dominant position of the language and Malawi's role in standardizing it. As can be seen below in my discussion of translated documents, Zambian translations indicated more variety in the choice of lexical items than Malawian translations, until the Zambian ones, too, became rather uniform. The competing notions in Zambia did not, however, represent clear alternatives to *ufulu wachibadwidwe*. *Danga* was perhaps the most common, sharing some of the semantic field with *mwayi* and *mpata,* all connoting "opportunity" and "occasion."

It has been only after specifically questioning Malawian and Zambian activists and academics that I have been given alternatives that are less tied to ideas of individual freedoms. One of these had been mentioned in the small circles of academics and activists in the early 1990s, but it was eventually rejected for defining rights as unduly concrete requirements. *Zoyenerera zachibadwidwe* is based on the verb *kuyenera,* "to deserve" or "to have to," and the construct refers to all those elements that a person deserves or needs as a human being.[6] The connotation, in other words, is *entitlements,* and it is revealing that not until 2003 did the notion reappear in a rare critique of freedoms *(maufulu)* as the dominant concept of human rights in Malawi (see Tenthani 2003). The author of this article, in a popular magazine, lamented that "only one side of human rights had changed" *(gawo limodzi lokha la human rights ndi lomwe linasintha),* calling attention to the fact that freedoms did not in themselves erase socioeconomic inequalities. Although the focus of the article was not on the choice of lexical items, its critical argument, by necessitating the use of *zoyenerera zachibadwidwe,* indicated how much may have been obscured by the single-minded reliance on *ufulu wachibadwidwe.*

Translation and Inequality

Despite its idiomatic value, *ufulu wachibadwidwe* would not have assumed a dominant position without supporting specific interests in the democratic transition. It is now widely accepted that the transition of the early 1990s in countries such as Malawi and Zambia put an emphasis on achieving political and civil freedoms.[7] In Malawi, many UDF leaders had held powerful positions in the MCP regime, which also made the emphasis on the new freedoms politically expedient. By quickly cloaking themselves in the garment of liberal democracy, these leaders preempted efforts to investigate their actions in the past (Ross 1998; Mapanje 2002). The MBC also switched its rhetoric virtually overnight, thereby remaining the mouthpiece of the ruling party (Kayambazinthu and Moyo 2002). The rhetoric of freedoms virtually replaced the rhetoric of unity and obedience.

My observations later in this book will show how Malawian elites, and those who mimic their ways, often assert the supremacy of English vis-à-vis Chichewa and other African languages. It is important to see the fallacy of the corollary that African languages are ill-equipped to express the idea of human rights. My discussion above not only indicates the challenge that African languages may pose to the abstract notions of human rights; it also demonstrates that both "freedoms" and "entitlements" as constitutive meanings of "rights" can be given Chichewa equivalents. If freedoms have come to dominate the Chichewa concept of human rights, it is not, therefore, because they are the only possible connotation the language can offer. Nor, as already alluded, is freedom as the individual's birthright the only connotation that the idea of freedom can evoke. The critical issue is why and how *this* connotation has imposed its individualizing context on the Chichewa/Chinyanja discourse on human rights.

The interface between political history and translation indicates that at issue is a somewhat different form of linguistic inequality than what theorists of translation have highlighted. Their focus has been on the inequality of languages, on the geopolitical reasons for the forcible transformation of "weak" languages by "strong" ones (Asad 1986; Venuti 1998; Yengoyan 2003). In opposition to that, critics have long advocated translators' openness to transform their own languages (see de Man 1986). In this regard, translation may give way to more appropriate metaphors of intercultural communication, such as "conversation" (Pálsson 1995), stressing the continuity of lived experience (Ingold 1993).[8] However, while these critics explore relations among languages (or cultures), the issue here is relations *within* a language group. The process whereby a particular translation has assumed a dominant position bespeaks linguistic inequality in which only some people have the power to determine what is worth saying (Maryns and Blommaert 2002). The possibility of a conversation within a language is curtailed by the particular interests that the powerful side has taken in the human rights discourse. In order to demonstrate that the powerful side does not consist only of politicians and state functionaries, I now turn to an analysis of key documents in the Chichewa/Chinyanja discourse on human rights.

Poor Translations for Poor People

Since the democratic transition in the early 1990s, a diverse group of institutions, employing an equally diverse group of translators, has been engaged in translating human rights documents and instruments in Malawi and Zambia. Both governmental and non-governmental organizations have taken up this task, with United Nations organizations also making a significant contribution. Translations into so-called local languages have provided one justification for many NGOs' existence, since the translations by government departments have generally been confined to very few documents. Translations have not, however, been a priority for most donors of aid, and the work of translation has often been linked to broader programs of civic education (see chapters 3 and 4) or, in the case of some organizations, abandoned in favor of other activities. One consequence of the lack of resources is the rather haphazard manner in which translations have been commissioned and carried out. While professional linguists and translators have been used in some cases, organizations have more often chosen to cut their expenditure by selecting translators among their own personnel or by hiring, for example, secondary school teachers, whose fees are relatively low. Why has not the quality of translations caused more concern in Malawi and Zambia?

My interviews with human rights activists in the two countries revealed that insufficient funds were not the only factor limiting the work of translation. While nobody would deny the need for translations in human rights advocacy, and many expressed the desire to see more effort in this area, few appeared to regard translation as a priority. On the one hand, many activists and officers in both governmental and non-governmental organizations shared the usual lay person's idea of translation as a straightforward matter of explaining an issue expressed in one language in the words of another. Any native speaker with sufficient knowledge of English would qualify for the task, an attitude that also accounts for activists' failure to see the relevance of lexicographical research before embarking on translating a new discourse. One officer in a Zambian NGO, for example, observed that after employing a Chinyanja expert at the Curriculum Development Centre,[9] she and her colleagues thought the expert's translation was too technical and decided to do the work themselves. On the other hand, the haphazard approach to translation also betrays a patronizing attitude. The subsequent chapters offer ethnographic witnessing to show how status distinctions toward the assumed recipients of human rights discourse influenced many activists' and officers' work. In other words, activists and officers saw their fluency in human rights discourse as an index of their own expertise. Translation as consultation or conversation with the impoverished recipients was, therefore, never given serious consideration.

By granting to themselves the tasks of both translation and its quality control, activists and officers risked producing inaccurate translations. Their assumed expertise, moreover, mitigated fears of a backlash, because those who were expected to receive the translations were rarely in a position to voice public criticism. In Malawi and Zambia, no mechanism existed to ensure that the translations were not as poor as the people who were supposed to read them. Chinyanja translations in Zambia are especially problematic because of the country's lack of a language policy encouraging the standardization and development of African languages. The situation in Malawi is better after decades of official promotion of Chichewa/Chinyanja as the sole national language. The now defunct Chichewa Board standardized, among other things, its orthography (see Chichewa Board 1990), which has been systematically implemented in schoolbooks and most works of fiction. Although Malawian and Zambian linguists have recently agreed on harmonizing the orthographies of the language in the two countries, their work still awaits official recognition and implementation (see, e.g., Bwanali 2001; Chisoni 2001; Mwale 2001).[10]

The lack of standardization is, however, a dubious excuse for careless production. One instance, particularly in Zambia, is texts that are internally inconsistent in their spelling. A glossy leaflet, designed to impress those who are unfamiliar with the language, prepared by the Zambia Civic Education Association on electing leaders,[11] for example, presents no fewer than three different versions of the expression "we the people of the country" (citizens) in its opening section: *anthu amuziko; ife anthu amudziko;* and *ise anthu amdziko.* The word for "country," *dziko,* appears in two different forms, as does the locative "in," *mu.* The pronoun "we," *ife,* also assumes the deviant form of *ise.* Throughout, the leaflet presents considerable inconsistencies in how words are divided, sometimes resulting in nonsensical constructions. Even the same sentence can include an inconsistency, such as *Tiyenera ku pennyetsetsa ndi kusankha* (we need to watch carefully and to choose). Here the sign of the infinitive form, *ku,* is first spelled separately *(ku pennyetsetsa)*[12] and then conjointly *(kusankha).* The pronoun prefixes show similar inconsistency, with the pronoun sometimes spelled separately *(ti sankhe,* let us choose), and other times, in accordance with conventional spelling, conjointly *(tidziwe,* let us know).

Another example of sheer negligence that hinders swift understanding comes from a text published by the Permanent Human Rights Commission, a governmental institution in Zambia. Its paper on ten human rights standards for law enforcement officials is based on a document by Amnesty International.[13] The internal inconsistencies of the Chinyanja translation are again extensive, with the same word roots appearing in different forms and contributing to an onerous reading experience. Not only has the translator coined a peculiar construct for "minorities," *timagulu tating'onoting'ono,* "tiny little groups"; its spelling is also rendered as *timagulu tin'go no ting'ono.* No appeal to a lack of standard orthography will explain the illogic of this spelling, even within the confines of this particular text. Moreover, the root *ng'ono,* "small, little," appears later as *ngono,* thereby losing its velar nasal *ng'* — in its simplicity a rather inexcusable mistake.

Many more phonetic and orthographic anomalies could be furnished as examples of careless translation and production. What makes them significant is their rare public scrutiny in Malawi and Zambia. It is hard to believe that such elementary and irritating mistakes would be accepted in documents published in English. When the language is the principal medium of a predominantly poor and uneducated population, attention to detail is apparently less crucial, for readers' difficulties in comprehending the texts can always be attributed to their limited skills in literacy.

Disempowerment through Translation

A comparison between different translations of the Universal Declaration of Human Rights reveals even more clearly how Chichewa/Chinyanja speakers can be disempowered by inaccurate translation. In the absence of coordination, at least two very different translations of the declaration exist, one provided by the United Nations Information Centre in Zambia and the other by the Malawi Human Rights Resource Centre, an NGO.[14] While somewhat abridged and simplified translations may be inevitable in a document meant for wide circulation, interesting questions are what translators omit from the original and how inaccurate translations may compromise readers' capacity for emancipatory interpretations. For instance, the subsection 4 of Article 23 reads,

Everyone has the right to form and to join trade unions for the protection of his interests.

Because Chichewa/Chinyanja does not distinguish between genders, it avoids the sexist connotation of "his interests" in the original. However, neither of the translations attempts to capture the notion of interest, and the Zambian translation even fails to specify the issue of workers' rights. The Malawian translation, followed by my free translation of it into English, reads,

Aliyense ali ndi ufulu woyambitsa kaya kulowa m'bungwe loimila antchito.

Everyone has the freedom to start or to join an organization that represents workers.

The Zambian translation, again followed by my free translation, reads,

Munthu aliyense ali ndi danga lokhala membala wa bungwe liri lonse lothandiza pa umoyo wake.

Every person has the opportunity to be a member of any organization that assists in his/her well-being.

While both translations omit "interests," the version provided by the Malawian NGO is clearly closer to the intent in the original than the Zambian version is. Yet both versions fail to give a specific equivalent to the economic and social right that workers are said to have, with the Malawian version using the generic *ufulu*, "freedom," and the Zambian version using *danga*, "opportunity," in its stead. Moreover, the Zambian version uses *umoyo*, which translates as "well-being" and "health," thereby obscuring what specific right is at issue in this particular subsection.

The translation of notions that touch on economic and social rights can be, as I discuss in more detail below, a particularly revealing instance of disempowerment. Article 22 of the Universal Declaration has this to say about economic, social, and cultural rights:

Everyone, as a member of society, has the right to social security and is entitled to realization, through national effort and international co-operation and in accordance with the organization and resources of each State, of the economic, social, and cultural rights indispensable for his dignity and the free development of his personality.

This formulation is complicated, calling for some simplification in a translation that is prepared for the widest possible audience. The official English version, moreover, contains notions that may confound any Chichewa/Chinyanja translator. "Social security," for example, properly belongs to a form of modern state that has the capacity to ensure its citizens' well-being when they face various obstacles to sustaining their livelihoods independently. "Social security," if it has any meaning at all in countries like Malawi and Zambia, denotes, in the first place, kin relations and other nonstate structures (Anders 2002). Similarly, "the free development of personality," despite appearing in an article on cultural rights, may not be a universally meaningful notion. While "personality" finds Chichewa/Chinyanja equivalents in *khalidwe*, connoting "conduct" and "behavior," and *umunthu*, connoting "humanity," its "free development" is likely to present a considerable challenge to a Chichewa/Chinyanja translator. The free development of personality is not necessarily a positive achievement in a cultural setting in which people gain their dignity not as mutually independent individuals but by attending to their social relationships.[15]

Translators even with the best intentions, therefore, face major challenges in expressing certain notions in their own languages. The Malawian and Zambian translations of the Universal Declaration have understandably omitted some aspects of the complicated Article 22. The interesting question for assessing its empowering potential is how, or whether, these translations seek to convey economic and social rights as "entitlements" that could permit making claims vis-à-vis the state and its foreign partners. This is how the Malawian version has rendered Article 22, followed by my free translation:

Aliyense ali ndi ufulu wopeza chithandizo cha boma pakakhala zosowetsetsa pa umoyo mowelekeza m'mene boma lingathe kuthandiza, komanso ufulu wa chuma ndi zomuthandiza pomusungila ulemu, chitukuko pa moyo ndi umunthu wake.

Everyone has the freedom to get assistance from the state when well-being is undermined in accordance with the extent to which the state can assist, as well as the freedom of economic activity and of what helps him/her to foster respect, development in life and his/her humanity.

While the omission of "social security" and "the free development of personality" is understandable in the light of the above discussion, it is remarkable how little effort the translator has made to convey a sense of entitlements in this article. The latter part of the translation, in particular, dilutes the original meaning of economic rights by effectively defending everyone's private economic activities. *Chuma* is not only a term for the concept of "economy"; it is also commonly used for "wealth" and "property." Combined with *ufulu,* "freedom," it hardly conveys an empowering notion that could be deployed to challenge social and economic inequalities. The assertiveness of the original formulation of economic and social rights as "indispensable" is also lost when the translation uses the generic *zomuthandiza pomusungila,* "that what helps him/her to foster." The prefix *zo-* refers to the word *zinthu,* "things," which is often unnecessary to mention in a sentence. Rather than specifying the entitlements that foster a person's development and humanity, the translation prefers to convey them as indefinite "things."

In one respect, however, the Malawian version does bear some resemblance to the original in English, allocating responsibility to the state, although failing to mention "international co-operation." The Zambian version, by contrast, not only omits the entire issue of the state, its foreign partners, and economic rights; it also muddles an already complicated text to the point of being incomprehensible:

Munthu aliyense pokhala nzika ya dziko ali ndi danga lolandira citetezo pa nchito za cisangalalo ca moyo wace ndi kuti ayenera kuzindikira za ufulu wace pa nchito za chuma, cisangalalo ndi miyambo cinthu comwe cili cofunikira kwambiri pa ubwino ndi citukuko ca moyo wace.

Every person as a citizen of a country has the opportunity to receive protection in improving his/her life, and he/she must understand his/her freedom in the

economy, entertainment and customs, a thing that is very important in the good-
ness and development of his/her life.[16]

"It is an established fact in Translation Studies," Susan Bassnett writes,
"that if a dozen translators tackle the same poem, they will produce a
dozen different versions" ([1980] 2002, 33). Yet beneath the variations, she
observes, ought to exist an invariant core that is common to all translations of a single work. Human rights discourse, while clearly not poetry,
must also allow for some flexibility in the work of translation. What the
above examples demonstrate, however, are unacceptable levels of careless
and inappropriate translation. The fact that translation into Chichewa/
Chinyanja and other African languages in Malawi and Zambia is not considered a priority, and hence is not allocated enough resources, makes
inaccuracies inevitable. For those who never have the opportunity to
compare the translations with the original texts, human rights discourse
risks becoming an alienating and irrelevant novelty. As has been seen, it
can also become a disempowering discourse, if translators omit its key features. Indeed, studying the extent to which *maufulu,* individual "freedoms," has established itself as the translation for all kinds of "rights" takes
us beyond inaccuracies in particular renderings. Whose interests are
served by this translation?

The Erasure of Alternatives

Human rights discourse gives rise to claims while setting a frame in which
those claims can be expressed. In this regard, how the discourse is introduced into particular languages is highly consequential, because this
also influences what kinds of claims people can make by using their languages. This is the conundrum that evokes the inequalities within a language that were mentioned above. The translation of human rights discourse is informed by the translator's interests. In Malawi and Zambia,
the recruitment of translators, as mentioned, was based less on their professional qualifications as translators than on the commissioning organizations' own interests. Consultation, or a systematic pretesting of translations before they were published, was not practiced in Malawi and
Zambia. Inequality had, as such, left its mark on the discourse even before
it had been deployed to address inequalities in society.

Translations do not frame local discourses on human rights simply
through their lexical choices. Also important are the kinds of documents

and instruments that have been chosen for translation. During at least the first ten years after the democratic transition, only the most general documents and instruments were translated into Chichewa/Chinyanja, such as the Universal Declaration of Human Rights, the African Charter on Human and People's Rights, the United Nations Convention on the Rights of the Child, and, only in Malawi, the new democratic constitution. More specific new laws, some of which stipulated progressive reforms in the field of social and economic rights, were available only in English.[17] This narrow selection of translations has also been conducive to civic educators' focus on political and civil freedoms, as the next two chapters will show.

In the interest of brevity, my discussion here must be confined to the translations of three instruments, namely, the African Charter, the Rights of the Child, and the Constitution of the Republic of Malawi, all prepared in Malawi. These documents demonstrate the dominant position that *maufulu,* individual "freedoms," has assumed as the equivalent of "rights." The particular interest of each of these documents revolves around a different issue. The African Charter presents an effort to express collective as well as individual rights. The Rights of the Child declares children legal and moral subjects on a par with adults. The Constitution, while by no means restricted to stipulating various individual freedoms, has been presented by most Malawian activists as a document that almost exclusively focuses on political and civil liberties. As an illustration, I also analyze a series of leaflets produced by a Malawian NGO. In fact, the predominance of *ufulu* appears so complete that even instruments stipulating economic rights, if translated, would be likely to entertain the notion of freedom. A leaflet by the Civil Liberties Committee, a Malawian NGO, has suggested this by referring to the International Covenant on Economic, Social, and Cultural Rights as *Pangano lokhudza ufulu pazachuma ndi chikhalidwe,* "agreement concerning freedom in the economy and culture."[18]

The African Charter, approved by the Organization of African Unity in 1981, has been hailed as a human rights instrument that takes the African cultural and political contexts seriously (see Lindholt 2001).[19] A major way in which this is done is by defining collective rights instead of merely individual rights. The notion of "peoples" appears frequently in the charter, granting attention to the possibility that persons may be exposed to injury not only as individuals but also as the bearers of particular social identities. The Chichewa translation, published by the Malawi Human Rights Resource Centre, fails to seize on this alternative way of conceiving rights. The title reads *Pangano la mu Africa la ufulu wachibadwidwe ndi wa anthu*, "African agreement on the freedom that one is born with and of the people." "Peoples" becomes the generic *anthu*, "people," with little to suggest an attempt to conceptualize social diversity. The only place where the translator follows the original intent is in translating Article 19, "All peoples shall be equal; they shall enjoy the same respect and shall have the same rights. Nothing shall justify the domination of a people by another":

Magulu onse a anthu ayenera kukhala ofanana ndi ulemu ofanana ndi ufulu wofanana. Palibe choyenereza kuponderezedwa kwa gulu limodzi ndi gulu lina.

All the groups of people must be equal with similar respect and similar freedom. There is no justification for one group to be repressed by another group.

Apart from the translation of this article, the five other articles on peoples' rights are translated with the word *anthu*, thus calling for individualistic interpretations. For example, the first subsection of Article 22 declares, "All peoples shall have the right to their economic, social, and cultural development with due regard to their freedom and identity, and in the equal enjoyment of the common heritage of mankind." The translation is as follows:

Anthu onse ali ndi ufulu wa ntchito yotukula chuma, ntchito zosamalira miyoyo ya anthu ndi chikhalidwe chawo.

All the people have the freedom to increase wealth, to care for people's lives and their culture.

The translation changes the intent of the article rather more than what simplification would warrant. Especially problematic is the replacement of "peoples" with "all the people," which, when combined with *ufulu*, becomes little else than a declaration of each individual's liberty to unrestrained economic activity. A similar individualizing effect is produced by the use of *ufulu* in the translation of the United Nations Convention of the Rights of Child, from 1989. Published by the United Nations Children's Fund (UNICEF) in Malawi, the translation is reasonably faithful to the original text. It uses, however, *ufulu* as the only equivalent of "right" and makes the child appear as a subject free from parental and other social constraints. The first subsection of Article 13, for example, declares, "The child shall have the right to freedom of expression." Since the Chichewa version uses *ufulu* for "right," it expresses the idea bluntly as "The child has the freedom to express his/her thoughts" (*mwana ali ndi ufulu wolankhula maganizo ake).* While the notion of a rights-bearing subject may always entail some individualizing potential, rights as individual freedoms inflate that potential far beyond the original intent in the declaration. For many Chichewa speakers, it is likely to be especially baffling that the subject of these freedoms is a child.

Documents are, of course, social artifacts, gathering new meanings as they are read and used by diverse subjects (Riles 2001). I discuss below how the emphasis on individual freedoms has led to counterdiscourses that criticize the new democratic era for bringing "too much freedom." Although the self-serving agenda of these counterdiscourses is often obvious, it is worth asking whether the translated human rights discourse actually facilitates such reactions. The idea of the moral person is at the heart of this controversy. Insofar as a person is thought to "grow" *(kukula)* throughout his or her life cycle (Englund 1999, 2002b), children embody prospective accomplishment rather than complete subjectivity in the present. The idea of moral personhood as something acquired rather than intrinsic has posed difficulties in envisaging and defending children's rights, not least in Africa (see, e.g., Last 2000).[20] Yet, the Rights of the Child is also the most widely ratified human rights convention (Lindholt 2001, 125). Whatever universal appeal its acute articles have, inappropriate translations may undermine its applicability in real-life situations. As can be seen below, when children and youths are proclaimed as unequivocally "free," a sense of a runaway world is easily created.

Selective Renderings of the Constitution

Translations require further interventions, such as "civic education" (the topic of the next two chapters), for their effects to be adverse. This can be demonstrated by considering how selective many Malawian activists have been in informing the public about the country's new constitution that came into force in 1995. Its 1997 translation[21] includes twenty-three chapters divided into over two hundred sections, covering, for example, institutions such as the National Assembly, the presidency, the ombudsman, the Human Rights Commission, the Law Commission, the police, the army, and the Reserve Bank. Yet it is chapter 4, entitled "Human Rights" and translated as *Ufulu Wa Anthu* (the freedom of people), that received most of the attention in activists' work during the first decade of democracy. Within this chapter, moreover, of its thirty-two sections only about eight were in the focus of activism and civic education. These eight sections stipulate the freedoms of association, conscience, opinion, expression, the media, information, assembly, and movement. Other sections, pertaining to the responsibilities of the state and to rights to economic and social justice, did not attract similar publicity.

Although the translation of the Constitution is relatively careful, it also subsumes various rights under the concept of *ufulu*. Neither *zoyenerera* nor *zomuyenereza za munthu,* either of which, as noted above, conveys a sense of rights as entitlements, appears in the translated Constitution. Even with this limitation, however, the translation is close enough to the intent of the original to permit activists with the appropriate inclination to challenge structural and historical inequalities in Malawi. The sections 30 and 31 in chapter 4, for example, declare that "all persons and people have a right to development," with the state being assigned the duty to realize this right by using measures such as "equality of opportunity for all in their access to basic resources, education, health services, food, shelter, employment, and infrastructure."[22] The state is also directed to "take measures to introduce reforms aimed at eradicating social injustices and inequalities," while every person is said to "have the right to fair and safe labor practices and to fair remuneration." Despite defining all rights as "freedoms," the translation gives activists enough material to reach beyond political and civil liberties in their advocacy and civic education.

The rare utilization of this material in Malawi can be demonstrated in several ways. While the next chapters base my argument on ethnographic witnessing of events and practices, examples of texts that some NGOs produced are also illuminating. The Centre for Human Rights and Rehabilitation (CHRR), a prominent Malawian human rights NGO, prepared and published a number of Chichewa leaflets and booklets on various constitutional provisions in the late 1990s. The booklet *Ufulu Wachibadwidwe Wa Munthu* (no date) presents a simplified and illustrated version of the Constitution's chapter 4. It provides a short paragraph and a cartoon of all the freedoms mentioned there, but, remarkably, section 30, stipulating the right to development and the duty of the state to realize that right, is wholly omitted. The NGO's series of leaflets, entitled Dziwani Ufulu Wanu (Know Your Freedom), includes some sixteen titles, of which not a single one focuses on issues of poverty and economic inequality. The leaflets cover topics such as various civil liberties, the freedoms *(maufulu)* of women and children, the rule of law, mob justice, and information on preparing a will.

The CHRR has made a major contribution by publishing all this information in Chichewa. However, what are the issues that the focus on civil and political liberties will *not* raise? The focus on individual freedoms may, in point of fact, disempower the vast majority of Malawians by depriving them of key concepts and legal provisions. Obscured is the fact that people generally pursue freedoms from unequal positions. The involvement of the CHRR in this process of disempowerment is both surprising and understandable. It is surprising because the NGO, led by intellectuals who had spent several years in exile, provided an independent and critical voice in Malawi after the political transition (see chapter 5). Yet it is also understandable, because its executive officers were themselves preoccupied with political and civil liberties. The more the ruling politicians appeared to violate these liberties, the more vocal the NGO became. Its high-profile interventions, sometimes in collaboration with other NGOs, were instrumental to subverting such unconstitutional initiatives as the state president's third term in office. At the same time, it also became apparent that these activists' own survival depended on the liberties they defended rather than on economic and social rights. Caught in the cross fire between activists and the government, the majority was left with few advocates of transformations that would eradicate their poverty and deprivation.

Controlling Freedoms

Television Malawi has broadcast a series of educational programs on human rights. One program, repeated several times in 2001 and 2002, showed a High Court judge explaining various freedoms to an audience of secondary school students in the northern town of Mzuzu. During the question time, a male student posed this question to the judge: "My question concerns education, those secondary schools that the government established, known as Community Day Secondary Schools. There are those secondary schools where some teachers are not really qualified, whereas in a school like ours almost all teachers have a degree or a diploma. Could we not say that the freedom of our friends at community schools to get sufficient education is ruined?"[23]

The question alluded to inequalities in education, to the fact that the Malawian government had, since the early 1990s, directed a flood of primary school graduates to so-called Distant Education Centers and, as they came to be known more recently, Community Day Secondary Schools. These students had not qualified to attend the few conventional government schools and were from families that could not afford private education. The proportion of candidates from Community Day Secondary Schools writing the final secondary school examinations rose from 1 percent in 1990 to 51 percent in 1999. Yet while the pass rate in conventional schools was 27.5 percent, only 3.6 percent of the students from these underresourced schools passed the final examinations in 1999.[24]

The above question was inspired by the concept of freedoms *(maufulu)*. It demonstrated that, whatever particular interest activists and state functionaries had attached to the concept, it could be used as a critical tool to expose inequalities from a young person's perspective. While the judge's response was an exercise in evasion, probably dictated by its broadcast in a state-controlled media, the question punctured authorities' attempts to control the application of *maufulu*.

Such reactions, opening up issues that were not necessarily anticipated by human rights activists and ruling politicians, became common in democratic Malawi. Yet the views they conveyed on democracy and freedoms could be extremely variable. The concept of *ufulu* could quite as well direct attention to unfulfilled promises as to apparently revolutionary consequences of the new era. Crucial for critical analysis, however, is how these counterdiscourses were controlled and what measures were taken to introduce limits to freedoms.

In Malawi, the potential in the translated human rights discourse to incite subversion became apparent in generational and gendered tensions. There is no doubt that the new discourse appealed to large segments of Malawi's young population. Their grievances over education and employment, discussed further in the next chapter, were a fertile ground for the idea of freedoms to flourish. Yet the translated discourse also confined its critical potential to disputes between youths and elders or youths and teachers, rather than facilitating a more profound analysis of structural inequalities.

In another episode of the above-mentioned TV program, the director of a prominent human rights NGO was cut short by her audience of secondary school students. She had begun to explain that if "government-school teachers do not teach you . . . if a violent headmaster or headmistress comes, you have the freedom . . ." when the crowd exploded in a deafening tumult.[25] While her words touched a raw nerve, some teachers associated the perceived rise in indiscipline in schools with the new discourse on freedoms. When some students were caught consuming alcohol during the National Education Day in 2001, one teacher said in despair, "There is just too much freedom in this country. If we discipline them [students] they will take us to court and we will be the losers."[26]

A discourse on "too much freedom" was quick to emerge in tandem with incidents of apparent indiscipline and protest. Striking was the ease with which influential persons laid the blame for obstacles in Malawi's transformation on such marginalized categories as youths and some women. The secretary of the Ministry of Education, for example, is reported to have bemoaned that "much talking on human rights has brought a chaotic situation into schools where even teachers are afraid of punishing pupils for fear of being accused of infringing their rights."[27] As for those young women who have embraced the new possibilities for unconventional clothing, the presidential adviser on women's affairs had this to say: "Some are wearing very tight clothes, revealing the belly, the thighs and so on. To reveal the body like that encourages men to rape."[28]

When the authorities entrusted to promote students and women were unable to offer better analysis than this, their own contribution to disempowerment was all too apparent. The discourse on "too much freedom" obscured the causes of discontent among marginalized Malawians and focused on the mere symptoms of a socioeconomic crisis. Just as students were taken to be responsible for a "chaotic situation," so too were young women made the causes of rape. A similar superficial analysis was evident in those comments that traced a perceived increase in crime to the democratic transition. It was a topic of heated discussion in democratic Malawi, finding its way even into schoolbooks. A short story in a Chichewa/ Chinyanja book for secondary schools, for example, involved elderly men complaining about youths who did "whatever they wanted without anyone preventing them" and wondering whether "stealing property, killing people" were examples of freedom (see Chilora and Kathewera 2000, 170–172).[29] A leading columnist alluded to widespread nostalgia by pronouncing, "[T]here has been an overindulgence of lawlessness in the name of democracy and human rights since the regimentation of the previous regime collapsed following the 1994 general elections."[30]

For ruling politicians and human rights activists in democratic Malawi, nostalgia for the one-party era was not an option. Instead, and despite major differences among themselves, they sought to dominate the public discourse by educating the populace on the concept of human rights. When she launched the Malawi Human Rights Youth Network in 2002, the presidential adviser on NGOs and civil society instructed her audience that "where one's rights end is where another one's rights begin. There is a tendency among the people to claim rights while impinging on other people's rights."[31] Responsibility, *udindo* in Chichewa, came to complement the emphasis on rights as freedoms. When exercising their freedoms, people were obliged to be mindful of the freedoms of others. Yet since the initial definition of human rights as *ufulu wachibadwidwe* had already made rights an individual's property, responsibilities could be established only in a reciprocal fashion among abstract individuals. In other words, subjects were thought to encounter one another as equals with the same rights and responsibilities, not as marginalized youths and privileged authorities or as young women and adult men. Obscured, once again, were power relations, structural inequalities that made the assumption of reciprocity a grievous error.

To insert responsibilities as an afterthought into a discourse on human rights is to commit the same mistake as those who have suggested the Universal Declaration of Human Responsibilities (see Falk 2000, 88; Hastrup 2001b). Rights and responsibilities are interdependent. The right to be free from slavery, for example, "obligates individuals and governments *not* to hold people as slaves, and further obligates governments to implement this right in domestic laws" (Hastrup 2001b, 67; emphasis in original). Rights and responsibilities are not related in a reciprocal fashion, as the presidential adviser quoted above would have it, as if one's claim could be matched by the other's responsibility. To have a right is to summon up a responsibility, with or without a claim taking place.

The focus of this chapter on translation and language use has disclosed how the issue of rights and responsibilities cannot be resolved in the abstract. By establishing a discourse confined to rights as freedoms, activists, politicians, and other self-proclaimed experts made it extremely difficult to express and pursue alternatives to the current disempowerment of the majority. As a proposed limitation to excess freedom, the concept of responsibility failed to provide an alternative, because it made individuals the responsible partners. As in abstract legalism in general, solutions to structural inequalities were thought to lie in the particular encounters of two or more aggrieved parties, preferably in a court of law (Kanyongolo 1998, 2004). The solutions were, in brief, piecemeal, however profound and widespread the abuses.

Political history is a key context for the preoccupation with rights as freedoms. A tacit alliance between politicians and politically independent activists, as improbable as it was real, was a consequence of this history, centered on a public discourse on freedoms. The discourse was introduced to the general public through inaccurate translations, sometimes omitting those notions and provisions that could qualify the single-minded focus on freedoms. This process of disempowerment was, at least for most human rights activists, entirely unforeseen. Activists' own interest in political and civil rights, understandable for historical reasons, was instrumental to the way in which freedoms came to dominate the public discourse, never quite qualified by the notion of responsibility.

This chapter has already alluded to a further factor in the entrenchment of the new discourse: the thinly veiled patronizing approach that enabled self-proclaimed experts to discount popular responses to their interventions. The next chapter probes this elitism further in order to explain why, despite their personal frustrations with politics and the economy, young people were usually the ones who spread this disempowering discourse through so-called civic education. This analysis will also disclose one more important factor in the entrenchment of the new discourse — the avoidance of overtly political issues by those donor agencies that fund NGOs and programs of civic education.

CHAPTER 3

The Hidden Lessons
of Civic Education

Training the Torchbearers

The translation of human rights documents is only a preliminary step in spreading the new messages. In countries where illiteracy is common and even the literate have limited access to reading materials, human rights advocates must devise various methods in order to get their messages across. These methods are deployed in civic education, a major component in the work of human rights advocates across Africa. Civic education during Malawi's first decade of democracy targeted ordinary people as citizens whose awareness of human rights was deemed to be deficient. Its methods attempted to create a spirit of informality, stressing the need to engage the audience in a dialogue or to entertain it through song, dance, and drama. Yet both the methods and the messages had often been established before activists entered the venue of their civic education.

Despite its promise of dialogue and empowerment, civic education on human rights in Malawi contributed to making distinctions between the grassroots and those who were privileged enough to spread the messages. The distinction would be irrelevant if civic education were to bring together people with diverse backgrounds to discuss human rights on equal terms. Nobody occupies, however, a social space where discussions proceed as if everybody there were equal. In 1998, James Tengatenga, a Malawian intellectual and more recently an Anglican bishop, was bold enough, if not heretical, to criticize the patronizing attitudes underlying the apparently participatory approaches to civic education in Malawi. Despite their democratic pretensions, he argued, these approaches "suggest *coming down* to the people. Even when [civic education] is referred to as blending or being one with the people, one can't help but notice the condescension" (Tengatenga 1998, 188; emphasis in original). Tengatenga's criticism may have been too much ahead of its time, or too politically incorrect, to attract the attention it deserved. This chapter takes his criticism a step further by showing how a leading civic education project marginalized people's own insights into their life situations. At the same time, well-meaning activists believed that their knowledge of rights had not yet touched the lives of the grassroots. Activists sought to "enlighten" the Malawians they considered as the grassroots, also known as the masses. They referred to this process with the Chichewa verb *kuwunikira,* which connotes the shedding of light. Activists saw themselves as the torchbearers, the ones who brought light to the darkness.

The distinction between those who need help and those who can provide help is familiar from the world of charity (see Bornstein 2003; Garland 1999). Here, as in civic education on human rights, the providers of assistance feel they have something that others lack. Moreover, the objective is not to upset the balance between those who receive help and those who provide it. Charity differs from structural change, whether by legislation or revolution, in that it presupposes a categorical distinction between the advantaged and the disadvantaged. The former help the latter to sustain themselves, while the distinction itself remains virtually intact. In a similar vein, the civic education project on human rights examined here involved little that would actually have enabled the disadvantaged to lift themselves from their predicament. That this troubling observation was largely unnoticed in Malawi indicated how natural the distinction had become even among human rights advocates.

The purpose of this chapter is to show how the distinction underlying civic education was a consequence of active effort, not a natural state of affairs. The crucial question, in effect, is not *who* did civic education but *how* they assumed their position. Nor is the objective of this book to lament the absence of equality in Malawian society. Rather than expecting human rights advocacy to facilitate the emergence of absolute equality, one might ask another crucial question: did it seek to lift the standards of living among the impoverished majority at all? In this chapter, representatives of a major civic education project in Malawi are the subjects of my ethnographic witnessing. The project had a nationwide network of salaried civic education officers, its reach was made even more comprehensive by a large number of volunteers, known as para–civic educators. Research on how these two groups of people were recruited and trained revealed an emphasis on status that few in the Malawian context could afford to resist. The differentiation of officers and volunteers from the targets of their civic education was a hidden lesson of civic educators' training. Through certificates, closed workshops, common appearance, and human rights jargon (often in English), a commitment to the project and its particular world-view was generated. Crucial to this emerging quasi-professional identity were those disadvantaged and poor Malawians — the grassroots — who were excluded from the group. The next chapter shows how civic educators put their exclusive knowledge into practice when they faced the expectations and disappointments of the grassroots.

Civic Education: Promises and Perils

Civic education is a relatively recent phenomenon in Malawi, one of those interventions that define the "new" Malawi. Ralph Kasambara (1998), a prominent Malawian human rights lawyer, has described how independent civic education could not take place in Kamuzu Banda's Malawi. Primary schools had a subject known as civics, giving a deliberately unspecific view of government, and the Malawi Young Pioneers visited villages to impose physical and agricultural training on adults. As with much else that took place in public, the glorification of the country's life president was an integral part of this activity. Significantly, the public protests that culminated in the 1993 referendum on the system of government needed little civic education to stir them. Although Kasambara describes the Catholic bishops' Lenten Letter in 1992 as "the first major attempt in civic education" (1998, 240), a more accurate description is that it gave a voice to the grievances that had long plagued the Malawian populace. Malawians hardly needed to be educated about "the growing gap between the rich and the poor" and other injustices. They lacked channels to make their complaints heard.

The referendum in 1993 and the general elections in 1994 introduced a need for new kinds of information delivery. The very idea of these, particularly the concept of free and fair elections, needed to be clarified, not least against persistent misinformation from the outgoing government.[1] Pressure groups, which eventually became political parties, and the Public Affairs Committee (PAC) were among the first to take up this challenge. PAC included representatives from churches and other religious organizations as well as from the Malawi Law Society and the Chamber of Commerce, and its primary task was to engage in dialogue with Banda's regime. Civic education was largely voter education. The independent press that began to emerge in 1991 quenched the thirst of literate Malawians, particularly in urban areas, for alternatives to the official rhetoric. The Malawi Broadcasting Corporation, then the only local radio station, spread voter education to an even larger audience.

The successful conduct of the elections raised the question of what role civic education would play in a country that had ostensibly achieved universal political and civil freedoms. As Kasambara (1998) has noted, political parties' civic education initiatives quickly degenerated into partisan campaigning. At the same time, there was no doubt that whatever democratic reforms the new government was able to launch, information about its new institutions and laws would not reach Malawians by itself. Particularly unfortunate was that the MBC once again became the mouthpiece of the ruling party, failing to be the objective conduit of information that many had hoped for; Television Malawi (TVM), established in 1999, had the same fate (see Kayambazinthu and Moyo 2002). A study of Malawians' awareness of their rights enshrined in the new constitution and other laws revealed, several years after the 1994 elections, widespread ignorance (HRRC 1999). A similar, more sophisticated study, also conducted several years after the transition, indicated comparable problems in Zambia (Chanda 1999).

The Malawian study has, however, a condescending approach that is absent from the Zambian study. Rather than being content to list the empirical results from a survey on Malawians' awareness of democratic rights, the study speculates on their intellectual capacities to gauge the idea of human rights in the first place. It laments that "the level of illiteracy in Malawi as in other Third World countries is quite high, so high that many people do not have the necessary intellectual competence and capacity needed to articulate such a subject as human rights" (HRRC 1999, 54, 68). While the study points out that human rights need not be incompatible with Malawian social and cultural realities, it conveys the need not only for more information on specific legal provisions but also for education of the masses on the idea of human rights. I return to the issue of illiteracy and ignorance in the next chapter. Here it is important to keep in mind that condescending attitudes are never far below the surface in the Malawian context of civic education. The evidence in this book shows how activists in human rights NGOs and projects forged a style that asserted their special status in several subtle ways. Their penchant for titles, formal credentials, and the English language, for example, resonated with both Banda's vanity (Phiri 1998) and the expressions of power elsewhere in postcolonial Africa (Mbembe 2001).

The contrast to Zambia must not be exaggerated, but it is illuminating to consider how the approaches in the two studies may lead to different notions of civic education. The Zambian study was written by Alfred Chanda (1999), chairman of the Foundation for Democratic Process (FODEP), who stressed the limited awareness of human rights among groups such as academics, teachers, and students.[2] FODEP worked, in effect, with these and other educated Zambians in an effort to create a nationwide network of experts who could facilitate others' claims and demands. The aim was not so much to educate millions of Zambians on abstract concepts, or even on specific laws, as to ensure that there were competent persons to monitor human rights violations. In Malawi, on the other hand, human rights NGOs and projects often assumed responsibility for training their own personnel, who were sent to villages and townships to conduct meetings, often very soon after their recruitment. A notion of "signposting" *(kulozera)* was developed in reference to a duty of civic educators, who, when they received questions, were to direct people to organizations and authorities, regardless of whether those organizations and authorities had the capacity to assist. Seen in a positive light, signposting at least gave poor Malawians the prospect of social or economic change. In practice, as my analysis in the next chapter shows, signposting could also be little else than a way in which the project disengaged from the predicament of exploitation and marginalization among the Malawian poor.

Human rights activists' tireless touring of Malawi to educate the populace on the concepts of democracy and human rights gave them a raison d'être between the elections. As such, civic education mitigated the confining concept of democracy as multipartyism and electoral competition. It contrasted with Kasambara's (1998) conclusion that civic education had reached an impasse. Had he written his review in 1999, when the second posttransition general elections were held, or thereafter, he would have noticed this new boom in civic education. Although several foreign donors supported these initiatives, Denmark and the wider European Union were particularly generous. The above-mentioned study on Malawians' awareness of human rights was conducted by the Human Rights Resource Centre (HRRC 1999), which had been known as the Danish Centre for Human Rights until 1997. The Danish involvement began in 1996 with training activities and various grants for Malawian NGOs. HRRC continued this work, becoming the resource center its name suggested, with its own library and other facilities. Its grants supported the emergence of a whole range of Malawian human rights NGOs, but the abrupt withdrawal of Denmark from Malawi in 2001 made HRRC dependent on a number of other donors.[3]

The single most important intervention in the field of civic education took place on the eve of the general elections in 1999. The European Union started to fund a comprehensive project of voter education, known as the National Initiative for Civic Education (NICE). While the Republic of Malawi was the official "owner" of the project, it was managed by the German Agency for Technical Cooperation (GTZ). It also claimed partnership with a number of organizations in Malawi and Germany, including PAC, but in practice NICE used its elaborate structure of officers to pursue its own civic education project. After the 1999 elections, NICE expanded to cover five thematic areas: local democracy, the environment, food security, gender development, and HIV/AIDS and health. According to its leaflet, the main objective was "to promote democratic values, attitudes and behavior at a grassroots level in both urban and rural Malawi through the provision of civic education services."[4] By the end of 2002, these "services" were provided by twenty-nine district offices, three regional offices, and a national office, employing over forty professionals and over ninety members of support staff. The reach of the project was greatly enhanced by over ten thousand volunteers, the para–civic educators mentioned previously.

Finding a NICE Job

With its systematic effort to have an office in every district, NICE was an outstanding example of a project whose coverage of the country was virtually equal to, if not greater than, that of the state. District offices ensured that this coverage extended to villages and townships through a network of volunteers, trained and closely supervised by full-time officers. "Every second village" belonged to the orbit of NICE, I was told by the project manager, a German expatriate leading the entire operation from the national office in Lilongwe. Although he and many others in NICE's professional staff emphasized their association with the grassroots, the fact is that NICE fitted uneasily into a vertical state/society opposition. This opposition — common in the minds of activists, scholars, donors, and the general public far beyond Malawi — situates the state "above" society, which, as a consequence, either challenges or supports it "from below" (for critiques, see Ferguson and Gupta 2002; Lewis 2002; Migdal 2001). Yet NICE, despite the apparent "ownership" by the Malawian people, was a transnational project that participated in governing Malawi with resources that in many cases exceeded those of government departments.[5]

Crucial to the work of governance that NICE performed, even despite itself, were the many subtle ways in which its officers and volunteers created a sense of belonging to an exclusive community of human rights experts. If vertical images are at all accurate in this context, it is the grassroots that was placed "below" NICE. Among salaried officers, the sense of exclusiveness began already at the recruitment stage. Vacancies for civic education officers prompted hundreds of applications, but only a few were selected for interviews. A university degree was not a requirement for civic education officers. Most of them had a background as teachers in primary schools, while others, for example, had experience as journalists. During the interviews, all the candidates received the same set of questions, which examined whether they understood the notions of democracy and human rights as defined by NICE. The recruitment process also included an assignment that tested the candidate's acumen in defusing difficult situations during civic education. These situations were typically politically charged, and the candidate was expected to show his or her skill in avoiding the expression of his or her own political views. According to the rules of NICE, political partisanship was one of the greatest mistakes that a civic education officer could make. Active members or officers of political parties were not, therefore, allowed to join NICE in any capacity.

After recruitment, several factors served as incentives to commit oneself to NICE. For civic education officers, for example, a competition had been established whereby they could earn a salary increase.[6] Each officer was evaluated by the national office every year, in practice by the expatriate project manager. Officers could earn up to one hundred points for excellence in civic education, twenty points for administrative skills, and five points for some innovation of their own. Every forty points brought a salary increase of forty kwacha (about fifty-five cents in U.S. currency). In 2001, the lowest overall score was sixty-three points, while a regional officer received the best result, ninety points. Para–civic educators, despite their position as volunteers, were likewise enticed to work for NICE through, for instance, competitions that tested their capacity to mobilize the grassroots for public meetings. Districts were divided into zones, some of which followed constituency boundaries; and others, the boundaries of chiefdoms. Different zones were occasionally asked to compete over the number of meetings organized there or over the number of participants in those meetings. The winners received prizes, usually cash, for their efforts.

Frequent workshops and seminars deepened officers' and volunteers' belonging to NICE. Their stated objective was "capacity building," but as my detailed account of workshops for volunteers shows later in this chapter, their immediate outcome was an appreciation of the distinction between NICE and the grassroots. Workshops served this purpose at every level of NICE's internal hierarchy, with officers spending a considerable amount of their time in attending them. National workshops, for example, were organized no fewer than four or five times a year. They were organized by one of NICE's three regional offices and attended by national, district, and regional officers. National workshops often had guest speakers, including academics from abroad, and their topics varied from the specific training and administrative skills needed in NICE's work to more general issues pertaining to its thematic areas. Regional workshops, on the other hand, were organized every second month, and they brought together national and regional officers. Regional officers, in turn, had the duty to conduct workshops with district officers. The combined effect of these workshops was that all officers were in constant collaboration with their peers and superiors in the NICE hierarchy.

Workshops had a monetary aspect that represented an interesting contrast to the meetings that officers and volunteers held with the grassroots. Officers attending workshops were not only reimbursed for their transport costs; they also received daily allowances whose total value, especially among high-ranking officers, could surpass their monthly salaries.[7] "We have to give them something," the expatriate project manager remarked to me, but critical to the constitution of hierarchies in NICE's work were the ways in which its officers dismissed similar claims for compensation among the grassroots. The highest-ranking officers developed a concept of "goat culture," which was intended to preempt any material demands they might encounter during civic education exercises. A regional officer began to explain the concept to me by saying that "not all is lost to Westernization." Malawian villages, he continued, still had a community spirit, which came to the fore during, for example, weddings. Villagers assisted one another by contributing firewood and food. In a similar vein, villagers who received NICE for a visit should not expect money; on the contrary, they should feed officers and volunteers. Eating together, the regional officer said, made people feel closer to NICE. It gave villagers, he concluded, a feeling of ownership.

The official information leaflet from NICE likewise defined "goat culture" as a practice that "intensifies team building by utilizing local resources at grassroots level by preparing and eating food together while discussing issues." Hidden in such statements was one of the ways in which officers and volunteers actually differentiated themselves from their hosts: they were to help the community in resolving its problems, and in turn the community was responsible for feeding and hosting them. Another example of such differentiation was officers' ability to travel to remote venues of civic education in hired vehicles, often large four-wheel drives, conspicuously arriving in villages where ownership of a simple bicycle was a sign of affluence. As the next chapter shows in more detail, officers also freely flaunted their mobile telephones, suits, elaborate hairdos, and high-heel shoes in front of impoverished village crowds. Under such circumstances, goat culture represented little else than an attempt by the well-off to manipulate local moral codes for their own benefit. Malawians have long been exposed to such manipulations, from the concept of *thangata* (assistance) during late colonialism (Kandawire 1979; Mandala 1990)[8] to various projects involving "community participation" in postcolonial times. Common to these initiatives was the use of idioms of "assistance" in mobilizing people for projects that, in many cases, were clearly exploitative.

NICE officers' access to allowances and various paraphernalia of smooth professional life was, in other words, in sharp contrast to how they saw their relationship to the grassroots. While ordinary Malawians were expected to assist NICE officers in carrying out their civic education "services," officers' sense of an exclusive professional community also presupposed their unquestioned devotion to certain hierarchies within NICE. The organogram for NICE, obtained from the national office, is explicit about different persons' responsibilities toward one another (see figure). It is a strikingly hierarchical structure, with consultation the prerogative of only the highest-ranking officers, and everyone accountable, in the last instance, to just one person, the project manager.[9] Hierarchical relations permeated the NICE structure from officers to volunteers. District officers reported to regional officers; office assistants, who since 2002 were also used in delivering civic education, were most directly controlled by district officers. The volunteers, or the para–civic educators, also had a hierarchy of coordinators and ordinary volunteers, who assumed different responsibilities in their zones.

One effect of frequent workshops and strict hierarchies was that top officers were able to closely monitor the messages that civic education put forward in NICE's name. This was particularly conducive to maintaining the nonpartisan status of NICE, which, as mentioned, was a recurrent theme during recruitment and subsequent training sessions. For example, when PAC and several other human rights watchdogs engaged in a heated debate with ruling politicians in 2002 over the question of a constitutional amendment to allow President Muluzi to stand for a third term in office,

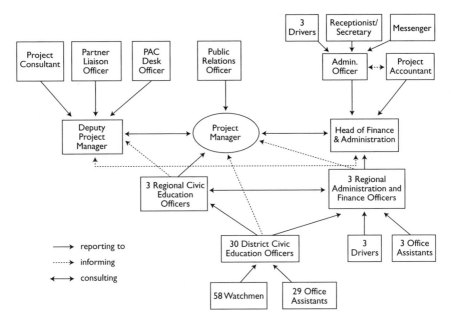

Organogram for the National Initiative for Civic Education (NICE).

NICE stayed quiet. Its highest-ranking officers convened internal work-shops to advise lower-level officers on how to react to questions about the issue from volunteers and the grassroots. Paradoxically, by insisting that officers and volunteers declined to participate in any such discussions, NICE merely served the interests of the ruling party that wanted to spread its own propaganda.[10] At issue was not only the contradiction between NICE officers' civic education messages exhorting participation in public life and their own timidity in addressing political disputes, but also the way in which NICE, an organization with a capacity to reach the majority of Malawians, contributed to undemocratic governance by remaining apolitical on issues that threatened to rip the nation apart.

The Pacification of Youth

A major challenge that NICE faced in its attempt to remain apolitical was the views and aspirations among its youthful volunteers. Although officially only those who were at least twenty years old could work as volunteers, it was difficult to control this requirement. I met volunteers who said, privately, that they were as young as seventeen, and the vast majority of volunteers were still in their early twenties. At every meeting or workshop I attended, about two-thirds of the volunteers were men.

Studies from elsewhere in Africa have shown that youths, particularly young men, are a volatile force in political developments, all too easily enticed into violence (Ellis 1999; O'Brien 1996; Richards 1996). Malawi's first two regimes after independence appeared to have understood this by creating special youth organizations in the ruling parties. During Banda's regime, the Youth League and the Malawi Young Pioneers safeguarded discipline and obedience in their neighborhoods and villages (Englund 1996). In Muluzi's Malawi, the Young Democrats, the youth wing of the United Democratic Front, grew increasingly important in enforcing loyalty to the head of state (Englund 2002c). In both cases, physical violence was integral to young people's political role. At the same time, both examples from Malawi also support the observations from elsewhere in Africa that rather than being a counterforce in society, youths are often manipulated by their elders (Bayart et al. 1992).

One of the differences between the one-party state and political pluralism was, however, the new opportunities for identification presented by the larger number of parties and organizations, such as NICE. Malawi's young population, on the other hand, also faced unprecedented frustrations as the divide between aspirations and opportunities became sharper. As mentioned in the introduction, the new dawn in politics in the early 1990s was not followed by prosperity. If anything, the new government fed unrealistic expectations by claiming to empower youths and women, in particular, through new educational and economic opportunities. The Youth Credit Scheme and various credit schemes for women, benefiting mainly those who were well-connected to the ruling elite or who already had profitable businesses, failed to establish small-scale enterprises as viable sources of income generation (Chinsinga 2002, 26). The introduction of free primary school education in 1994 created chaotic scenes throughout the country, because the number of teachers did not keep pace with the increasing numbers of pupils, with unqualified teachers and a lack of teaching materials making quality education a distant dream in most schools at both primary and secondary levels. The pass rate for the school-leaving examinations in secondary schools was particularly dismal from the mid-1990s onward. While the pass rate was 48 percent in 1990, by 1999 it had fallen to just under 14 percent.[11]

Under such circumstances, NICE's demand for a vast pool of volunteers was bound to be welcomed by youths, who found their prospects for educational and economic success shattered. NICE participated in the pacification of youth as a volatile political force by requiring nonpartisanship, on the one hand, and by offering them both symbolic and material trappings to enhance their status and self-esteem, on the other. Although volunteers received monetary rewards usually only when they attended workshops outside their own areas, the mere belonging to NICE distinguished them from the rest of the country's poor. All NICE volunteers received a letter of introduction allowing them to approach local dignitaries such as village headmen, church elders, and party officials directly. They conducted civic education and obtained from NICE certain crucial symbols of their special position, such as a gleaming white T-shirt that bore NICE's emblem. Moreover, at some workshops regional or district officers presented them with certificates. One regional officer described these certificates to me, with neither irony nor apology, as "symbols of power." By flaunting certificates and official letters in their houses and during civic education, volunteers participated in their own small way in the display of power that used such documents as resources for status distinctions, as in much of postcolonial Africa (Mbembe 2001; Simpson 2003).

At the same time, NICE also created distinctions among the youths who were associated with it. Salaried officers were better-placed than volunteers to pursue the lifestyle of professionals. These distinctions recall a frequent observation in the study of African societies — biological age can be a poor indicator of a person's social status (see Fortes 1984). The processes by which NICE contributed to distinctions among young people were also a part of wider shifts in power and authority in the lifeworlds of its officers and volunteers (Durham 2004). The government's unfulfilled promises to volunteers had diluted their enthusiasm to be identified with the category of "youths" *(anyamata)*. What many of these school-leavers wanted was recognition as *adults,* both in their capability to assume responsibilities in their own lives and in distinction to the uneducated multitudes, whose poverty was all too reminiscent of their own. While less successful than officers in achieving adulthood, however, volunteers experienced enough enhancement of status to contain their explosive frustrations.

The Making of Self-Regulating Subjects

Before we consider how NICE's internal workshops contributed to the inculcation of certain values and beliefs among its officers and volunteers, it is important to note the wider social world in which they lived. Insofar as membership in NICE presupposed a measure of self-regulation, particularly toward overtly political issues, it was a precarious achievement, always threatened by the critical ideas that the expatriate project manager and Malawians alike harbored. The expatriate manager had worked in Africa for several years and took a passionate interest in democratization in various African countries. He had worked in Zimbabwe before Malawi, and in privacy he would often explain politics in one country in terms of the other. He appeared to me to be mistaken in his comparison of Robert Mugabe and Bakili Muluzi because of the two leaders' investment in radically different rhetorics, but his inclination to see dictatorial tendencies in an ostensibly democratic president was interesting. A combination of linguistic and economic factors had made his social network among Malawians very narrow, largely confined to his work. While his managerial status made it difficult for him to develop rapport among Malawians, other expatriates provided a community in which he could express his views among like-minded peers.

What was striking about these confidential exchanges among expatriates, most of whom worked for development projects and private enterprises, was the inversion of the views they expressed otherwise. Expatriates were moderate and cautious at work or resolutely impartial when Malawians, particularly representatives of the Malawi government, were present. When at expatriate-only parties or meetings, they became fierce critics of the government. Muluzi's desire to change the Constitution to allow him a third term in office was roundly condemned, and many expatriates admired the resolve of the clergy to oppose the move. NICE's expatriate manager, however, was able to hold apparently contradictory points of view. On the one hand, he joined his expatriate peers in deploring the setback in Malawi's democratization. On the other hand, much of his work during this period consisted in ensuring that nobody associated with NICE would express opinions on the issue. He issued directives to officers and convened internal workshops to train them to defuse excitement about the debate among volunteers.

The expatriate manager's contradictory conduct was partly informed by his understanding of what the project's survival depended on. He felt that the project was under constant surveillance by the Malawi government, and the presidential adviser on NGOs and civil society was a particularly potent source of anxiety. Much as the project manager would use this anxiety to gain personal credibility and respect among his critical expatriate peers, the practical effect was to depoliticize NICE. Yet this effect would not have been profound without the expatriate manager's own belief in the content of NICE's work. To be sure, the survival of the project served his personal interests as its unquestioned leader, whatever the formal arrangement of "ownership." Equally important, however, was the expatriate manager's embrace of the notion that democratization is predicated on a transformation in values and attitudes. He was eager to question the view that poverty poses an obstacle to democratization, and Malawi had clearly become a test case for him, an experiment to show that by adopting the right values and attitudes, the grassroots would deliver a democracy. As a subject, the expatriate manager was as much self-regulating as he was constrained by the Malawi government. His belief in the power of attitudes and values maintained the nature of power in Malawi. The impoverished majority was depicted as the source of thwarted democratization, asked by NICE to transform the society by the mere force of attitudes.

The life-worlds of NICE's Malawian officers and volunteers were riddled with comparable contradictions. Fluent critics of the government in private, they would in public place the onus of democratic change on the grassroots. Although activism in political parties was proscribed among officers and volunteers, some had previously been involved in the local organizations of various parties. Many others had always been unwilling to work for political parties, viewing party politics as the deceitful pursuit that the Chichewa term for "politics," *ndale,* suggests.[12] Participation in the activities of NICE, in any case, heralded the end of political activism, but it could not eliminate political opinions. Yet, the identification with NICE often seemed to elevate officers and volunteers to a position above party politics, the reach of NICE being virtually equal to that of the ruling party and, as such, offering them an alternative moral high ground. Through this position, it became possible for officers and volunteers to observe party politics with studied detachment. The position was associated with connections to foreign donors, and it graced its occupants with righteousness. Political disputes were rare among the officers and volunteers I worked with, because those who were too obviously partisan were quickly dismissed from NICE. Whatever they might learn about democracy and human rights through their work for NICE, it was clear that their interest in public life had not emerged because of NICE. If anything, it had arisen *despite* NICE, assuming an increasingly depoliticized content once they began to work for the organization.

Material considerations influenced the conduct of officers and volunteers, just as they did with the project manager. For primary school teachers, employment with NICE could entail a tenfold increase in their salaries. As mentioned previously, regional and district officers were able to sustain the lifestyles of Malawian professionals, involving obligations as the providers of extended families. Married with children, many officers also accommodated nephews and nieces in their houses and paid their school fees. Among even those who were relatively young, officers had often acquired positions of considerable authority in their families. Their opinions were sought when illnesses or funerals occurred, they offered advice on businesses and sometimes entered joint commercial ventures with their relatives, and they were in demand as the guardians (*nkhoswe*) of new marriages. Crucial to these multiple roles and obligations were the connections, widespread among Malawians virtually regardless of their class (Englund 2002d), that urban dwellers cultivated in their rural areas of origin. The village was the ultimate home; both "village" and "home" were spoken of with the same concept of *mudzi*. My observations indicated that home villagers saw little difference between NICE and other "top jobs" (*ntchito za pamwamba*) that successful relatives in towns were seen to occupy. On the other hand, there was little in officers' conduct to suggest that the messages of NICE had any relevance outside their working hours. Civic education was a professional duty, separate from the life-world of familial obligations.

Human rights discourse in Malawi, with its emphasis on individual freedoms, was less consequential in officers' own lives than subtle notions of honor (Iliffe 2005). As urban villagers, salaried officers were deeply involved in rural relations while pursuing careers in other districts or in towns.[13] Although often only marginally older in age than volunteers, officers had achieved a decisive break from the confines of "youth" as a social category. Volunteers' situation was more ambiguous, largely because of their greater material insecurity. As mentioned above, volunteers also enjoyed access to some paraphernalia of an enhanced status and even access to cash through competitions or participation in workshops outside their own areas. Without regular income, however, they were unable to become full adults, the trappings offered them by NICE sufficient for mere courtship in contrast with officers' more respectable obligations. As such, civic education itself became a resource to negotiate a new status. Volunteers were less eager than officers to make a distinction between civic education and personal life. While both came to absorb the lessons of civic education as self-regulating subjects, volunteers appeared to discover in them grounds for challenging aspects of the established order in local settings. For officers and their project manager, a major preoccupation was to prevent these challenges from rocking the status quo.

The Desire for Status

In order to gain a deeper insight into the process by which youthful volunteers came to take apolitical civic education for granted, their training workshops must be considered. For ease of reading, I focus here on one workshop, but the conclusions I draw from my participation in it apply, in my experience, to other NICE workshops as well. The example workshop was held in 2002 to train volunteers, known as para–civic educators, or PCEs. Both a regional and a district officer were in attendance and directed the proceedings. Thirty-one volunteers participated, out of whom twenty-one were men and ten were women. With the exception of four volunteers who were over thirty years old, all were in their early twenties or even younger.

The workshop was one in a series of meetings between officers and volunteers, its purpose to equip the volunteers with skills to carry out civic education, known as *maphunziro,* "studies." Most volunteers had already conducted civic education for several months, even years. As such, the impact of the workshop was not simply the acquisition of new skills but also the renewal of the commitment to NICE as an organization. By coming together, volunteers from different zones and full-time officers could negotiate, explicitly and implicitly, what it meant to belong to NICE. As my analysis below shows, crucial to this negotiation was the production of certain hierarchies and status distinctions, both among NICE representatives themselves and, above all, in relation to the assumed targets of civic education.

The language of democracy was on everyone's lips during the workshop. It was used to steer the workshop itself, as when the regional officer, who dominated the event, frequently referred to the need to do things in a "transparent" manner, sometimes saying it in English, sometimes as *moonekera* in Chichewa. Any item on the agenda that required a decision became a solemn occasion for self-consciously democratic debate, with the regional officer addressing the gathering as *nyumba* (house), from Nyumba Ya Malamulo (house of laws), the Chichewa term for Parliament. He also solicited views from women, always regarded as a separate group, as a routine aspect of the deliberations. The items calling for decisions included what expectations the participants had toward the workshop and the rules by which they should conduct themselves during it.

In practice, however, various hierarchies guided the proceedings. Hierarchies and the unremarked desire for status distinctions were evident, for example, in the seating arrangement in which the officers and myself were seated before a half-circle of volunteers. The officers were the only participants with mobile telephones, and although one of the rules stated that they should be switched off, the officers kept them on, displaying them on the table before them and frequently taking calls. Volunteers, for their part, wrote their names on cards and placed them on their desks. Some added improbable titles such as "Hon." and "Doctor" before their names. While no reference was made to me during the deliberations, as the only white person and foreigner, I became the guest of honor, an inescapable feature of almost any public event in Malawi. It was in this role that I was asked to say a few words both in the beginning and at the end of the workshop.

My presence facilitated, in fact, an early display of status distinctions at the workshop. Although I had known and worked with the district officer and several volunteers for a number of weeks, this was the first time I met the regional officer. When he arrived, several minutes later than everyone else, he at first ignored the others and rushed to greet me. He then pulled aside the district officer, but the two stayed within an easy hearing distance from me. The district officer explained my presence as a part of the research I was currently conducting in Malawi. The regional officer looked displeased and said that I should have sought permission from NICE's national office. The district officer pointed out that I had a letter of introduction from the University of Malawi. The regional officer asked her to fetch it from me. After taking his time to peruse the letter, with the group of volunteers watching us, he went outside to make a phone call to the national office. He came back, smiling, and explained that the national office had given me permission to stay, because my project was not considered to be political. Later during a break I wanted the regional officer to see the irony of the incident. Deploying the current discourse, I remarked that I had thought NICE was a decentralized organization. He responded, in all seriousness, that, while NICE was decentralized, it had to be wary of politics.

The avoidance of politics was a central preoccupation during the workshop. Yet the politics of officers' and volunteers' own conduct passed unremarked. My attendance at the workshop without the regional officer's prior knowledge violated the entrenched habit in Malawi, from offices to villages, whereby subordinates must not assume initiative without consulting their superiors. The district officer may have been too intimidated by my own status as a white man to question my motives to study her work. On the other hand, because she had not discussed my presence with the regional officer, she may also have begun to take it for granted. In any case, the regional officer's reaction was not a mere demonstration of the proper protocol within NICE. He could certainly have made the decision about my participation on his own, but by considering the case in front of an audience of volunteers he gave an indication of his own superior status. In this sense, his phone call to the national office was not so much an act of submission as a proof of his direct access to the top of NICE's hierarchy.

As the workshop progressed, the status distinction between the two officers took more serious forms. The regional officer interrupted his colleague on several occasions to correct her or, again significantly before an audience, to instruct her on how to conduct the workshop. Toward the end of the workshop he had virtually taken over as the chairperson. On several other occasions, however, the two officers appeared as one unit in relation to the volunteers. The officers referred to themselves and were addressed by volunteers as *a kuofesi,* "people from the office." The volunteers, in turn, were the ones responsible for "villages" *(midzi).* During the workshop, status distinctions among the volunteers also became apparent in the extent to which, for example, some disagreed with their peers or simply felt able to express opinions. On the whole, however, the sentiment at the workshop was amiable and clearly encouraged everyone's identification with NICE. The meal allowance of MK 150 (just over US$2), which could have bought a volunteer at least three meals, was generous for a one-day workshop, as were the complimentary soft drinks and cookies served during the day. Every volunteer was also given a pen and a notepad, items that were gratefully taken back to the poverty from which the volunteers had come.

Learning to Be Special

Implicit in the proceedings was the effort to construct the grassroots as the object of civic education. This was achieved through an explicit focus on volunteers as resourceful individuals who possessed knowledge and skills that could benefit the grassroots. Volunteers, in other words, were *made* to appear as those who could assist the grassroots. The distinction between volunteers and the grassroots did not exist prior to the arrival of organizations such as NICE. All volunteers were from the same social setting as the people they were supposed to assist, embedded in many complex ways in local social relationships. Moreover, the distinction between the volunteers and the grassroots was achieved at the workshop not through a discussion of the messages that civic education spread but by training the volunteers to understand *how* the messages should be presented to their audiences in villages and townships.[14] Volunteers' previous knowledge about their social world, including their facility with basic courtesies, was made into "skills" *(luso)* and codified in exotic-sounding English concepts.

The first item on the agenda, after the opening prayer and a discussion on workshop rules and expectations, was the question, "What is NICE?" *(NICE ndi chiyani?)*. Although most volunteers had heard the answer to this question at virtually all the workshops they had attended before, its purpose was clearly to reaffirm both the official answer and the volunteers' commitment to NICE. A volunteer drew the NICE emblem on a flip-chart, and the officers explained at length the involvement of the European Union and the German agency GTZ. This apparently direct link to the outside world, where affluent white people funded NICE, was crucial to volunteers' identification with the specific role assigned to them in the organization's hierarchy. Volunteers were able to imagine their belonging to a transnational community. It was, moreover, a transnational community that promised an alternative to the networks of patronage that ruling politicians maintained by exploiting foreign aid. Yet a similar desire for access to external links, a similar salience attributed to what Jean-François Bayart (2000) calls "extraversion," underlay both the governmental and the non-governmental strategies.[15]

Another initial theme, repeated over and over during the workshop, was the nonpartisanship of NICE. The district officer, for example, announced that "we are not politicians" *(ife sindife andale ayi)* and "we do not have a party" *(tilibe chipani)*. She and the regional officer, on several occasions during the workshop, used the verb *kuwunikira* to describe the purpose of NICE's civic education. Its most appropriate translation in this context is "to enlighten," from the basic meaning "to shed light on a spot with a lamp or fire to see a thing" *(walitsa pumulo ndi nyali kapena nsakali kuti uwone chinthu)* (Centre for Language Studies 2000, 349). They stressed the need to invite local party functionaries to civic education sessions and to show them equal respect by applauding them when they spoke. The officers also explained that the colors in the NICE emblem resembled those that the Malawi Congress Party used, but it was every volunteer's responsibility to prevent misunderstandings among the grassroots. In a similar vein, the regional officer later rejected a suggestion from one volunteer to hoist flags on the location that NICE held meetings. Because Malawi's political parties also used flags, he explained, ordinary villagers would be confused if NICE also had a flag.

This effort to avoid identification with political parties — from specific parties to the general manner in which they conducted rallies in Malawi — had an immediately obvious reason. Many areas were sharply contested in Malawi's multiparty politics, and the Young Democrats of the UDF had intimidated and assaulted supporters of other parties across the country. Yet the stress on nonpartisanship, coupled with the idiom of enlightenment, also contributed to a distinction in another sense. The representatives of NICE sought to convey the impression that they were not consumed by the passions underlying political squabbles. In effect, they were not only outside politics but also *above* it. It was NICE that could invite all the parties to its meetings, giving their officials equal representation while reserving to itself the privilege of distributing nonpartisan information. As can be seen in the next chapter, this nonpartisanship provided little "enlightenment" when the impoverished crowds confronted NICE representatives with questions about the causes of their predicament.

The audiences that civic education officers and volunteers encountered were diverse and often vociferous. Workshops like the one discussed here were, therefore, important in inculcating self-esteem and self-confidence in NICE representatives. In addition to the imagined external links and their position above politics, volunteers were introduced to certain personal characteristics that set them apart from the grassroots. These characteristics of individual volunteers (*zomuyenereza munthu kukhala PCE*) were initially identified in small groups that subsequently presented their findings to the two officers. A recurrent theme was education, the need for a volunteer to be "educated" (*wophunzira*), "someone who has been to school" (*wopita kusukulu*), and "smart" (*wozindikira*). Each time the regional officer asked the others to endorse these characteristics presented by small groups, the response was invariably a loud and enthusiastic "yes!" *(ee!)*. The issue of education clearly struck a chord with the youthful gathering of volunteers. Although volunteers were formally required to have only the primary school graduation certificate, most of them belonged to the category of young people who had, as mentioned, unsuccessfully pursued secondary education. By offering a context in which youths could feel that their education had not been wasted, NICE also ensured commitment to its cause.

The emphasis on education was not, of course, merely a consequence of the current crisis in Malawi. It resonated with the unrivaled channel to personal advancement that formal, Western-style education had represented in both colonial and postcolonial Africa (Serpell 1993; Simpson 2003; Stambach 2000). The crisis of expectations and opportunities in Malawi made the quest for academic success more desperate than ever. During the workshop, another aspect of education, first introduced by Christian missions, also received a great deal of attention. Volunteers' self-esteem was enhanced by frequent references to the neat and clean appearance as one of their defining characteristics. Several participants emphasized the need to "take care of oneself" (kudzisamala), particularly by washing oneself frequently (kusambasamba). The emphasis was also on smart clothes, with nobody mentioning modesty in dressing that would suit village settings.

This fascination with appearance, with personal cleanliness, not only gave the impression that the grassroots had particular problems with hygiene; it also resonated with another legacy of colonialism as a "civilizing" mission. Several scholars writing about southern Africa, for example, have demonstrated a close correspondence between ideas of hygiene and self-improvement in the patterns of consumption, medical work, and domestic relations that various colonial agents introduced (see, e.g., Burke 1996; Comaroff and Comaroff 1997; Vaughan 1991). In Malawi, such patterns have continued to symbolize progress, embodied no less by Banda's puritan style of dressing than by Muluzi's flamboyant one. Few volunteers could afford suits or elaborate dresses, but many of them wore at the workshop fashionable jeans and the kind of sports gear that African-American youth culture has made popular across the globe. The regional and district officers embodied success by clothing themselves in a suit and a dazzling white dress, respectively.

To situate the emphasis on cleanliness within wider colonial and postcolonial processes is not to produce a far-fetched historical analogy. Large-scale historical processes boil down to such mundane and taken-for-granted dispositions as the emphasis on personal hygiene. It consolidates existing inequalities. As my fieldwork in rural Malawi has taught me, villagers generally do take a bath once or twice every day, but their poverty does not allow for patterns of consumption that distinguish the well-off as heavily perfumed and fashionable citizens. However unlikely NICE's volunteers were to attain these patterns of consumption, the emphasis on cleanliness at the workshop expressed the *desire* for a status that would set them apart from those who were considered in need of civic education. By imagining themselves as particularly clean, the volunteers also imagined themselves as belonging to the category of Malawians who had historically had the power to define what progress and development consist of.

The Supremacy of English

Another mechanism of status distinction, also resonating with wider colonial and postcolonial processes, concerns linguistic resources. Most participants, and especially the regional officer, spoke a language that was a mixture of English and Chichewa. While English expressions and words often appear in the spoken language of urban dwellers in the region (see, e.g., Kashoki 1972; Kayambazinthu 1998; Moto 2001), the regional officer's discourse made a notion of "code switching" between different languages and registers somewhat spurious. Consider, for example, how he responded to a volunteer's question about involvement in conflicts that occur in villages:

Izi zikachitika inu mukapereke lipoti kuofesi. A kuofesi akaona nkhaniyo ndi yofunikadi kuti pakakhala mediation . . . *chifukwa m'mene mukakambirane nkhani ija . . . ambirife sitinapange* training *ya kufield ya* conflict resolution.

When these things happen, you should report to the office. When people in the office see that the issue is important, that there should be mediation . . . because how you could discuss that issue . . . many of us have not done training in the field of conflict resolution.[16]

Although Chichewa could have expressed the substance of the regional officer's reply, which suggested that conflicts were to be reported to district offices because few volunteers had been trained to mediate them, he chose to include a few English words in formulating his reply. The impact was to make Chichewa seem like a language that lacked the vocabulary used in "conflict resolution," with even "discussing" *(kukambirana)* becoming a technical procedure that could be performed only by those who were specifically trained.

Another common strategy among Chichewa speakers who want to use English is to introduce English expressions with the verb *kupanga,* "to do" or "to make." In the above extract the regional officer used this verb to refer to "training in the field of conflict resolution." The next extract is from his explanation of the difference between "dominant participants" and "docile participants."

Amafunikanso pamsonkhano, koma kofunika ndi kupanga notice, *kupanga* control. *Pali ena amati madocile kapena* timid participants, *anthu ofatsa, ali phee. Amenewa kofunika ndi kupanga* jack-up.

They [dominant participants] are also needed at the meeting, but it is necessary to notice [them], to control [them]. There are others who are called docile or timid participants, quiet people. It is necessary to jack-up [them].

In order to express the activity at issue in English, the regional officer used the verb *kupanga* three times in this short extract. Such uses of English, commonly followed by all participants at the workshop, were based on linguistic patterns that were widespread in the region.[17] They had developed independently of the official Anglo-American standards of English and were inadequate communicative tools for, for example, African immigrants in Europe (Blommaert 2001, 2002). Yet their specific effect in the Malawian setting was to create distinctions that contributed to local inequalities.

Several studies have shown the high esteem that Malawian elites attach to English, with many insisting that their children speak only English (see Matiki 2001; Mtenje 2002a, 2002b; and Moto 2003).[18] To be sure, a person's recruitment to a formal occupation usually presupposes good knowledge of English. Malawians who are in the habit of using English in their everyday interactions with other Malawians often seek, consciously or unconsciously, to associate themselves with those few who have succeeded in their educational and professional life. Here they maintain another colonial legacy that had its most extreme postcolonial result in Kamuzu Banda's Anglophilia. He never spoke Malawian languages in public, he always dressed in the most conservative costume to be found in the modern English wardrobe, and he established the "Eton of Africa," Kamuzu Academy (see Short 1974). However detested he is among contemporary human rights activists in Malawi, his thirty years of rule did much to entrench the colonial legacy of regarding England and the English language as the prime sources and symbols of progress.[19]

The frequent use of English during the workshop supported two tacit objectives. On the one hand, by referring in English to various skills and methods in civic education, the participants were able to make them seem like elements of an exclusive body of knowledge. The participants were, for example, taught that "open air technology" referred to the use of materials and facilities that were available in the venue of civic education. "Information market," in turn, describes the method whereby the audience was asked to write down their preferred topics on cards and to display them as in a market. When NICE representatives were unwilling to consider some of the chosen topics, they either ignored them or gave the audience "signposts" to other organizations (see the next chapter). "Edutainment" and "energizers" were also among the technical English terms the volunteers were asked to learn. Both referred to the importance of entertainment in civic education.

On the other hand, the participants could also detach themselves from the grassroots, understood to be dependent on Chichewa and other Malawian languages, by bemoaning the problems of translation. These problems appeared time and again during the workshop, because, for reasons that were never explained, the regional and district officers used English concepts as the foundation for their discourse. For example, they first mentioned concepts in English, such as "poster," "report," "sitting plan *[sic]*," and "experience," and then asked the audience to suggest equivalents in Chichewa. While for some concepts the equivalents were quickly identified, many others prompted volunteers to lament the poverty of Chichewa, exclaiming, for example, that "Chichewa is problematic!" *(Chichewa ndi chovuta!)*. For example, despite the existence of *chidziwitso* for "poster" and *kaundula* for "report," *positala* and *lipoti,* respectively, were established as the translations.

These attitudes toward translation were another indication of the desire to associate civic education with symbols and resources that were external to the reality of the grassroots. Volunteers, under the officers' leadership, moved between two languages, one associated with quality education and opportunities, the other with impoverishment, disadvantage, and ignorance. The assumed civilizing and progressive undercurrents become apparent when one realizes that the movement between the languages was one way. In their efforts to find word-for-word rather than idiomatic translations for English concepts, the participants saw English as the unquestioned source of discourse. If Chichewa equivalents were not forthcoming, the problem was necessarily in this language, not in English. Here the workshop upheld the inequality of translation that also underlay the official translations of human rights discourses in Malawi and Zambia. The embrace of the same inequalities by Malawians who had no background in translation was a measure of the similarity of these inequalities to wider historical processes.

Educating Elders

The tacit teachings at the workshop, from personal cleanliness to language use, were crucial to the transmission of more explicit messages. The overt theme was to train the volunteers to acquire skills *(luso)* to be deployed in civic education. While issues such as cleanliness and language served to enhance volunteers' status and self-esteem, the issue of skills revealed in a more obvious way that the volunteers' recognized distinction between themselves and the grassroots was a precondition for civic education. A central item on the agenda was "the skill to teach elders" *(luso lophunzitsa anthu akuluakulu)*. This item recognized the challenges of conducting civic education among adults, particularly elders, who were customarily seen as the embodiments of wisdom and authority. The very idiom of "teaching" *(kuphunzitsa)*, rather than, for instance, "discussing" *(kukambirana)*, betrayed NICE representatives as the ones with knowledge.

The challenges of imparting this knowledge received somewhat ironic remarks from both the volunteers and the officers, often provoking laughter. A volunteer, reporting from a small-group discussion, observed that "elders do not make mistakes, they merely forget" *(akuluakulu salakwa, amangoiwala)*. The district officer also stressed that "we do not disagree, we only add a little bit" *(sititsutsa, timangoonjezerapo)*. The meaning of elders "forgetting" and NICE representatives "adding" something was immediately apparent to the volunteers. Their "skills" included subtle ways of making elders agree with civic education experts' indisputable knowledge.

The idea that elders' knowledge was somewhat deficient was expressed in various ways. The most common strategy, for both volunteers and officers, was to shift the deficiency from the category of elders to the category of villages *(midzi)* and to give examples of ignorance and false beliefs there. "In villages they believe that AIDS is caused by witches!" *(Kumidzi amakhulupirira kuti edzi imachokera kwa afiti!)*, one volunteer exclaimed. The officers warned, however, against embarrassing elders in public. A better strategy was to solicit several viewpoints on the same issue, and when the right answer appeared, the civic educator would start repeating it in different forms. The intent would be to make the crowd accept the message without appearing to impose it on them. Elders, in turn, would seek to avoid embarrassment by aligning themselves with the emerging dominant view. In their work of gradually overcoming resistance, volunteers would also encourage those individuals in the crowd who appeared to understand the civic education message quickly.

Several techniques were at civic education officers' disposal to persuade the crowd to accept their viewpoints and messages. Adults differed from children, it was observed during the workshop, in that they wanted to feel equal to their teachers. In this respect, the volunteers were advised to perfect the skill of "lowering oneself" *(kudzitsitsa)* in order to adopt the "level" appropriate to the crowd. For example, when teaching youths they should "take the level of youths" *(kutenga level ya anyamata)*, and when teaching chiefs they should "take the level of chiefs" *(kutenga level ya mafumu)*. As with politicians, so too with other social categories — civic educators moved among different categories at will, enlightening those who remained trapped in their particular world-views and roles. This workshop was one among many to induce the volunteers to regard themselves as being outside and above "culture" *(chikhalidwe)* no less than politics. The grassroots, also known as villages, existed as the audience of messages that only civic education officers fully understood.

Several aspects of their training contributed, therefore, to youthful volunteers' identification with NICE and its practice of civic education. These disillusioned school-leavers had found an organization that improved their self-esteem by defining them as intrinsically different from the impoverished multitudes. Certificates confirming participation in training workshops, formal letters, personal appearance, linguistic resources, and various "skills" distinguished them from the grassroots. Consistent with their new status, they would categorically condemn, for instance, villagers' erroneous ideas of the causation of afflictions such as AIDS while conveniently ignoring the extent to which witchcraft gripped the imagination of educated Malawians (see Lwanda 2002). Volunteers' particular concern was to *teach* elders, betraying a generational tension that had increased in the region as youngsters faced greater constraints to advancement than their parents had experienced. Here NICE's pacification of youth also controlled interpersonal and intergenerational tensions. These tensions have occasionally culminated in the harassment and killing of suspected witches, especially in the context of rapid economic recession and political upheaval, with elderly people accused of holding back prosperity (see Ashforth 2005, 256–257; Niehaus 2001, 154–155). By using the messages on democracy and human rights as their swords, civic educators were unlikely to unleash physical force against elders.

Revelations and Hidden Agendas

"Centre for Human Rights and Rehabilitation is like a lamp in the darkness" *(ACentre for Human Rights and Rehabilitation ali ngati nyali m'mdima)*. These words ended an audio tape on which a Malawian NGO, through the performances of the popular comedians Izeki and Jacob, informed citizens about their constitutional rights.[20] The idioms of "light" and "darkness," of "enlightenment," were by no means confined to NICE. Civic education programs in Malawi on human rights commonly used them to convey how radical the new message was. While the above quote identified the NGO itself as the source of light, activists generally considered their civic education on new laws and democratic principles as having this revelatory potential. There can be little doubt about the need for such revelations. In a country where the only mass media worthy of the designation, namely, the radio, continued to be a tool of misinformation after the democratic transition, information on new laws and rights was not easily available. The paramount task of organizations providing civic education was to carve out a space where the substance and implications of human rights could be debated.

This chapter has raised doubts about the success of civic education in Malawi in carrying out this necessary task. Civic education on rights and democracy gained new momentum after 1999, but its relation to taken-for-granted hierarchies in society remained poorly recognized. Although the youths associated with NICE were often genuinely concerned about the state of democracy in their country, an effect of their training workshops was that identification with certain quasi-professional markers overrode identification with the targets of their civic education. The allure of status distinctions was irresistible in a country where youths faced an unprecedented divide between their aspirations and opportunities. After having been fed on a diet of hopes for progress and personal advancement during their school years, the last thing Malawian youths expected was to be identified with the poverty and disadvantage from which they had started. NICE provided one context to satisfy the desire for status.

The social and economic crisis in which NICE operated was only one reason why its civic education may not have empowered the rural and urban poor. The crisis undermined the radical potential of civic education when it was combined, first, with a specific view on education and, second, with the impact of the Malawian state on civic education programs. As mentioned, NICE announced in its public relations materials that its main objective was "to promote democratic values, attitudes, and behavior at grassroots level." It is this emphasis on values and attitudes that most directly contributed to the possibility that civic education on rights merely maintained entrenched inequalities. NICE's objective, calling for behavioral change, may be seen to address the need to educate citizens both *about* and *for* human rights (Engelbronner-Kolff 1998, 14). Yet it fell short of enhancing the capacity of the disadvantaged to confront the power relations that underlay human rights violations. No Freirean "pedagogy of the oppressed" (Freire 1970) was involved in the idealistic belief that the right values and attitudes, in the absence of transformative action against structural inequalities, were enough to institute democracy. Especially disturbing was NICE's assignment of the duty of changing attitudes to the grassroots. As the next chapter discusses in more detail, it was a subtle way of avoiding mention of the wider power relations that had made the grassroots the audience of civic education in the first place.

This avoidance of mentioning power, already seen in NICE's insistence on nonpartisanship, was essential to the smooth running of the project. The state in Malawi retained considerable influence over the precise content and capacity of foreign-funded projects. As explained earlier in this chapter, the state was not "above" the donor-sponsored "civil society" as a more encompassing structure. Some NGOs were superior to the state in their capacity to reach the populace and to offer their employees considerably more attractive salaries and transnational links. Yet the balance between the state and the nonstate was precarious, forever subject to negotiation. As discussed in the introduction, a law requiring the registration of NGOs came into force in 2001, giving the state the final say in defining legitimate organizations. Diplomatic confrontations were also important weapons in the arsenal of the state to control and curtail the operations of organizations whose foreign donors were represented in the country.

This tension was particularly apparent in NICE's case, because its status as a "project initiative" was a constant source of ambiguity. While its donors emphasized its "ownership" by the Republic of Malawi, cabinet ministers and senior government officials often interrogated NICE's expatriate project manager about its true identity. A presidential adviser had reportedly accused NICE of acting "like an NGO" without being registered as such. Paradoxically, among expatriate donors and Malawian civil society activists, such accusations served to strengthen the belief that civic education projects were politically consequential. Rather than these accusations and threats being seen as one way of cowing human rights NGOs and projects into nonpolitical themes, they were taken as evidence for the impact of civic education. "We must be getting it right, since the government wants to close us," NICE's expatriate manager remarked to me.

NICE is, in point of fact, an example of how a civic education project with transnational links contributes to undemocratic governance. As Dorothy Hodgson (2002, 1093) has noted in a Tanzanian context, while the "donor community" encompasses a wide range of actors — some secular, others religious; some willing to challenge the state, others acquiescent — most donors prefer to sustain themselves by depoliticizing the interventions they sponsor. The trend is common among externally funded NGOs and projects, with the initial excitement with "empowerment" in new democracies changing into "service delivery" (Fisher 1997,

454). Note, for instance, NICE's promise to provide "civic education services." From the content of its messages to the ways in which it channeled popular frustrations into distinctions regarding the grassroots, NICE depoliticized civic education and controlled popular challenges to the state and transnational governance (Howell and Pearce 2001; Jenkins 2001). The next chapter takes a closer look at the content of these messages and how civic education officers responded to the demands they encountered among the grassroots.

CHAPTER 4

Watchdogs Unleashed?

Encountering "the Grassroots"

During the time I conducted the fieldwork for this book, the National Initiative for Civic Education held public meetings on its five thematic areas (local democracy, the environment, food security, gender development, and HIV/AIDS and health), led by its representatives but actively soliciting contributions from participants, known as the grassroots. Few could deny that the five themes appeared to be of immense relevance to Malawi. Food security was precarious in many rural and urban households, partly because of adverse environmental and climatic conditions and partly because of new agricultural policies that had removed subsidies. The country's incidence of HIV/AIDS was one of the worst in the African pandemic, with the imbalanced power relations between the sexes partly accounting for its spread (Lwanda 2002). All these problems culminated in the need to institute a democracy in which all citizens would be treated with dignity and downtrodden Malawians' claims would be heard.

How did the officers and volunteers of NICE respond to these challenges? As was seen in the previous chapter, most of them were young people, themselves frustrated by the economic and political impasse at which Malawi appeared to be after a decade of democratic experimentation. The previous chapter also indicated, however, that NICE created an organization of quasi-professionals who were taught to think of themselves as separate from the grassroots. Identification with the organization, rather than with the concerns of the grassroots, became paramount. This process stemmed from the imperative that the sponsors and managers of NICE faced in order to sustain the project. It could not appear to challenge the prevailing political relations in the country. The five relevant themes, each profoundly political, were pursued by an organization that was supposed to function apolitically. How did NICE cope with this contradiction?

NICE could not quite erase the political content of its themes, but it relegated politics to a sphere that posed no threat to wider power relations. The sphere was "the grassroots," often understood as a synonym for "community." It was the grassroots/community that was asked to assume responsibility for its development in a political and economic sense. This chapter shows how NICE's civic education defined political problems as if they were reducible to communities and, by so doing, made communities the problem. The strategy, even if poorly understood by activists themselves, was not unique to NICE or to Malawi. It belonged to a trend in development aid that called for, in the name of "participatory methods," communities' greater input to their development.

Its severely confined notion of politics did not, of course, pass unnoticed among the targets of NICE's civic education, themselves embedded in complex social relationships that made an easy definition of a community impossible. I show in this chapter how NICE's civic education was challenged on the ground as people expressed their actual concerns and demands, many of which NICE was unable to consider. Toward the end of the chapter, I also indicate how civic education on human rights and democracy has begun to be a topic of critical reflection in Malawian popular culture.

Community as a Problem

Although at their internal training workshops NICE representatives used teaching *(kuphunzitsa)* as the Chichewa concept for civic education, they usually employed other concepts and idioms in their direct encounters with the beneficiaries of civic education. The verb for these encounters became, for example, "to discuss" *(kukambirana)* or "to share ideas" *(kugawana nzeru)*. This shift in concepts was consistent with the task that NICE had set for itself. Its objective was to empower the populace, and civic education officers and volunteers were aware that this objective would not be fulfilled without a sense of ownership and participation among the grassroots. Just as "discussion" replaced "teaching" in the official jargon, so too did civic education officers prefer to see themselves as "facilitators" rather than as "teachers."[1]

Because the recipients of civic education were usually adults, NICE recognized the need to make them accept the extra demand on their time. High-ranking officers explained to me that "the community" had to realize that "it" had problems and, moreover, that NICE could assist it in solving those problems. Among the strategies that NICE representatives used to reach this goal were references to proverbs and folktales. One useful tale depicted a house in which a husband and a wife were sleeping. When they woke up they realized that a snake had entered the house. They shouted for help, and a passerby, a stranger to the couple, heard them. He broke into the house and killed the snake. The officers and volunteers of NICE used this tale for various purposes. Two of the most common were to demonstrate to the grassroots how outsiders could sometimes be instrumental in solving a problem and to enable the officers and volunteers themselves to resist any demands to share their resources with the community. If NICE was helping the community to overcome problems, it was rather unreasonable to expect further favors from the civic educators. As in folklore and popular fiction, such as Willie Zingani's 1984 novel, assistance from an outsider was expected to prompt a generous response from the assisted instead of pleas for more assistance.[2]

My analysis will consider in more detail below the limited extent to which officers and volunteers permitted any qualification of their preconceived sense of what the problems were. What should be understood at the outset is the way in which NICE's focus on the community was compatible with its apolitical stance. Deeper issues of power and injustice did not need to be addressed because the community was the one that both had problems and was provided with solutions through civic education. NICE's work on food security, for example, involved teaching the community to utilize various products of its land to avert hunger. The flour that was needed for cooking *nsima,* the staple porridge, could be obtained from cassava and potatoes if the maize harvest was poor. Yet, instead of following this advice, people sold part of their produce for cash, according to NICE officers' complaint to me.

This complaint carried the assumption that some households in Malawi do not need cash. The assumption was absurd, as anyone with experience of poverty in Malawi could attest. Even food producers need cash in contemporary Malawi, if only to sustain their livelihood in the first place by buying fertilizer, tools, and seeds. By making hunger a consequence of the community's lack of enthusiasm for NICE's advice, civic education officers were able to obscure the unjust political economy in which food insecurity and poverty were the fate of the majority of Malawians.

The focus on community as the unit of various developmental interventions is not new in Africa. Community development was already a concern for the British Colonial Office in the 1940s, when measures were taken to curb the perceived disintegration of rural societies and the threat to the colonial order posed by urbanization and nationalism (see Hickey and Mohan 2005, 239–240). The idea of participatory development could assume potentially radical forms under some postindependence regimes. However, Malawi was among those countries in which paternalism combined with a tendency to carry out large-scale projects from the top down. It was in response to such currents in international aid that participatory development returned to the agenda of some governments and NGOs in the 1980s. Chambers (1994, 1997), in particular, devised methods to assess the needs and priorities among the actual recipients of aid. Rapid Rural Assessment and, more recently, Participatory Rural Appraisal have carried the promise of involving the poor as partners in defining the objectives of aid. The demise of autocratic regimes in sub-Saharan Africa made the promise all the more plausible. In Malawi, for example, "community empowerment" became an essential part of the new regime's agenda.

The problems outlined above, however, suggest how quickly "community talk" degenerated into self-serving rhetoric among donors and politicians. What began as a noble effort to include the disenfranchised in the debate on development evolved into making that group the problem itself, as now happens far too often. Scholars and critics have highlighted various aspects of this trend in "developing" countries. They have emphasized the unfortunate corollary that both the source of and the solution to poverty can be found within the community (see, e.g., Bornstein 2003; Cooke and Kothari 2001; Goebel 1998). They have also raised doubts, on historical and sociological grounds, about the assumption that communities are entities with one will and one voice (see, e.g., Geschiere 2004). Fundamental to these critiques is the attempt to identify the historical context in which the perceived problems of poverty and deprivation have emerged. The scale of the critique may also be extended from communities to countries. As James Ferguson (1990) has asked in his study of development in Lesotho, Why are countries seen as the sources of their own successes or failures? Why, for example, is Lesotho labeled a less-developed country rather than a South African labor reserve? The designation, entrenched as the result of World Bank reports, deflects our attention from the exploitative and racist historical processes that made Lesotho a country in the first place.

When I posed questions inspired by these critical considerations to top

NICE officials, their response was typically to dismiss talk about the wider political economy as an excuse for inertia. People should learn, they remarked, to work for their development without waiting for the world around them to change first. Implicit in such responses were condescending assumptions about impoverished Malawians' disinclination to work and about their lack of awareness of their duties and responsibilities as citizens. As I show later in this chapter, these assumptions had particularly insidious effects when they combined with assumptions about ignorance and general backwardness among illiterate or semiliterate rural folks. The previous chapter described how officers and volunteers were trained to elicit "right answers" from the audiences of their civic education, making "participation" an appalling misnomer. The nature of the Malawian experiment with democracy became alarmingly elitist when the realm of the conceivable was defined even before the impoverished majority entered the debate. Yet elitism did not diminish complexity. When civic education involved actual encounters among variously situated persons, it did bring to the fore some of the contradictions in community talk.

Community as an Abstraction

One of the paradoxes involved in community talk is that, despite its promise that ordinary people's viewpoints and priorities will be appreciated, its notion of community is too abstract for significant differences in real life to be discerned. This paradox had serious consequences for the interactions between civic education officers and their interlocutors. Yet it was compatible with the apolitical approach that NICE, among others, pursued in civic education. If the targets of civic education were simply a community, civic education officers did not need to consider the actual differences among and within communities that might be political in nature. The civic education message, as a consequence, could be delivered as a standard everywhere, adjusted only to the "level" of the audience, as NICE officers and volunteers learned.

The effects of abstraction became clear when I followed civic education officers on their field trips in a predominantly rural district in Malawi. My ethnographic witnessing here is based on the observations I made during several such trips. The officers' trips were sponsored by a foreign donor agency. It supported adult literacy classes in the area and wanted NICE to provide guest speakers in the classes. Such requests were a major chance for NICE's salaried officers to conduct civic education outside the programs that received funding on the eve of elections. During the periods between elections, NICE volunteers had the main responsibility for conducting civic education at the local level. Officers welcomed external donors' invitations as opportunities to get out of the office and to enhance district offices' economy — and their own — with the fees, transport costs, and allowances that they were able to extract from the donors.

Certain patterns recurred during our visits to villages. Officers' mode of dressing was one conspicuous feature that clearly distinguished them from the people they encountered in the villages. In this district I traveled with two civic education officers, a man and a woman, both in their twenties. Neither of them made an effort to adjust their appearances before embarking on these field trips. They wore the same clothes both in the office and in the field, with the man preferring a slightly more casual look than the woman. He always wore safari-style clothes and a pair of fashionable trainers. She, on the other hand, displayed her taste for high-heeled shoes and knockoff designer dresses. Even in the dustiest village, her hair was elaborately done with chemicals, a bundle of dreadlocks on top, and large round earrings completed the impression of a city woman. She looked strikingly different from her audience, in which every woman wore a *chitenje* (a wrap-up skirt), and most were barefooted. The male officer had only a marginally more modest appearance, his style also betraying access to fashionable imports. He also carried a mobile phone even when conducting civic education, proudly taking calls in those villages that were within the network.

Civic education officers, as described in the previous chapter, maintained close ties to their own rural areas of origin. Respectable and resourceful members of extended families, they spoke the language of individual freedoms only in their professional contexts. A corollary was a certain detachment from those rural settings where they conducted civic education. The two officers described here, for example, never spent more time in villages than it took to deliver their messages. The visits included very little casual chatting with members of the audience, and the persons whom the officers greeted on arrival and thanked at departure were local notables, such as village headmen, the instructors of literacy classes, and the headmasters of local schools. When the officers stayed long enough to eat, in accordance with the goat culture, their hosts were selected from these local dignitaries. Civic education officers did not, in other words, challenge existing hierarchies but became firmly placed within them. Their position within local hierarchies was, moreover, different from the one in their own villages, where their superior status entailed obligations and engagement. The approach was, of course, consistent with the abstract notion of community that informed their civic education. If communities were all similar and internally undifferentiated, then their leaders must be the best persons to represent them.

Abstraction took almost tragic forms during our visits. After cruising into the villages in a hired four-wheel drive, the officers shook hands with the dignitaries and conducted opening prayers. Even in areas where the majority of villagers were Muslims, the officers invariably said Christian prayers, betraying their own religious outlook. The body language of the crowd indicated that very few took part in these prayers. In a similar fashion, the officers displayed little sensitivity to the linguistic situation and spoke only Chichewa during the visits. In several villages the main language was Chiyao, and when members of the audience spoke it, the officers could clearly understand what was said. Yet instead of actively encouraging people to speak their own language, the officers stubbornly continued with Chichewa. Particularly inconsiderate was forgetting the name of the village where civic education was taking place. On some occasions, before proceeding with his or her speech, the civic education officer had to pause to ask for the name from a notable sitting nearby.

All these problems might be seen as a result of having inexperienced or untrained persons conducting civic education. Yet this was not the case. The sessions were conducted by NICE's district officers, not volunteers, and both of them had worked in this capacity for at least a year. The apparent insensitivity to context was, rather, a consequence of the notion that "community" was the target of civic education. Community could be, in effect, any community in rural Malawi, because NICE had developed its approach to civic education as a universal blueprint. The frequent internal workshops kept officers and volunteers at all levels abreast of one another's work and enabled top officials to monitor NICE representatives' performance. Throughout the country, a standard message was being delivered to a standard audience. Abstract universalism obscured the situation of human rights.

One unintended consequence of this approach, as is described below, was the apparent disappointment that many in the audience felt when they realized that NICE's messages had little relevance to their particular predicaments. The majority often sank into silence, clearly bored with the proceedings, and others who tried to pose questions were often quieted with the message that their questions were diversions from the theme the officers had introduced. The lack of active responses from the audiences was a major concern to the officers, who repeatedly asked the crowd *tikumvana?* (do we understand each other?) or *tili limodzi?* (are we together?). Every session also contained invitations to the women who were present to sing something. Alternatively, people were invited to participate in short plays, which, in the NICE jargon, were called energizers. For example, the officer would mention different animals in rapid succession, and the crowd would utter *nyama* (meat) after every animal that was edible. Those who made a mistake were excluded from the play. With their background in teaching primary and secondary school students, the officers were skillful in managing the crowd and helping the participants to enjoy such moments of entertainment. It was apparent, however, that the energizers and songs were just that — entertainment that was not supposed to elicit more of the crowd's responses to the topic.[3]

The Meaning of Democracy

A sponsoring agency had ordered NICE to provide civic education on two topics: democracy and human rights. The audiences were female-dominated adult literacy classes, but anyone else who was interested could participate. Local dignitaries were always present, and the sessions would not begin before they had arrived. The delivery of the messages took a standard form that varied only according to the amount of time the officers had at their disposal. The topic *demokalase ndi mfundo zake* (democracy and its principles), for example, had been divided into four subthemes or "objectives" *(zolinga):* "the meaning of democracy" *(tanthauzo la demokalase);* "the cornerstones of democracy" *(ngodya za demokalase);* "the problems that are caused by misunderstanding democracy" *(mavuto omwe ali pano chifukwa chosamvetsa demokalase);* and "how we can help others to understand democracy" *(m'mene tingathandizire anzathu kumvetsetsa demokalase).* In a standard pattern, some of these subthemes were first discussed in small groups, followed by the officer's lecture.

After the opening prayer and general introduction, the officer divided the audience into small groups of four or five persons. Each group was given a pen and a sheet from the officer's flip-chart for writing down the results of their discussion. The groups then presented their points to the others. In every village there was a remarkable consistency in the way in which the groups defined the meaning of democracy. With only minor variations, the most commonly listed items were "talking without fear" *(kulankhula mosaopa),* "living freely" *(kukhala momasuka),* "free schools" *(sukulu za ulere),* "change in politics" *(kusintha kwa ndale),* "deterioration in security" *(kusokoneza kwa chitetezo),* and "inflation" *(kudula kwa zinthu).* Rather than discussing these responses, the officer invariably only thanked the participants. He or she would give the definition of democracy with no reference to what had just been said, typically, "Thank you very much. Let me explain the meaning of democracy in brief. Democracy means a government which is run by the people."[4] The officer would proceed to trace the origins of the term in Greek (Chigiriki), emphasizing the association of "power" or "rule" *(mphamvu)* with the people (see also Nyamilandu 1999).

There was, in other words, an unremarked assumption that the question of democracy could have only one right answer. The issue of "misunderstanding democracy" *(kusamvetsetsa demokalase)* was addressed later during the session, and only then would the officer comment on the participants' own views. Throughout the session, despite the officer's idioms of "discussing" *(kukambirana)* and "sharing ideas" *(kugawana nzeru),* he or she asked the audience only to confirm that they had understood the officer or, if not, to seek clarification: "Does anyone have a question? Is there anybody who has not understood properly?"[5] I will later describe how civic education officers reacted when someone did have a question or comment that did not indicate acceptance of the officer's viewpoint. Crucial to understand here is that officers' preoccupation with "right answers" gave them little chance to actually listen to what transpired during the small-group discussions.[6]

Participants voiced widespread ambivalence among Malawians about their experiences with democratization. "Fear" *(mantha)* in everyday life had been replaced by freedom *(ufulu),* if only in theory, because *demokalase* had also come with countertendencies that undermined the positive changes. Breakdown in security affected both the poor and the well-off, with the violence of "mob justice" and witch cleansing being the poor people's equivalent of armed robberies among the wealthy. Underlying all these concerns was the economic crisis that had increased the cost of living in both villages and towns. Under these circumstances, ancient Greece was decisively less relevant to the meaning of *demokalase* than Malawians' personal experiences of an ambivalent historical rupture.

In spite of ignoring or devaluing these experiences, NICE's civic education officers contributed to the popular juxtaposition of the one-party and the multiparty eras in Malawi. They used the concept of a cornerstone, *ngodya,* to refine the definition of democracy. The one-party regime of the Malawi Congress Party had been built on the four cornerstones of unity, loyalty, discipline, and obedience. The officer was explicit that multiparty democracy also had its cornerstones, in this case six of them: tolerance, citizens' participation, free and fair elections, human rights, the rule of law, and transparent leadership. Once again, there was no attempt to find out the extent to which these cornerstones resonated with the experiences of the audience. The participants were simply expected to accept them as the definition of *demokalase*. The juxtaposition between the two types of cornerstones implied, moreover, that the transition from one to the other had already been achieved. Not only did this strategy of civic education disregard participants' own expertise in defining what democracy meant to them; it also offered them a neat one-to-one comparison between the two eras. Not surprisingly, the strategy actually fed popular nostalgia for some aspects of the old era, particularly discipline that would ease the general feeling of insecurity.

Elections and Participation

Two aspects of the civic education messages on democracy revealed especially clearly the tension between officers' abstractions and villagers' experiences: elections and citizens' participation. Throughout the sessions, the officers were at pains to emphasize democracy as "the rule of the people." They would often provide both the questions and the answers:

When we say that government is based on the rule of the people, what do we mean? We mean a government that is run by the people, and the people are us in the villages. If such a government is run by the people, what do we mean? We choose the leaders, we the people of the villages. Thus all the work that these people do derives from us. The meaning of democracy is a government that is accepted by everyone, because it is the people who choose the leaders.[7]

"We the people of the villages" were, in this view, entrusted with the quintessentially democratic duty of choosing the leaders who managed the government. The topic also prompted the officers to talk about the need to have free and fair elections, about the need for an "equal chance" (*mwayi wofanana*) both during the period of campaigning and on the day of voting itself. They warned against voting under the influence of fear (*mantha*) or "bribes" (*ziphuphu*).

When NICE and other such organizations conduct civic education during elections, they offer Malawians an important source of unbiased information on voting procedures and principles. NICE's messages on the topic at other than election times, however, were abstract, unlikely to strike a chord with the actual experiences of multipartyism in villages and townships. The claim that all the work of the leaders derives from the people of the villages was at best wishful thinking and at worst obscured the politics of patronage in contemporary Malawi. Not only had the country been divided into distinct power bases of the three main parties since the 1994 elections, but also the national-level leaders of these parties had initiated and discarded alliances across the party lines without consulting their local-level supporters (Englund 2002c). Worse still, in many areas access to development projects had been conditional on voting for the ruling party, with the state president threatening that no development *(chitukuko)* would occur in those constituencies that elected opposition candidates. Conversely, clean water, new schools, bridges, and whatever else defined *chitukuko* in particular local settings could also be used as patronage that obliged the electorate to be grateful to the ruling party rather than to expect outlays for needed improvements in poverty-stricken areas.

It was the reality of their situation that made the crowds withdraw into indifferent silence when the officers expounded the theory that villagers were in charge of running the country. Open challenges to the official rhetoric remained rare in Malawi, especially when the rhetoric was spoken by apparently sophisticated civic education officers and when it occurred in an area that was ostensibly within the orbit of a United Democratic Front power base, which was the case in these example villages. Yet there were, and had been even during the one-party era, ways in which disenfranchised Malawians reflected on politics without appearing to criticize power. Songs have historically been major channels of resistance in Malawi and the region (see Vail and White 1991). It was interesting to note that this tradition of resistance had not disappeared with multipartyism when a group of women began, immediately after an officer had lectured them about elections, to sing the following song:

Bungwe, bungwe ilo
Bungwe ilo la chitukuko
X
X kubweretsa sukulu ee
X tidzavotera
Ndalama tilibe

Agency, that agency
That agency of development
X[8]
X bringing schools yeah
We'll vote for X
We have no money

The song, while causing some laughter, was not commented on, and it was considered as one of the energizers by the civic education officers. Yet it offered a perspective on electoral politics that clearly challenged the officers' message. Rather than trusting Malawian politicians, the women intended, according to the song, to vote for the foreign development agency that sponsored their adult literacy classes. The song expressed a desire for a direct link to the agencies that funded Malawi's development. The civic education officers, on the other hand, asked their audience to believe that it was ordinary villagers who were responsible for running the country. This stance appeared implausible to the villagers, because, since the transition to multipartyism, they had seen how members of Parliament and cabinet ministers were often more accountable to national leaders than to their constituents. These civic education sessions took place, moreover, when the entire ruling party was being herded into supporting the state president's unconstitutional third term in office. Under these circumstances, the message on villagers' power to choose their leaders was far removed from the reality of their situation.

Other than the song, the lack of response that civic education on elections drew from the crowd was another indication of how little impact the freedoms of multipartyism had on people's willingness to discuss in public issues that touched on party politics. Even in these strongholds of the ruling party, villagers were all too aware of the violence that followed those who appeared to challenge their leaders. The issue of "participation" (*kutenga mbali*, literally "taking part or a side"), on the other hand, provoked overt reactions, because the civic education officers implicitly scolded the audience for not providing free labor. The officers acknowledged the history of forced labor in Malawi, from *thangata* in the colonial period (Kandawire 1979; Mandala 1990; see also the previous chapter) to the so-called youth weeks and other forms of forced labor during the one-party era. Yet they wanted the audience to understand that villagers themselves benefited from their own work: "Why do many people say that 'oh, I think it's *thangata?*' Isn't that how we say free things have gone; time to work for free went with Kamuzu, right? Nowadays all work is paid for. But we forget that the work we do, especially development work, helps ourselves."[9] Words such as these clearly touched a raw nerve among the audiences. It was by no means the first time that villagers were being urged to work more, and the issue had been discussed in various contexts before the civic education officers arrived to teach them. Striking was the lack of any effort the officers made to find out the specific experiences with development work that each village had had. They showed little interest to engage with villagers' own views on the matter. The officers spoke, instead, the same rhetoric of participation as that spoken by Malawian elites.

Between 1994 and 2004, a major policy initiative to foster poor people's participation was the Malawi Social Action Fund (MASAF), which supported various projects of community development with materials and expertise if the recipients provided labor. While it resulted in several completed school blocks, bridges, clinics, and other developments across the country, it was also the subject of many local controversies, in some cases fueling suspicions of forced labor.

Villagers attempted to make the civic education officers understand these concrete experiences. In one village a woman posed the question, "There are some organizations that choose [workers], that recruit. How can we participate if we are not chosen?"[10] She pointed out that not all villagers were able to participate in development work, and when the representatives of organizations exercised their discretion in choosing participants, misgivings about favoritism arose. In another village a more serious situation awaited the education officers. Abruptly interrupting the officer's speech on the benefits of participation, a woman blurted out, "This village is big, but there is no clinic."[11] The officer smiled and said, "Perhaps these words should go to the agency X [that sponsored the literacy classes]."[12] The practice of referring people to other organizations was called signposting *(kulozera)* in NICE's jargon. As I discuss below, it deflected attention from NICE's own actions without considering whether the other organizations actually had the capacity to assist. In this case, the other agency had neither the mandate nor the funds to build clinics.

What the woman in the audience wanted to express were the villagers' disappointments in their attempts to attract development. The departure of the civic educators enabled me to engage in another facet of ethnographic witnessing, probing the situation in the village that the civic educators were not interested in seeing. My inquiries revealed that the villagers had built a house on their own in the hope that the government would open a clinic in it. This hope was never realized, and the building housed a Community Day Secondary School during my visit, one of the many dismal Malawian schools with no qualified teachers or adequate learning materials. The lack of interest the civic education officers had in finding out about such concrete instances of "participation" was highly frustrating to the villagers. Yet the officers' approach was consistent with their abstract notions of community and participation. Just as they did not appear to respect the local linguistic and religious situation, so too did they work on the assumption that villagers everywhere had unfounded suspicions about participation. Investigations into actual experiences and aspirations never replaced the urge to teach abstract principles to an abstract community, with condescending assumptions about villagers' ignorance and laziness never far below the surface.

Misunderstanding Democracy

The abstract notion of community was compatible with civic education officers' awareness of critical views on democratization in Malawi. "Misunderstanding democracy" *(kusamvetsa demokalase)* was a regular item on their agenda. During the sessions I attended, this topic occasioned more divisions of the crowd into small groups, this time to discuss "problems that are coming because people do not understand democracy" *(mavuto amene akubwera chifukwa choti anthu sakumvetsetsa demokalase)*. Villagers' participation in this discussion as a genuine dialogue between themselves and the civic education officers was circumscribed by the officers' initial statement on what had caused the problems. It was misunderstanding, a false consciousness, that produced problems. Moreover, they deemed that misunderstanding haunted the people, the community itself, all the while avoiding any question of whether political leaders' understanding of democracy was satisfactory. This definition of cause precluded a more open discussion of the political challenges of instituting democracy in the Malawian society. Villagers' own experiences and understandings were, once again, devalued and largely erased from the public domain.

It was striking that in every village the responses to the question of misunderstanding democracy contained some of the observations that had been made in the earlier small-group discussions on the meaning of "democracy." Insecurity and inflation, for example, were frequently mentioned as both the "meaning" *(tanthauzo)* and the "problems" *(mavuto)* of democracy. Problems also generally included "children who did not obey their parents, rudeness, women who wore shorts, not listening to the complaints of the people in the village, lack of access to credit, lack of money."[13] These meanings and diverse problems of democracy not only indicated villagers' ambivalence about the new era; they also suggested that misunderstanding inhibited authorities no less than youths and some women.[14] If authorities did not hear the complaints of their people, had they not also misunderstood democracy?

The civic education officers, for their part, were highly selective in hearing what villagers listed as the problems of misunderstanding democracy. The officers usually began their own accounts of misunderstanding by saying something to the effect of "I choose rudeness, disobedience toward parents, and deteriorating security."[15] The focus became, therefore, those problems that the officer could trace to the villagers' own shortcomings. The officer seldom offered new information at this point, simply returning to what he or she had taught the crowd about the meaning of democracy in the beginning of the session. The crowd had to accept that the problems did not belong to the definition of democracy. The limited extent to which the officer's teaching convinced them was apparent in long silences and forced expressions of consent, as the extract below illustrates:

Civic education officer: But we who are here today, we know the meaning of democracy, right? [silence of six seconds] We also know the principles of democracy, the way in which things should be in a government that is democratic. We can't say that (problems) happen because of democracy, right? [silence of three seconds] You don't answer with force. [silence of five seconds]

Literacy class instructor: [in a quiet voice] Well, the way I have understood today's lesson, perhaps they don't happen because of democracy.[16]

The instructor's cautious endorsement of the officer's point of view, coupled with the officer's difficulties to elicit any response at all, revealed a contrast between the lessons of civic education and the experiences of villagers. While some audiences were less silent than others, villagers' reluctance to respond and lack of enthusiasm marked exchanges on misunderstanding democracy on every occasion. The officers' stubborn insistence on an abstract meaning of democracy, stripped of any actual problems, bypassed two important issues. First, despite asking the audience to suggest problems created by misunderstanding democracy, the officers were not prepared to discuss those problems. Instead of engaging with all the recurring concerns that people expressed, the officers effectively silenced those concerns that did not fit their focus on "the community." Second, this strategy of civic education deprived people of a chance to explain what democracy meant *to them*. The possibility that their current experiences of democracy were ambivalent, with positive developments combining with a deep sense of disempowerment, received no serious consideration. The crowds were left to observe, often in silence, how they were being fed a notion of democracy that did not resonate with their own experiences.

Freedom and Poverty

The villagers' views on the inseparability of the meaning of democracy from the actual political and economic reforms in their country became even more apparent during the sessions on *ufulu wachibadwidwe,* the translation for "human rights" that defines them as freedoms *(maufulu).* The small-group discussions on the meaning of democracy had already listed some reforms that clearly associated democracy with the advent of the UDF government. "Free schools" *(sukulu za ulere)* and "speaking without fear" *(kulankhula mosaopa)* were the most common aspects of popular definitions of democracy. In a similar vein, when the civic education officers asked the crowds to discuss, again in small groups, the meaning of *ufulu wachibadwidwe,* villagers demonstrated their mastery of the current rhetoric. They typically cataloged various freedoms, from the freedoms of speech and dress to the freedom of moving one's household. One group's account amused everyone for being so direct in its rhetoric: "Freedom of speech, freedom of studying, freedom to dress in a self-respecting way, freedom of man and woman to abstain, we thank Bakili."[17] The group had included key elements of the new rhetoric, including the emphasis on free speech and schooling, as well as abstaining *(kupewa)* in this time of AIDS. As if to ensure that their account was politically correct, the group finished by thanking President Bakili Muluzi.

I show below how, in many villages, people began to express their impatience with the messages of civic education, especially when human rights were discussed. The initial challenge for the civic education officers was, however, to distinguish an abstract notion of human rights from the political rhetoric in which most villagers had placed it. A key strategy was to emphasize that freedom *(ufulu)* belonged to each individual irrespective of the political system in which the individual lived. The following exchange illustrates the civic education officers' challenges to get their message across:

> *Officer:* When did this freedom begin? For a person to have freedom, when did this freedom begin?
>
> *Woman 1:* It started in 1994.
>
> *Officer:* 1994. We hear that lady, right? 1994. How about you, sister in the back? When did your freedom begin?

Woman 2: It's the same.

   Officer: It's the same, right? 1994. Here, sister?

Woman 3: '94.

   Officer: '94. When we are able to understand these freedoms, they begin even before the person has been born.[18]

Ufulu, in its shift of meaning from national independence to individual freedom, was so much associated with the UDF government's ascension to power that the question "When did your freedom begin?" was politically loaded. In this UDF heartland, a villager suggested other origins for freedom at his or her own peril. As with civic education on democracy, the officers were not interested in understanding the reasons for villagers' apparently mistaken views but proceeded to expound an abstract notion. Particularly bewildering was the idea that the person possessed freedom even before he or she was born: "Freedom begins before the person is born, when the mother has an image of the child. . . . When the child is born, that's when he or she just continues with other freedoms."[19] Although the officers merely wanted to extend rights to fetuses, the idea that one is a person even before one's birth hardly resonated with local concepts of personhood. As was mentioned in chapter 2, Malawian and regional cosmologies posit persons as social beings who grow throughout their life cycles (Englund 1999). Pregnancies are certainly taken seriously, but the emphasis on the freedom of an unborn baby is unlikely to strike people as relevant during civic education.

It was during these sessions that the officers were often interrupted by questions and comments that appeared unrelated to what they were saying. These interruptions typically concerned villagers' disappointments with credit facilities. In one village, for example, an officer was interrupted when he was expounding the theory of individual freedom with these words: "I said that freedom begins even before the person is born; when he or she is born it just continues, right?"[20] A woman in the crowd seized the opportunity and pointed out that villagers needed credit to start businesses, exclaiming, "We don't have anything at all!" *(Tilibe chili chonse!).* The officer was flexible enough to acknowledge the woman's complaint, but he used it as an excuse to demand more sponsorship for civic education: "I believe that the senior officials who are here [pointing to the representatives of the donor agency that sponsored the literacy classes] will plan with us another visit, so that we'll bring only those studies that show how you can run small businesses. When those who lend money come back, you will not get lost with that money."[21] The officer's response was a remarkable example of avoiding the political issues surrounding the inequality alluded to in the woman's exclamation "we don't have anything at all!" The officer recommended more civic education, implying that the problem was villagers who "get lost with their money." At the same time, the officer was also able to suggest he himself would be the one to deliver these studies — funded by the donor agency that, as we saw in the officer's earlier attempts to "signpost" villagers to this agency, in reality had no mandate to work on this particular issue.

Women in these villages were eager to have NICE's civic education officers understand their negative experiences with microcredit. They complained, in particular, about the policies of the Foundation for International Community Assistance (FINCA), a lending institution that had arrived in Malawi in 1994 as a part of the boom in microcredits created by the new government's program of poverty alleviation. FINCA's loans were available to women, who were expected to form groups that took collective responsibility for paying them back. If one member defaulted, others would be obliged to make her payments as well.[22] An especially onerous requirement was the repayment of the loan by weekly installments. This requirement placed considerable pressure on women to have a cash flow that was impervious to fluctuations in business, not to mention impervious to such problems as funerals and illness.

Women in different villages presented strikingly similar complaints to the NICE officers. For example, when an officer was explaining that "we have the freedom to speak" (tili ndi ufulu wolankhula), "every person has the freedom to join any religion he or she wants" (munthu wina aliyense ali ndi ufulu wolowa chipembedzo china chili chonse chimene iyeyo akuchifuna), and other freedoms that were likely to be, at least in rhetoric, already familiar to all the adults who were present, a woman interrupted him with a concrete problem: "The organization that my friends mentioned [lends] insufficient money, since you can borrow three thousand [kwacha]. What kind of business can you start with three thousand [kwacha]?"[23] FINCA's policies had already been mentioned during this session, but the officer had continued his speech on freedoms after he had recommended that the women receive civic education on small-scale businesses. This woman's question indicated that the issue was far from resolved.

The officer responded to her question by appealing again to the aid agency that had brought NICE to the village and quickly said, "So let us continue to look at those freedoms" (Ndiye tipitirire kuona maufulu aja). The women, however, were not prepared to discard the topic. Before the officer could continue, another woman began to complain about membership fees: "And also, those who borrow money are the poor like us, but before you have borrowed money from that organization, they say that those who want to take money should give three hundred [kwacha], perhaps two hundred [kwacha], others four hundred [kwacha]. We want money; should we also give two hundred [kwacha] to find money?"[24] In this case the officer consistently appealed to the aid agency and continuing civic education until the women ceased to interrupt him with their complaints. In another village, however, a different officer used the concept of freedom to respond to similar grievances: "We have the freedom to choose an organization; if FINCA has bad policies, leave it" *(Tili ndi ufulu wosankha bungwe; ngati FINCA ili ndi mfundo zoipa, siyeni).* Although this statement received some applause, it was, in practice, as inconsequential as the other responses. Impoverished villagers were hardly in a bargaining position with lending institutions that operated on commercial principles. The neoliberal vision of free choice entailed by the officer's appeal to freedom bore little relevance to the local predicament.

The above examples illustrate how participants in civic education on democracy and human rights refused, often in subtle ways, the role that officers assigned to them. Instead of being the recipients of knowledge, the women in these examples wanted to inform the officers about the injustices they had experienced. NICE's promise to encourage dialogue was revealed as mere rhetoric by these popular grievances, which were never the starting points for civic education. It became apparent, as in civic education on democracy, that the officers solicited people's views on human rights only in order to expose ways in which an abstract notion of rights could be misunderstood. The officers began, in other words, with a preconceived idea of rights, whose relevance to local realities was not an issue to be discussed. Women registered their impatience with this approach by interrupting the officers with complaints about microcredits. For these women, the interesting issue was the actual reforms and circumstances that influenced their lives. Persisting with their abstract notion of rights, the officers failed to act as intermediaries between the women and the institutions that had caused their injury.

Whose Knowledge Counts?

Civic education officers' encounters with the grassroots show how they pursued an apolitical agenda on topics that were, in point of fact, profoundly political. A major way in which NICE attempted to resolve this paradox was by placing the onus of securing democracy and development on an imagined "local community." It was the community that had a key responsibility for its own well-being, and the problems that hindered its development were, to a great extent, caused by its own "misunderstandings." The assumption that problems with democracy and development could be traced to the poor themselves called for civic education and "capacity building." As, for instance, two recent studies from Tanzania have argued, such interventions treat consciousness in a vacuum. Tim Kelsall (2002, 601) has written about a "liberal-developmental" subjectivity as an objective of these programs, and Maia Green has pointed out how "individual agents are empowered at the level of consciousness, in a vacuum divorced from actual social and political action" (2000, 68; emphasis omitted).

This chapter has given substance to the argument in chapter 1 that the currently influential version of human rights discourse involves a certain contempt for the reality of situations (Badiou 2001). This contempt is informed by human rights activists' belief in universal subjectivity that they alone can redeem. They are propelled to act by the abstract victimhood of the downtrodden and the marginalized. Although participatory citizenship is promised in rhetoric, the contempt for the situation of human rights keeps it below the horizon. The actual citizenship offered is one-dimensional in its scope, a guarantee of political freedoms, and even then the object of constant concern that subjects submit to the right attitudes and values (Lazar 2004). The forms of contemporary neoliberal governance vary, but they share remarkable affinities across the world. As Julia Paley (2004) has shown with respect to Chile, much as the neoliberal definitions of democracy champion the free and critical expression of public opinion, it is another matter entirely whether that opinion can influence public policy. The stress is on procedure rather than outcome, something that NICE's abstract principles promoted in the Malawian context.

The ethnographic witnessing in this and the previous chapter facilitates understanding of two crucial issues in regard to NICE's work. First, the state's continuing stranglehold on non-governmental interventions makes it understandable *why* the managers of NICE consistently trained their staff and volunteers to sidestep politics. Through its monopoly on legislation and the means of violence, the state controlled the definition of democracy in Malawi. Second, the evidence presented here and in the previous chapter also demonstrates *how* the apolitical imperative was sustained by NICE's civic education officers and volunteers. A conundrum that requires more attention, however, is that the irrelevant and abstract messages of civic education rarely, if ever, provoked Malawian officers and volunteers to critically reflect on their own work. This prompts the critical question, Why did they so readily assume this apolitical disposition despite their own frustrations with Malawi's economic and political impasse?

The immediate answer is that they enjoyed the status distinctions that civic education maintained in democratic Malawi. The previous chapter showed how NICE's officers and volunteers came to think of themselves as a privileged class, equipped with symbolic and material accoutrements that resonated, however modestly, with colonial and postcolonial relations of inequality. They objectified the targets of civic education, despite the rhetoric of participation and responsibility, as anonymous and abstract "communities." The "misunderstandings of democracy" persisted as an item on the civic educators' agenda, a reminder to themselves how unfinished the process of absorbing new values and attitudes was. Insofar as new subjectivities were emerging, the civic educators themselves were their likeliest embodiments, defined as such by objectifying others. The abstract notion of human rights was quite compatible with these inequalities: it made civic educators the bearers of truth, while it erased from purview specific political and historical conditions.

It is particularly apposite that my fieldwork on the encounters between civic education officers and the grassroots focused on adult literacy classes. The Malawian elites, and those who aspire to become part of them, see illiteracy as one of the most obvious indices of backwardness and ignorance. Note that disadvantage in an economic and social sense is not the only issue. Illiteracy also equals ignorance, underdeveloped intellectual faculties that frequently result in mistaken beliefs and misunderstandings. In 2003, for example, when I attended the International Adult Literacy Day celebrations in Malawi, I observed that both governmental and non-governmental representatives frequently referred to illiteracy with the Chichewa term for "ignorance," *umbuli*. Its dictionary meaning is "disposition or conduct where one knows nothing" *(khalidwe kapena machitidwe osadziwa zinthu)* (Centre for Language Studies 2000, 348). The minister of gender and community services, who graced the occasion as the guest of honor, declared in her halting English to Television Malawi: "Anybody who is illiterate cannot do anything, even in the family. You cannot do anything, because the understanding, the understanding level is low. So anything cannot go well, even HIV/AIDS. Anybody cannot understand if he or she is illiterate. You need to know what you are doing or what you want to do."[25]

It will be recalled that the 1999 Human Rights Needs Assessment Survey stated that because of high levels of illiteracy, many Malawians "do not have the necessary intellectual competence and capacity needed to articulate such a subject as human rights" (HRRC 1999, 54). Two more public statements demonstrate the extent to which this discourse is shared across political divides. The first is by an executive member of the ruling UDF; the other, by the executive director of the Civil Liberties Committee, a leading Malawian human rights NGO:

In a democracy you have to think for yourself. Now when you have over 60 percent of a population that is illiterate, they are guided constantly, and it is difficult for them to perceive what is the way ahead and what path we should follow.[26]

When you have an illiterate society, politicians take advantage.[27]

While the lack of literacy skills is an indisputable disadvantage in contemporary Malawi, important in these statements is the assumption that illiterate Malawians are incapable of thinking for themselves. Quite apart from the UDF representative's exaggerated statistics on illiteracy,[28] the claim that illiterates need to be "guided constantly" betrays a patronizing attitude, a self-serving assumption of inferiority that obliges others to lead the chronically misguided subjects. Since it is difficult for them to perceive the way ahead, politicians may also take advantage of them.

What these assumptions ignore is the possibility that people, whether literate or not, have insights into their own life situations and cogent reasons for acting on those insights. The assumptions also ignore the fact that few Malawians acquire knowledge about current affairs through reading. News travels orally, and the blanket condemnation of illiterates obscures important differences among those who claim to be literate. In Malawi as elsewhere, it may be useful to think of "literacies" in the plural, with the elites socialized to an interpretative relation to texts and nonelites to a submissive relation to texts (Collins 1995, 84).

The critical issue is whose knowledge counts. By conjuring up an image of intellectually inferior masses, civic educators ignored the possibility that people considered their civic education messages as irrelevant. I must stress that I do not see that a deliberate plan informed these processes. Just as NICE's volunteers came to think of themselves as separate from the grassroots through a subtle identification with the symbols of progress, so too did officers have little reason to question their assumptions about inferiority; after long historical processes, those assumptions merely appeared to affirm the natural state of affairs. Everything appears natural when the distinctions and inequalities are also a part of the landscape, spatialized by locating the masses in villages *(midzi)*. While the rural village often signifies in Malawi the idealized home of tradition (Englund 2002d; Ribohn 2002), the flip side of its image summons up backwardness. A prominent urban-based private school, for example, advertised itself by declaring, "You do not have to send your children to the middle of nowhere back into the eighteenth century."[29] Note how a spatialized image combines with a temporal one. It is a prime example of an enduring colonial mentality, sheer contempt, "the middle of nowhere" seen as "the eighteenth century" in a country of discrete pockets of modernity. Colonial agents and their critics have endlessly debated these images (see Dirks 1992). "For Conrad's Marlow," Simon Gikandi writes about the novel *Heart of Darkness,* "going up the River Congo was like going back in time" (2002, 148). For the would-be elites of postcolonial Malawi, the rural masses are not only ignorant but also scarcely their contemporaries.

Those who are relegated to the status of inferiors have, of course, their own views on civic education that devalues their experiences. This chapter has indicated how civic education officers' assumptions of "misunderstandings" served to obscure popular ambivalence about the experiments with democratization in Malawi. Inadvertently, NICE ended up contributing to negative discourses on democracy precisely by confining the concept. If "democracy" means exhortations to participate and single-minded veneration of individual freedoms, it loses its critical edge to address questions such as why villagers may not see development despite their participation, or why the rhetoric about economic empowerment through microcredit may not ease their poverty. The concepts of democracy and human rights, it should be recalled, are formidable tools of critique. The question is whether the civic education described in this chapter allows Malawians to use these tools.

One emerging form of popular critique in Malawi attacks human rights NGOs for being elitist and greedy. This critique carries the danger of being unduly useful to the government, which would not mind curtailing the independence of certain NGOs. Yet if the capacity of human rights NGOs to identify with the concerns of the poor is as limited as NICE's, they have only themselves to blame for popular doubts. During my other projects of ethnographic fieldwork, I have frequently witnessed attempts by impoverished Malawians, expressing their frustration with economic and political reforms, to create networks that bypass both political parties and secular NGOs (see, e.g., Englund 2000, 2001b, 2002a, 2003, 2004a). The frustrations underlying these attempts are also topics in Malawian popular culture. A character in Ken Kalonde's novel, for example, exclaims, "What should I eat with the current freedom?" *(Ndizidya chiyani ndi ufulu wa masiku anowu?)* (Kalonde 2000, 42). Charles Sinetre's song takes a swipe at local NGOs that claim to defend children's rights. It describes how NGO executives pass children engaged in petty trading on the roadside as they themselves proceed to collect hefty allowances for attending a seminar in the capital.[30] The tools of subversive critique cannot so easily be seized from the hands of the disempowered. Nor, as especially chapter 7 will show, is the critique necessarily confined to the idioms of individual freedoms.

CHAPTER 5

Legal Aid for Abused Labor

Individualizing Grievances

Civic education is by no means the only domain of human rights discourse worth critical consideration in Malawi and Zambia. In both countries, human rights NGOs and projects often combine awareness-raising efforts with more tangible interventions. Some of these interventions are highly visible in the public sphere, while others are less dramatic actions taken on behalf of particular disadvantaged individuals. The most high-profile interventions have included press releases and public demonstrations against ruling politicians' attempts to undermine democratization. As has already been mentioned, NGOs, in collaboration with church and other religious groups, voiced public protests that subverted the ruling party's desire to allow the state president to stand for an unconstitutional third term in office in both Malawi and Zambia. While the NGOs appeared to have popular sentiment on their side, the outcome of these protests was not obvious. The protests bore testimony to activists' commitment to their cause despite widespread intimidation and propaganda by the agents of the state.

Free legal aid is an example of human rights NGOs' less conspicuous interventions. Many NGOs have been established by lawyers, and they have subscribed to the idea that human rights abuses are best rectified through the legal domain. A remarkably consistent pattern characterized the legal aid of human rights NGOs in Malawi and Zambia during the first decade of democratization. Often their initial interest was to monitor and defend human rights in general, from various civil and political freedoms to prison conditions and the conduct of the police to gender relations. After opening centers for legal aid where citizens and refugees could present their complaints, these NGOs were, however, generally overwhelmed with labor-related disputes. Appalling conditions of work, including poor pay and arbitrary dismissals without compensation, gave complaints a tone not quite anticipated by activists' preoccupation with freedoms. These complaints exposed the actual socioeconomic inequalities that existed in the areas where human rights were being pursued. This and the next chapter investigate whether NGOs' legal aid provided an effective answer to these inequalities.

In Malawi, the legal aid of NGOs has complemented similar efforts by several governmental institutions. Labor disputes, for example, were considered in regional and district labor offices even before the democratic transition. The procedures of these offices were notoriously slow and generally seen as being prone to corruption through employers' bribes. The new constitution in 1995 obliged the state to establish more institutions to safeguard human rights, and one of them was the office of the ombudsman. Despite this office's mandate to investigate misconduct in various types of public activity, it received mainly labor-related complaints until 2002, when these disputes were defined as the prerogative of the Industrial Relations Court, another institution established by the new constitution. At the time of this clarification in responsibilities, about 70 percent of all cases thus far presented to the ombudsman were reported to be labor disputes.[1]

Non-governmental centers for legal aid have attracted clients because their services have been offered free of charge. The Industrial Relations Court, by contrast, has held its clients liable for paying the costs of witnesses.[2] The governmental Department of Legal Aid has offered free legal advice and representation, but its lack of resources and personnel has made the procedures very slow and inefficient (WLSA 2000, 81–85). NGOs have provided, by contrast, a rather swift and personal conduct of those cases that they have decided to pursue. In Malawi, two NGOs were particularly prominent in offering free legal aid during the first decade after the democratic transition: the Malawi Centre for Advice, Research, and Education on Rights (Malawi CARER) and the Centre for Human Rights and Rehabilitation (CHRR). Both also witnessed high demand for legal aid on labor disputes. The CHRR, which was the primary setting of my fieldwork on legal aid, stated in its biannual report for April–October in 2000 that, out of a total of 360 cases, 232 cases (64 percent) concerned labor relations. The biannual report for the same months in 2001 stated that, out of a total of 212 cases, 160 cases (75 percent) were labor-related.[3]

Despite being free to clients, legal aid has been costly and has competed with other priorities in NGOs' work. Malawi CARER has engaged two lawyers at its head office (Chirwa 2000b, 27), while the CHRR has had only one lawyer at a time. The impact of status distinctions on legal aid has been considerable, and this chapter shows how an NGO failed to narrow enormous gaps in income even among its own personnel. Lawyers' salaries, in particular, placed a major burden on the CHRR's budget. It relied on the work of paralegal officers when its funds were insufficient to attract qualified lawyers. Paralegal officers received training, provided by NGOs themselves, on laws and legal procedures, but they could not represent clients in court. In most cases, therefore, the aim of legal aid was to achieve redress through mediation between clients and their adversaries.[4] My analysis in this and the next chapter shows how "legal aid" was often a misnomer for this mediation. NGO personnel had to engage in personal and piecemeal bargaining with abusive employers, with adverse consequences for both the rule of law and the welfare of workers.

The scarcity of resources, coupled with the fact that the tedium of legal aid has not offered NGOs as much publicity as high-profile interventions have, has severely constrained NGOs' commitment to legal advocacy as a means of social and economic transformation. Instead, legal aid has often been reduced to a technical management of grievances, seen as individual rather than collective predicaments. One of the disconcerting findings discussed in this and the next chapter is the extent to which an NGO's legal officers used their apparently exclusive legal knowledge to avoid confronting the exploitation that many Malawians endured. It is important to understand why this finding should be so disconcerting. As mentioned, this study is not based on a particular vision of democracy; nor is the propagation of absolute equality its aim. Its task is to investigate whether "democracy" and "human rights" were allowed to exist as contested concepts, amenable to the expression and negotiation of diverse interests. Legal aid offers insights into this issue, not because it ought to level all inequalities, but because it promised to defend the minimal legal provisions for decent living.

Wonderful Laws, Appalling Conditions

A sharp contrast between appearance and reality strikes the observer of workers' rights in Malawi. On the one hand, the democratic transition heralded progressive reforms in legislation, resulting in, for example, the

Labor Relations Act in 1996 and the Employment Act in 1999. On the other hand, the provisions that these laws make for workers' organizations and the conditions of their employment have not, on the whole, been translated into practice. The observer might expect politically independent NGOs to champion a scrupulous application of the new laws. Yet as this and the next chapter show, legal aid on behalf of workers' rights was compromised by legal officers' lack of commitment to a structural transformation in society.

Taken at face value, the new laws represented a major step forward from the labor and employment laws of the one-party regime. Not only were the old laws largely a continuation of colonial legislation; the one-party regime also integrated the Trade Union Congress within the ruling party (McCracken 1988). While the Malawi Congress Party supported strikes for political reasons before independence, labor militancy had no legal basis after it. The Labor Relations Act of 1996 separated labor organizations from political parties and created the legal basis for a remarkably independent labor movement.

Even before the new Labor Relations Act had been passed in Parliament, workers in both public and private-sector organizations took advantage of the more permissive setting. The same fifty-four organizations that reported only four strikes for the period of 1966–91 reported seventy-five strikes for the period of 1992–99 (Dzimbiri 2002, 133). Trade unions, some dormant and others disbanded by the one-party regime, were resuscitated or formed anew, with the number of registered unions rising from twelve to twenty-one between 1994 and 2000 (Dzimbiri 2002, 238). The Labor Relations Act came to support this resurgent activism through its provisions for the freedom of association, collective bargaining, and dispute settlement. Section 5, moreover, provides the right of an organization to affiliate with and participate in the activities of international workers' and employers' associations. The provisions in sections 42–54 control the powers of the minister of labor and the registrar of trade unions by stipulating the rules of dispute settlement and the right to strike.

The new government did not take long, however, before indicating that its commitment to workers' rights was only superficial. Various tactics, some subtle and others intimidating, were at the ruling politicians' disposal. For example, as the biggest source of employment in Malawi, the civil service had demonstrated in 1993–94 its capacity to paralyze the country through strike action. The leadership in the Malawi Congress of Trade Unions (MCTU) developed remarkably independent and critical views on the country's economy and labor relations. They were, however, countered by the submissive views of the Congress of Malawi Trade Unions, which came into existence in 2000 (Anders 2002, 47). It was, in principle, a splinter group of the MCTU, but few failed to notice the complicity of the state in founding this second labor federation, particularly when some of its leaders were seen to acquire considerable material benefits. The effort to mislead the public already began, of course, with the name of the federation, violating the stipulation in the Labor Relations Act that the registrar registers a union only when the name "does not so closely resemble that of another trade union or employer's organization so as to mislead and cause confusion."[5]

Before this shadow federation was established, the government had already sought to defuse the threat posed by critical leaders in teachers' and civil servants' unions by posting them to different parts of the country and abroad (Manda 2000, 69). President Muluzi also used his public speeches to warn trade unions that he would "deal with them" if they opposed his government (Manda 2000, 64). Under such circumstances, trade unions faced great difficulties in consolidating themselves and pursuing reforms in labor relations. By the late 1990s, it had become common for the police to use tear gas to disrupt strikes (Dzimbiri 2002, 157).

The workers who brought their grievances to centers for legal aid did not usually belong to unions. In their cases, the Employment Act of 1999 was more relevant than the Labor Relations Act. Again, a comparison between the old and new laws creates the impression of great strides. The one-party regime did have an employment act, but it applied to a very small proportion of the working population (Banda 1995, 49). The new employment act, by contrast, was universal in its application and contained provisions regarding, for example, antidiscrimination, forced labor, child labor, hazardous work, termination of contracts, maximum daily working hours, payment of wages, and minimum wage. The act was remarkably worker-friendly and stipulated, in its sections on the termination of contracts, the minimum period of notice in writing and the level of payment in lieu of notice.[6] Various forms of contract were taken into account, such as those in which the worker was paid on a monthly, fortnightly, weekly, daily, and hourly basis.

The stipulation of minimum wage must be hailed as a particularly progressive move in a country with an authoritarian past. Subsection 3 of section 54 began, moreover, by requiring the minister to consider "the needs of workers and their families, the general level of wages, the cost of living, social security benefits and the relative living standards of other social groups." Subsection 4 of section 54 provided a clear framework for prescribing minimum wages by stipulating that "the Minister shall, in consultation with representative organizations of workers and employers, reconsider the level of the minimum wage at least once every three years."

The Limits of Legalism

New laws such as the Employment Act of 1999 would seem to offer human rights activists a sound basis for both civic education and direct interventions on behalf of disgruntled workers. The rare occurrence of these interventions during the first ten years of democracy left ruling politicians without a serious challenge to their self-congratulatory rhetoric on workers' rights. When the ubiquitous discourse on individual freedoms marginalized the systematic promotion of socioeconomic rights, ruling politicians were given a free hand in claiming that the new laws reflected their commitment to their subjects' welfare. In 2001, for instance, the vice president of Malawi declared that "the law should be used as an instrument for sustaining social and economic development."[7] With its progressive legislation, Malawi could, in this rhetoric, bask in the glory of empowering its citizens.

The vice president's comment was not, however, mere self-congratulatory rhetoric. It also contained a profound assumption about the power of law to effect, virtually by itself, social and economic transformation, an assumption that also informed NGOs' legal aid. Such an assumption has recently come under scathing critique by Fidelis Edge Kanyongolo (2004), a Malawian legal scholar. The crux of his critique is twofold. For one thing, Kanyongolo questions the assumption that the judiciary and other legal experts can be entrusted to monitor and enforce social justice, however progressive the legislation. Legal experts do not occupy a political and cultural vacuum, and their interpretations and arguments can serve specific interests in society. For another, Kanyongolo criticizes the illusion that comprehensive transformations take place through the cumulative effects of particular court cases. Although transformation could happen in the very long term, the illusion leads in practice to a focus on individuals. Rather than discerning a collective grievance in several individual cases, those who work under this illusion remain content with particular solutions.

Kanyongolo's critical perspective is a lone voice in Malawi. Human rights NGOs have not devised strategies of collective action similar to those that characterized the successful campaign against the state president's third term in office. Legal aid, despite its potential benefits to particular individuals, has represented a belief in piecemeal and technical solutions to widespread exploitation. No mobilization of workers to demand their rights as enshrined in laws has appeared on NGOs' agenda. Instead, representation, lobbying, and organized disobedience have been left to weak trade unions, whose membership covers only a fraction of Malawi's employed population. Centers for legal aid have been frequented by security guards, domestic servants, semiskilled and unskilled laborers, and others at the very bottom of the workforce. Treated as individuals by NGOs' legal officers, these workers have been denied an opportunity to voice their grievances as a collective force demanding structural transformations. At the same time, a certain objectification of claimants has informed the work of the NGO that is in the focus of this and the next chapter. While claimants have been led to believe that their grievances are particular, they have also been treated as generic representatives of ignorant and irresponsible masses. Individualization has not involved respect for clients as resourceful persons. Contempt for their victimhood has made each appear as a saboteur of his or her own freedom.

Minimum wage is a good example of the discrepancy between appearance and reality in Malawian labor relations. As mentioned, the Employment Act of 1999 stipulated that the level of the minimum wage is reconsidered "at least once every three years." Over three years after the act came into force, Malawians were yet to witness such a review. While the violation of the act thus appeared to begin with the very state that had introduced it, another serious issue was the level at which minimum wage had been set since the new act came into force. It was MK 50 (about US$0.52 in 2003) per day in the urban areas of Lilongwe, Blantyre, Zomba, and Mzuzu. The figure excluded a housing allowance of MK 5 per day. In rural areas, the minimum wage was MK 37 (about US$0.39 in 2003) per day, with a housing allowance of MK 3.70. Thus the minimum wage in an urban area for a thirty-day month was MK 1,500 (about US$16 in 2003), with a housing allowance of MK 150 (about US$1.60 in 2003).

It is difficult to decide what was the most appalling aspect of the Malawian minimum wage. Could it be, for example, that many of the workers whom I met at a center for legal aid had been paid wages far below the minimum level?[8] Or is it that I rarely witnessed a legal officer investigating this breach of law, the officer instead focusing on some other grievance? Or is the most appalling aspect, rather, the level of the actual legal minimum wage? First, to find accommodation for MK 150 per month in an urban area was likely to send one to a shack or to a kraal shared with goats. In Lilongwe in 2003, the rent of even the cheapest house without electricity and running water was seldom under MK 600 per month. Add to this monthly costs such as MK 600 for a bag of maize for a family of six, MK 450 for relish, and so on, and the pitiful inadequacy of the legal minimum wage is all too evident.

Entrenched Authoritarianism

Trade unions remained weak and human rights NGOs had other priorities during the time of my research, so strikes again became rare and often unsuccessful. I frequently discussed with the rural and urban poor the reasons for labor docility in Malawi. The most common reason that emerged in these discussions was that jobs were scarce, with a large pool of unemployed or underemployed individuals always prepared to fill the gap left by dismissed employees. The incidence of unemployment was difficult to ascertain, since the state had no provisions for those who were without formal employment. Such individuals tended to sustain themselves as criminals, beggars, petty traders, or pieceworkers. Yet, as my interlocutors indicated, regular income, however small, was very attractive under the conditions of poverty, in many cases seen as the foundation of household economy on which complementary income-generating activities could be built.[9]

Under such circumstances, few were prepared to endanger their income by participating in strikes. Without a solid collective force to represent their interests, striking workers were often dismissed, a new contingent of workers only too pleased to take their place with unchanged conditions of service. Few strikes had a positive and sustained impact on workers' welfare. Civil servants, for example, organized several strikes in various departments, without much success in realizing their demands, except in 1994, when a substantial salary increase for junior officers was secured (Anders 2002, 47).

Labor activism at David Whitehead and Sons, a Malawian textile manufacturer and retailer, was particularly illuminating. While the company's workers spearheaded the transition to the new era with a strike in 1992, they staged another, less successful strike in 2003 to protest against the selling of the company at a low price. Although their strike was one reason for instituting a presidential commission of inquiry, the ultimate result was that the sale proceeded on virtually the same terms as before. The decade that had passed between the two strikes had turned the company's work-force from a vanguard of positive change to an ultimately insignificant voice of protest in the quest for profits and foreign investment.

The events at David Whitehead and Sons also illustrate the extent to which labor activism is confined to particular workplaces. Solidarity, join-ing together workers under similar conditions in different companies, is yet to enter the vocabulary of Malawian discourse on rights. The same lack of solidarity accounts, of course, for the fact that those in relatively good positions of employment do not stage protests against the exploita-tion of others, including the appalling level of the minimum wage. For this reason, managers are often able to conduct their companies and workplaces as if they were distinct worlds.

Authoritarianism, no doubt influenced by the political culture of an earlier era, is never far from the surface in Malawian labor relations. Workers at the Lilongwe Water Board, for example, threatened to go on strike in 2001, because the water tariff had been increased twice within a year without any change in their meager wages. Meanwhile, board mem-bers were purportedly buying themselves expensive cars. After the threat of a strike had been issued, the clerk to the board had this to say: "We are still looking into those issues and a decision has not been made yet. Once it is made it shall be communicated to the workers and the press of course."[10] The workers were, in other words, expected to wait until the board reached a decision at a convenient time. Rather than representing the process as negotiation, moreover, the board gave the impression that it had the power to make unilateral decisions that would subsequently be communicated to the workers.

The Politics of Complexion

Authoritarianism in Malawian labor relations during the first decade of democracy was nowhere more apparent than in some businesses run by persons of European and Asian origin. The popular resentment against the yawning gap between their wealth and their workers' conditions was palpable to anyone who was trusted enough to be told such opinions. The problem was also touched on in the 2001 National Human Development Report prepared by the United Nations Development Programme (UNDP). It traced the sources of income inequality in Malawi to, among other things, the fact that the trade sector was "heavily dominated by the

Asian community, with indigenous traders participating on the margins and their operations not growing to the levels attained by the Asian traders" (UNDP 2001, 20). A newsletter from the Malawi Congress of Trade Unions went even further by offering the headline "Asians Exploiting Malawians."[11] It reported that workers at Asian-owned businesses had formed a trade union called the Asian Workers Union, a rather misleading name, because it represented Malawians who worked for employers of Asian origin. Little has been heard of this union since, and the case study in the next chapter, revolving around a conflict between an Asian employer and a Malawian worker, will show some of the challenges in organizing labor in these enterprises.

The actual numbers of foreign nationals have always been very low in Malawi. At independence in 1964, British and other European nationals constituted fewer than 0.2 percent of the total population (Pryor 1990, 24). The figure contrasted with their proportion in the settler society of Southern Rhodesia (now Zimbabwe), where it was 4.8 percent in 1964. The British government had also brought Asians, primarily Indians, as soldiers to Malawi during late colonialism, and many of them remained as merchants. Their proportion of the total population was a mere 0.3 percent at independence (Pryor 1990, 26). During the 1970s in Malawi as in some other African countries, the Asian business community came under fire, and Kamuzu Banda's regime forced it to relinquish its businesses in rural areas. Some Asians acquired Malawian nationality and have sought to enjoy the patronage of the government of the day ever since. The 1998 Population and Housing Census was the first to collect data on nationality, and it revealed that 99 percent, or 9.9 million people, of the enumerated population were Malawians (National Statistical Office 2002, 28). The largest group of foreign nationals was Mozambicans, but even they constituted a mere 0.3 percent of the total population. Of the Indian nationals, 37 percent lived in Lilongwe and 52 percent in Blantyre (National Statistical Office 2002, 31). After 1994, Malawians living in urban areas were also able to observe the arrival of new entrepreneurs. Apparently encouraged by President Muluzi's Muslim identity, these entrepreneurs came from the Middle East and North Africa to compete or collaborate with earlier migrants from India and Pakistan.

Foreign nationals and Asians naturalized in Malawi thus wield considerably greater economic power than their numbers suggest. Complexion remains an index of wealth and opportunity, with most Europeans and Asians enjoying vastly higher standards of living than most black Malawians. Virtually all expatriates, as well as those Asians who have acquired Malawian citizenship and the black elite, live in urban residential areas that the impoverished majority visit only as servants, guards, petty traders, laborers, and, occasionally, armed robbers. Although apartheid was never formally instituted in Malawi, segregation is also evident in diet, modes of transport, pastimes, and numerous other everyday contexts. Foreign professionals also tend to be paid more than similarly qualified Malawians.[12] Expatriate aid workers, in turn, usually wallow in their luxury, exempt from tax and employing domestic servants and other support personnel.

In order for us to gain insight into the rather patronizing environment in which Malawians working for employers of European and Asian origin were supposed to defend their rights during the first decade of democratization, an examination of the market in domestic servants is revealing. In the close-knit expatriate communities, Malawian servants circulated on the basis of personal recommendations. One source of information was the advertisements that were displayed in shops frequented by expatriates. Although servants may have requested such ads at the end of their service, they were usually composed by expatriate employers themselves. Statements such as "His present salary is only MK 4,000" were the closest one could get to price tags on people in a country that proscribed slavery.

The servant's character was also a central issue in these ads; for instance, "He is a hard-working, kind, and very modest man." Modesty, hardly a key feature of the expatriate lifestyle, was clearly expected of both the servant and his or her family: "Mr. Pondelani has a lovely wife, Jennifer, who is equally kind and modest." The ever-present fears that poor servants might steal from their masters or madams were best allayed with personal experiences: "On several occasions I have entrusted Mr. Phiri with my property and money, and I have never had any reason to doubt his honesty." Many ads included photographs of the people being advertised, and when a servant decided to wear spectacles in his picture, the expatriate author of the ad included this qualification: "Mr. Kadzuwa has an excellent eyesight. He only found that wearing specs would make him look nicer in the photo!"

The misunderstanding over the significance of spectacles is a rather harmless example of the distinct perspectives of servants and their employers. In this picture, the servant had dressed up in a formal suit, complete with spectacles, as many Malawian men do when they want to create an impression of sophistication; never mind that the spectacles are usually made of plain glass. The desire for sophistication was likely to be similar to that of those civic educators who, as seen in chapter 3, stressed personal hygiene as their distinctive characteristic. In the labor market controlled by expatriates, however, such apparent sophistication became an object of suspicion. Instead of admiring the servant's appearance as indicating a clean and intelligent person, his potential new employers could take the spectacles to indicate poor eyesight. And poor eyesight, of course, made a bad servant.

More serious differences came to the fore during complaints and conflicts. In such cases, the patronizing attitude of expatriate employers could transform from a benevolent position into a ruthless display of power. As an illustration, consider this correspondence in a leading Malawian newspaper in 2003. A Malawian employee, calling him- or herself Worried Malawian, began by drawing attention to his or her boss, "a Boer": "[W]e are slaves in our own country. We are not allowed to attend funerals."[13] Moreover, the worker went on to complain, "Just imagine being shouted at from 7.30 A.M. to 5 P.M. for unknown reasons. This boss has completely failed to run the company and instead heaps the blame on us."

After a few days, Worried Expatriate appeared with a letter on the same page.[14] The first objective of the letter was to rebuke Worried Malawian for using the term "Boer," which, the expatriate felt, was "derogatory and racist." Without pausing to assess who had introduced a racist vocabulary to Malawians, Worried Expatriate went on to explain the ban on attending funerals: "This is just a way of ensuring high productivity." Pointing out that Malawi was in an economic crisis in which businesses needed to operate efficiently, Worried Expatriate finished the letter by offering this piece of advice: "I would suggest to the complainant [that] he or she sits down and discuss[es] these issues with the manager, [and] perhaps both parties will be able to understand and appreciate each others' concerns and fears."

Ethnographic witnessing in this and the next chapter demonstrates the unequal positions in which employers and employees would sit down and discuss as recommended by Worried Expatriate. Left to defend their rights without an organized force to support them, Malawian workers generally have few prospects to enter into a genuine dialogue with their employers. Protest and resistance take subtle forms, such as absenteeism, laziness, and stealing.[15] They may be, alas, all too subtle, misunderstood by employers as weaknesses and inefficiency rather than as protest and resistance. A cycle of dismissals and appalling conditions thereby continues, unbroken by collective and public expressions of grievance.

From Radicalism to Exclusion

Complaints at centers for legal aid are attempts to break the vicious cycle of Malawian labor relations. Clients who seek legal aid have often endured considerable exploitation before meeting an NGO's lawyer or paralegal officer. For disgruntled workers, seeking legal aid often presupposes some resolve in the context of patronizing and authoritarian labor relations. Moreover, most clients enter centers for legal aid on their own, representing themselves in disputes against powerful adversaries. As mentioned, few clients belong to labor unions, and the procedures of village courts, such as having a guardian to argue one's case, do not apply in legal aid. Village courts, following the principles of "customary" law, hear cases that typically involve disputes over land or family relations. Labor disputes are, therefore, confined to the other pole of the legal dualism, the one whose jurisdiction is defined by the country's written laws. Within this legal sphere, NGOs' legal aid attracts clients through its accessible and cost-free procedures. Not only are its services free, moreover, but the redress it provides also often takes the form of monetary compensation.

The Centre for Human Rights and Rehabilitation has offered legal aid in Lilongwe, Malawi's capital, with funding from various foreign agencies, particularly the Norwegian government. It was one of the first Malawian human rights NGOs to be established after the 1994 elections. Its founders spent several years in exile before returning to Malawi during the democratic transition. They were exiles in East Africa, eastern Europe, and the Soviet Union, developing political opinions that were clearly at odds with Kamuzu Banda's conservative regime. Despite studying social sciences in these countries, the founders did not attempt to apply socialist ideas in Malawi. They were, instead, receptive to the general thrust of the human rights discourse of the post–Cold War era and focused on political and civil freedoms, an emphasis that kept this NGO in the Malawian limelight.[16] This emphasis also indicates why legal aid never became its major preoccupation, employing at best three paralegals and one consulting lawyer. By 2003, the CHRR had suspended legal aid in favor of other programs, carried out under four "core areas": public awareness and community safety; civic education on human rights and democracy; training and research; and capacity building and networking (CHRR 2003, 11).

The temporary shift in program areas was not the result of a mere whim in donors' priorities. By 2005, the Norwegian government and other donors had persuaded the CHRR to resume legal aid, but it remained the responsibility of a paralegal officer who also performed other duties in the NGO's office. The pool of donors expanded, with involvement in campaigns against HIV/AIDS, in particular, bringing in new personnel. Although the high cost of legal expertise was a major reason for the management to give a low priority to legal aid, this success in expansion, coupled with donor sympathies toward legal aid, suggested that the commitment to address actual grievances was also rather subdued. To be sure, whatever its founders' radical inclinations, the CHRR found itself deeply embedded in the status distinctions and hierarchies of the Malawian society. Within its own organization, it failed to overcome the rampant income inequalities in the wider Malawi context. In 2002, a lawyer who provided legal aid had a monthly salary of about one hundred thousand kwacha, while a paralegal officer received fifteen thousand kwacha per month. The receptionist, who often took the first statement from clients, received twenty-five hundred kwacha per month. The difference in income was nearly sevenfold between the lawyer and the paralegal officer, and it was sixfold between the paralegal and the receptionist. Between the lawyer and the receptionist, the difference was fortyfold.

At the same time, contempt, as understood in Badiou's 2001 critique of human rights, made legal aid a realm of tedium. Both lawyers and paralegal officers, despite the attempts by abused clients to engage them in the reality of their situations, preferred to present themselves as impassive professionals rather than as impassioned activists. Their conduct was consistent with the belief in piecemeal and technical solutions that the expert knowledge of law appeared to reveal. Even more, the exclusiveness of professional knowledge, as also noted elsewhere (see, e.g., Goodwin 1994 and Philips 1998), was created in various semiotic ways. An obvious example was various elitist hierarchies in client-officer interactions, starting with their modes of address. Whereas the officer would use the client's name in address, the client would often use such honorific titles as *bwana* (master) or "sir" and, for female officers, "madam" or *mayi* (mother). A similar effect was created by the organization of office space. As in Malawian offices in general, a receptionist received visitors before they were allowed to meet the professional staff. Alternatives to entrenched Malawian hierarchies were also curtailed by legal officers' clothes, which were usually more formal and more expensive that what their clients were wearing.

The officers' room for maneuver between impoverished claimants and corrupt employers was often so narrow that a certain quasi-professional detachment from clients appeared inevitable, if only because of the chosen emphasis on piecemeal and individualized mediation. The above-mentioned signs of status distinction also recall what was earlier described for civic educators. Moreover, among the legal experts pursuing human rights, the officers at the CHRR were not alone in their failure to distance themselves from the preoccupation with status. Similar concerns, albeit on a different scale, informed the establishment of the office of the ombudsman. Explaining the ombudsman's need for an expensive vehicle, the first annual report stated that "public transport is risky to the Ombudsman and not conforming with his status. In the region all Ombudsmen run a Mercedes Benz except in the Republic of South Africa where the Ombudsman has chosen a BMW."[17] The notion that it was inappropriate for legal professionals to mix with the general public was also explicit in an editorial that lamented magistrates' low income: "Society expects the magistrate to dress in a way befitting the office, to live in a house that imparts that aura of status and to socialise in certain circles which bespeak dignity."[18]

As the above quotes indicate, status symbols in a professional's lifestyle may be expected by the society at large and not merely by the professional him- or herself. In Malawi, the hierarchies that these symbols reinforced were evident in virtually all workplaces. Inequality at death is a revealing example, with many employers assisting the bereaved according to the deceased's status. A report in 2000 on the impact of HIV/AIDS on Malawi's civil service, for example, noted that "the cost of coffins ranges between MK5,000 and MK65,000. More expensive coffins are bought for senior officers and cheaper ones are bought for junior officers."[19] High status all too readily became an index of superior intellect, as an irate director of public prosecutions demonstrated in 2002, when he countered journalists' criticism by declaring, "You can only have a person of my wisdom to occupy the office."[20] The legal experts working for the CHRR displayed a somewhat similar tendency toward exclusion. Legal discourse was often a marker of their professional identity and, as such, a means to discredit some clients' perspectives on their own situations.

Oracles and Supplicants at a Legal Clinic

During my fieldwork on legal aid in 2001–2, the CHRR referred to its office of legal aid as the Legal Clinic. I never detected irony in this designation. The clinical metaphor provided, rather, a description of legal officers' mandate. In their attempts to explain why only some aspects of clients' complaints deserved attention, officers would often have recourse to the division of skills and expertise in the medical domain. For example, when a client had narrated several abuses that he had endured at work, an officer likened his or her own legal assistance to medical specializations in order to illustrate that some of the abuses had to be eliminated from their discussion.[21]

Officer: It's like in a hospital, right?

Client: Yes.

Officer: I say it again, right? You can go to a hospital, to a doctor, "I am having problems with eyes," but the doctor you found is not an eye doctor. Is he/she going to make an eye operation?

Client: It's not possible.[22]

The clinical metaphor for legal aid served three important functions. First, it associated legal officers with medical experts, with similar pretensions to unchallenged authority. Second, it portrayed clients as individuals in one-to-one interaction with the adversaries who had caused their afflictions, rather than as a collection of people whose experiences of abuse stemmed from similar structural problems. Third, and consistent with the other two functions, the metaphor made officers' legal instruments seem like medicine, which, when properly administered, assuaged, perhaps even eliminated, clients' grievances. Broader questions about power relations and inequalities were thereby erased, a technical approach replacing politically consequential engagement.

A tension between clients' initial narratives and legal officers' subsequent interrogation lays bare the fallacy of the clinical metaphor. Clients were asked to narrate all the details that pertained to their complaints, at first to the receptionist, who considered whether the case could be referred further, and then to a legal officer. Although the legal officer could reject a case even after the initial screening, common to virtually all cases was the way in which they were pruned of details once subjected to officers' scrutiny. The process is familiar in legal discourse, with experts' preoccupation with rules overriding clients' concern with complex relationships (see Conley and O'Barr 1990). Complaints about labor relations, for example, often included a whole range of grievances that touched on not only relationships in a workplace but also the impact of abuse on a client's life in general. While unfair dismissals and employers' failure to pay terminal benefits constituted the most common grievances from a legal point of view, clients' narratives often elaborated both on the events that had led to their specific complaint and on the consequences of abuse. Confined to their role as legal technicians, officers usually failed to consider the wider moral and political implications of these narratives.[23]

In order to do justice to clients' complex narratives, only one representative case can be analyzed in some detail in the next chapter. Before we embark on this analysis, however, it is important to identify general features in the encounters at the Legal Clinic. Some aspects of officers' approach were common to legal work everywhere, such as the demand for evidence, while others indicated more specifically Malawian conditions of legal aid. Their approach included the lack of resources to investigate cases. Yet both the general and the specific aspects of officers' approach were embedded in hierarchies that frequently circumscribed clients' empowerment through legal aid. The very individualization of grievances was predicated on objectifying clients as the ones who lacked relevant knowledge. More often than not, even in those cases that were successfully completed with paid compensation, the status quo prevailed.

The Burden of Proof

After hearing a client's narrative, one of the legal officer's first tasks was usually to indicate that much of the detail furnished in the narrative was irrelevant and that the true prospects of the case could be established only through proper investigation. Since the Legal Clinic remained a low priority, legal officers had few opportunities to leave their office to investigate the validity of clients' claims. Officers had limited funds to travel within the city of Lilongwe but not beyond, and witnesses were very rarely summoned because their expenses could not be reimbursed. Such problems with resources placed a considerable burden on clients either to provide officers with appropriate funds or to produce written evidence as required by officers. In neither case did officers seem prepared to admit failure because of their own deprivation. They appeared more anxious to defend their status as professionals, even if it would paradoxically involve convenient misinformation about existing legislation.

The Employment Act of 1999, as mentioned earlier, clearly stipulated the procedures for an employee's dismissal. After pruning clients' narratives of their details, officers found in many cases that complainants had been dismissed without a notice or a payment in lieu of notice. If the client's workplace was too far away for the officer to visit, or if the case involved so much conflict that the employer's cooperation seemed unlikely, the officer could demand the client's written evidence on the level of payment in lieu of notice. The practice ignored the provisions in the Employment Act in a whole range of possible cases, with a legal officer having the right to determine the level of compensation even without leaving his or her office. In one case in which the client presented his appointment letter as evidence of the conditions of his employment, the officer was sarcastic about the client's demand for compensation.

Officer: You, how many days' notice pay do you want? That's what I am asking you.

Client: Master, I claim a one-month's notice pay.

Officer: Why one month? Did I say so?

Client: No, Sir.

Officer: So where does one month come from? You just dreamed about it?[24]

In this case, the officer played on his and the client's unequal positions in order to place the burden of evidence on the client. Yet sufficient evidence had already been provided in the form of an appointment letter that indicated the date when the client had started his employment and the amount of the monthly salary. Instead of referring to the Employment Act, the officer questioned the client's claim for a month's notice pay with the sarcastic *mwangoilota?* (You just dreamed about it?), uttered with an equally sarcastic smile. The client's submissive modes of address, such as *bwana* (master) and "sir," indicated the limited extent to which an overt challenge to the officer's authority was feasible in this encounter.

Another reason why officers were seldom challenged was that few clients were aware of the legal provisions that applied in their cases. As mentioned in chapter 2, only the most general human rights instruments had been translated into Chichewa during the first ten years of democracy, while the more specific labor and employment laws, for example, were available only in English. Literacy in English became, in this context, one of the preconditions of legal redress. Yet legal officers guarded their status as experts by defining the limits of what could be said and claimed in particular cases (Maryns and Blommaert 2002). The issue of evidence played a crucial role in this tacit work of demarcating the scope of cases. The following reprimand, expressing frustration over a client's failure to produce the required evidence, was rather typical.

Officer: You came here as if to a legal office.

Client: Yes.

Officer: We don't want mere words/talk.

Client: Yes.

Officer: We want information, material [to show how] these things are.

Client: But =

Officer: = We can't just act on a thing, but there isn't what — evidence for us. If you leave your place to come to complain, you have sufficient evidence, is that right?[25]

Mawu, translating as both "words" and "talk," contrasted with the written evidence that the officer desired. The criteria for evidence, in point of fact, were often strikingly different among legal officers and their clients. While clients' narratives could marshal numerous personal and circumstantial pieces of evidence for compelling moral arguments, officers could always disparage them by demanding written evidence. In yet another case of dismissal without a notice or a payment in lieu of notice, the client's best evidence came from previous cases at the same workplace.

Officer: When someone wants to leave the job or is dismissed, how many days' notice do they give?

Client: For example how they gave the driver who =

Officer: = You, I am asking about you, not about your friends.[26]

This refusal to consider circumstantial evidence was consistent with officers' attempts to represent claimants as individuals. No matter how common clients' complaints were, officers would not begin to pursue them as collective grievances demanding collective action. Each case was considered as if it were unique, as if the officer had forgotten the countless instances in which he or she had heard about similar violations of workers' rights. Legal aid did not, as a consequence, threaten the status quo in labor relations, because the focus on individuals rendered structural abuse and inequality invisible within the parameters of discourse. The procedure served officers' interests to convey impassive professionalism, unquestioned authority that would not be qualified by a close identification with the plight of exploited workers.

Poverty and Professionalism

When I asked officers at the Legal Clinic about their often ruthless interrogation, they replied by pointing out that some clients were mere impostors looking for easy money. Although this was a real concern in a town where underemployment fed various forms of trickery, officers could not explain why they sometimes dismissed cases that seemed to merit further investigation. It is only when officers' aspirations and challenges are considered as a whole that such apparently erratic procedures can be understood. Much like the civic educators discussed before, legal officers assumed a distinction between themselves and those whom they were expected to assist. The distinction provided them with a professional identity, but a major challenge was to maintain that identity under the conditions of the underfunded Legal Clinic. It had neither a vehicle nor a computer, and even basic stationery was often scarce. Rather than admitting to clients that meager resources prevented assistance in some cases, officers often preferred to take advantage of clients' less powerful position and ignorance. The deprivation the officers endured was not allowed to detract from a professional identity.

While the demand for written evidence was one important method to discredit clients' claims, another common method was to apportion some of the blame for weak cases to clients themselves. The responsibility for successful redress came, therefore, to rest on clients' shoulders. One example of this was the retrospective complaints that dismissed workers made, with the expectation that a legal officer would investigate and retrieve what the client had lost during his or her employment. When a client complained about an employer who had not paid for the work that the client had performed after the agreed working hours, an officer found fault with the client.

Officer: They didn't give you [compensation for] overtime?

Client: No, we are not given.

Officer: How come you did not complain before you left [the job]?

Client: Oh, master, there wasn't a reason for me to complain, I was expecting that =

Officer: = So now, how does it work when you did that overtime, when a person does overtime this month, next month you still continue, they don't give you [compensation for] overtime. You are still working [overtime], still working, still working. Now they dismiss you, "I want my [compensation for] overtime for the past eleven months." Does it make sense?[27]

The officer's reaction was remarkable for its disregard of the actual labor relations in which most Malawians worked. The client may have been too intimidated to claim compensation for working overtime, content that he was employed at all. In a country where even the mildest protest could lead to a dismissal, the legal aid of a human rights NGO was likely to appear as one of the few trustworthy sources of assistance and advocacy. Yet some clients discovered hierarchical bureaucratic practices that bore a close resemblance to virtually any other Malawian office. It seemed as if officers provided legal aid less because of their concern for social justice than because of an apparent need to curb claimants' demands.

In some cases, legal officers also sought monetary support from their clients. I never heard bribes being requested or offered at the Legal Clinic, but the success of some cases became conditional upon clients' capacity to cover the costs of investigation. This applied, in particular, to cases outside the city of Lilongwe and in which correspondence or telephone calls were deemed necessary. Although it was a measure of the Legal Clinic's low esteem at the CHRR that such basic administrative costs could not be covered by legal aid, officers used idioms of mutual assistance to solicit support from clients. "If you do not help us, we cannot help you" *(ngati simutithandiza sitingakuthandizeni)* was a common statement in these efforts. "Helping each other" *(kuthandizana)* is an idiom that in a subtle way transferred some of the responsibility for successful investigation to the clients themselves. Because clients were often unable to give any money to officers, poverty appeared as clients' predicament, not as a factor damaging officers' professional identity. The involvement of no fees could also be taken to mean that self-sacrificing officers offered their expertise without any pay whatsoever, as the following extract from an officer's comments to a client illustrates.

Officer: This is an organization without money. It is not a governmental organization, because perhaps many think that maybe government gives us money to assist people, but no. Just to help like volunteers. But it is up to the person who comes with complaints to find a way that we do what, that we help him/her. That's the only fee. "The case is yours, give one thousand," no, we don't do that, but if there's a phone call or envelopes when we write letters, go and buy the envelope, give [us].[28]

My conversations with clients before and after their meetings with legal officers revealed that the swiftness with which officers assessed the merits of cases, as compared with the inefficiency of the governmental labor offices, was widely appreciated. Yet, inevitably, disappointment was the result of many cases, both when officers were seen to omit crucial details and when their requests for assistance prevented a further consideration of cases. Clients' disappointment could be detected in several subtle instances of discourse during their meetings with legal officers, alluding to their frustration with the rules as stipulated by legal officers and to their experiences as disgruntled and poor claimants (see Englund 2004c). Outside the Legal Clinic, some clients would express disillusion over human rights NGOs because of their failure to pursue their claims. Some clients accused these "organizations" *(mabungwe)* of "not helping us" *(satithandiza)*. It was apparent that, in these experiences, labor discontent had discovered the limits of its expression within the current discourse of human rights in Malawi.

Clients' perspectives and experiences receive more analysis in the next chapter's study of a seemingly successful case against an employer of Asian origin. Yet the general patterns of officer-client interactions at the Legal Clinic indicate the constraints of an NGO's legal aid. Legal aid was, for this prominent Malawian NGO, one showcase to highlight in annual reports and mission statements; never mind the paucity of attention that it was given in practice. Whatever its emancipatory aims, legal aid, no less than civic education, became an answer to educated Malawians' desire to find occupations that brought them status. Elitism reigned even though most legal officers and civic educators shared critical and well-informed views on Malawi's current ills. Such were the entrenched inequalities in their society that any assistance presupposed a clear status distinction toward those deemed to be in need of such attention.

The objectification of claimants at the Legal Clinic could result in a display of power reminiscent of any Malawian encounter with authority. As such, claimants' moves between abusive employers and legal officers were between two sets of unquestionable authorities. Disillusion found expression in private or in covert criticisms, never in collective protests. The individualization of grievances, in point of fact, also served legal officers' professional status in a less obvious sense than what was discussed above. With each case considered in isolation from all other cases of abuse, each claimant was also left to endure disillusion alone, facing a legal officer's judgment as a mere individual.

CHAPTER 6

Crimes of Exploitation

Dehumanizing a Lorry Boy

Legal-aid officers at the Centre for Human Rights and Rehabilitation assumed elitist habits in their interactions with clients, but there was no conspiracy to maintain the exploitation and abuse of Malawian workers. Officers shared with other activists at the CHRR a strong rhetoric against injustice in Malawi. They were keen to hear, in particular, cases involving disputes with employers of Asian origin. There was no shortage of such cases, because vast tracts of Lilongwe were owned by shopkeepers and investors whose forefathers had come from India and Pakistan. "We show no mercy to them," an officer insisted to me at the early stage of the case I am about to analyze.

Critical analysis subverts its own objectives if it does not include activists' contradictory position in regard to human rights. Non-governmental legal-aid officers, for example, were often outraged by the cases they chose to pursue, even if they showed little of their indignation to clients. At the same time, officers' contributions were not, in a strict sense, *legal* aid, be-cause few cases could be settled by following the letter of the law. Exploited workers brought officers into contact with relatively affluent and influential employers, whose corrupt ways could easily make a mockery of legal aid, buying off either the officer or the client. Yet it was precisely the nature of legal aid as *mediation* that compromised officers' private passion for justice. By entering into deliberations with employers as if their crimes of exploita-tion were isolated incidents, officers lost their cases from the outset. Rational debate was not an option when money spoke louder than laws and when the CHRR's resources for legal aid could never threaten the might of successful entrepreneurs. A sorry convergence of interests took place. On the one hand, officers, stimulated by their belief that human rights were individual freedoms, could create the impression that justice was being pursued case by case. On the other hand, employers avoided collective action against their regime, treated as they were as individuals whose freedom was equal to that of their workers.

A case study is essential to a proper understanding of these intricacies of legal aid. Ethnographic witnessing made it possible to consider what constituted "success" in the procedures of an NGO's legal aid. Even when a client was made to believe that his or her injuries had been addressed in full, my analysis shows that the status quo could prevail. Such cases were filed as "successfully completed," even though they had, more often than not, touched on only a fraction of a client's complaints. The case presented here, including its resolution, was by no means uncommon among the cases I heard at the Legal Clinic. It involved extensive abuse and copious crimes of exploitation at the hands of a ruthless employer. Yet by the time the case was closed, most of the injuries had never been considered by the legal officer, and a petty compensation constituted the final redress.

The case also presents an opportunity to recall the broadest questions raised by this book. What are the prospects for human rights to be universal in the actual situations in which they are evoked? How do historical inequalities influence both the popular understandings and the actual scope of human rights? The various aspects of human rights discourse considered in this book — from translation to civic education to legal aid — have demonstrated the extent to which the very idea of human rights may, despite its universalist pretensions, assume a highly particular content. No argument about cultural difference was at stake when, for example, Malawians were taught to regard rights as individual freedoms and to claim their rights through piecemeal legal redress. The discourse was universalist, not culturalist, and yet it masked the highly specific interests that it served. By making individual freedoms the essence of rights, it marginalized other grounds for making claims. Moreover, by disengaging from the reality of situations, it provided no means to imagine the universal in the situation of human rights. A case involving some of the worst forms of exploitation in contemporary Malawi suggests that engaged universals remain a mirage as long as collaboration between activists and the marginalized is sacrificed to depoliticized mediation.

The case is harrowing also because it lays bare the naïveté in the expectations that countries like Malawi are on their way toward a genuine democracy. "The achievement of social justice," to recall Sen's words, "depends not only on institutional forms (including democratic rules and

regulations), but also on effective practice" (1999, 159). The uncomfortable reality that confronts us after the case is analyzed, and indeed after
the findings of this book are considered as a whole, relates to effective
practice. To be sure, free subjects would seem to have abounded in
Malawi. Not only were "democratic rules and regulations" in place in the
form of new laws and an enlightened constitution, but also effective practice, while certainly not fully attained yet, would seem to have been within
reach. Both governmental and non-governmental institutions safeguarded the new democracy. Some NGOs, in particular, were veritable
forces of opposition, incessantly monitoring ruling politicians' backslid-
ing into undemocratic habits.

The practice of democracy, once the appropriate institutions exist,
would thus appear to have been intensifying, its consolidation a matter
of time. Since the case in this chapter revolves around labor relations, the
implicit teleology of these expectations is best considered within that
domain. Sen refers to Karl Marx when he presents the freedom of
employment as a decisive step toward democracy and development
(1999, 29). For Marx, the transition from slavery to wage labor represented a progressive change, despite the cruel exploitation that characterized labor relations in industrializing countries. The parameters of
emancipatory struggle, at any rate, were laid out by this acknowledgment
of the freedom of labor.

In Malawi, the formal freedom of employment might be taken to
promise a similar triumph of democratic labor relations in the future. With
new institutions in place, including non-governmental legal aid, this goal
would seem to have been attainable, in small steps if not in great leaps forward. The sobering finding of this chapter is, however, that the very institutions that were expected to consolidate democracy could actually maintain the illusion that Malawi was on a path of improvement. Everything
took place as if a progressive change were under way, with new labor legislation expanding the freedom of employment, new organizations providing legal assistance, and workers themselves seeking redress. Yet the
actual parameters of making claims were not reducible to such positive
developments. The situation of human rights was, instead, embedded in
historical inequalities that showed no sign of disappearing or even of becoming the objects of critical reflection. Claiming human rights as individual freedoms could, in point of fact, consolidate those inequalities.

Just as the officers at the CHRR's Legal Clinic offered not so much legal
aid as mediation, so too did their work, at least in principle, pertain to
labor laws rather than to human rights in general. However, exploitation
could continue precisely because the officers' particular human rights dis-

course displaced the recognition of labor laws. This demonstration of how legal officers' formal commitment to human rights failed to challenge exploitation is an instance of ethnography as witnessing. I was present each time the protagonists in the case visited the Legal Clinic and recorded their conversations with legal officers. I was, therefore, able to follow the development of the case from the client's first visit to his former employer's payment of the final compensation. In order to verify some of the details narrated in the client's accounts, I also made observations and interviewed people at the client's home and his former workplace. My investigations indicated that the client's accounts at the Legal Clinic were, on the whole, reliable representations of what had happened.

Because the proceedings at the Legal Clinic were, in some respects, *extralegal* aid, if not outright illegal aid, ethnographic witnessing could not evade complicity. The fact that I allowed the events described here to happen is hardly made any more acceptable by my efforts to pose critical questions to legal officers or by my investigation of the details of the case. Nothing alters the outcome that an exploited worker became the casualty of a dubious agreement between a legal officer and an entrepreneur. Yet complicity itself is a complex affair, linked to the purpose of witnessing. The instrumentalist sense in which ethnographers seek complicity in order to build rapport that provides them with data, most eloquently outlined by Clifford Geertz (1973, 412–453), has long been contested in anthropology. Another sense of complicity revolves around the existential conditions of ethnographic witnessing, the "affinity" that emerges between the ethnographer and his or her interlocutors and directs the ensuing representations (Marcus 1999, 122). Geertz's wry remarks on "unbearably earnest fieldworkers" aside (1988, 97), the serious intellectual-cum-political issue is the extent to which the ethnographer expects his or her work to become a part of the situations in which fieldwork takes place. Not only do I expect this book to be read and discussed in Malawi, but also *I* will return, armed with reflections on what I saw, if only because I never left "the field" as an existential aspect of myself. The full significance of my complicity will accrue only in due course.

Hard Work, Little Pay

Yamikani Chikondi worked for Hassam Patel for three months in 2001–2.[1] One of their many disagreements concerned the exact length of Chikondi's employment, with Patel insisting that Chikondi had been dismissed after working for two months and twenty-six days. For Chikondi, a twenty-five-year-old father of two who lived with his family in the high-density township of Area 23,[2] it was one of the many insecure, lowly paid, odd jobs that he had been able to find after moving from his village to the capital some six years earlier. Without so much as a full primary-school certificate in hand, he had to sustain his family as a laborer, never able to break the cycle of small pay and abrupt dismissals with his own commercial venture, which he had dreamed of. Start-up capital remained elusive when his salary was often spent on basic necessities even before the next payday.

Chikondi found work at Patel's hardware store soon after his dismissal from another hardware store owned by another businessman of Indian origin. Patel was a prominent entrepreneur in his fifties and lived with his family in the low-density Area 3, in a spacious house surrounded by a magnificent garden and a group of black servants. His decision to concentrate on hardware for builders and building contractors had been an answer to the diminishing profits in his previous trade in textiles, clothes, and various household items. These commodities had largely become the prerogatives of small-scale Malawian entrepreneurs and hawkers, who traded in imported or smuggled secondhand goods after the economic liberalization that accompanied the democratic transition.[3] Patel's store, coupled with other investments, whose extent I was not allowed to verify, ensured the continuation of a comfortable lifestyle involving regular holidays abroad, the education of some of his children in India and the United Kingdom, and a Mercedes Benz. Crucially, such success depended on both Patel's business acumen and his efforts to keep the labor costs low.

Chikondi's first disappointment as Patel's employee was the level of his salary. Chikondi had received MK 1,450 (US$20) per month at the previous hardware store, but Patel announced that his salary would be only MK 900 (US$13) per month. Although it was far below the minimum wage of MK 1,500, this aspect of the situation appeared neither in Chikondi's complaints, who was unaware of labor legislation, nor in legal officers' interventions. Yet when Chikondi did try to protest against the low salary, Patel told him that its level could be revised only after some time. Thus started Chikondi's ill-fated employment, in which he served mainly as a porter who carried goods, such as heavy bags of cement, within the store or to customers' vehicles outside it. Another important dimension of his job was to act as, in Patel's words, a "lorry boy," who accompanied the store's lorry driver in the delivery of hardware to remote parts of the country. Ironically, a major source of income for this exploitative enterprise was the Malawi Social Action Fund, which, as mentioned previously, was an initiative of the new government and the World Bank to provide funds and material assistance to communities that were prepared to work for the development of their areas. These communities were taught to sing the MASAF's motto: *mavuto achepa,* "problems have become fewer."

Chikondi's problems, however, did not become fewer with the new employment. He was distressed every time he was abruptly called to accompany the lorry on its journeys to "the field." A family man, Chikondi was given no chance to inform his wife of the absence, to leave some money with her, or to collect additional clothes for the journey. He made three such trips during his short employment, each time ordered by Patel to load and board the lorry with no forewarning of the journey. The first journey was to Nkhata Bay in the Northern Region, some 320 kilometers from Lilongwe, where he stayed for two weeks. The second journey, to Dedza, some ninety kilometers from Lilongwe, took two days. The final journey was to Mzimba, again in the Northern Region, some 240 kilometers from Lilongwe, also keeping him away for two weeks. There appeared to be no limit to Chikondi's tribulations during such journeys. In addition to having no chance to prepare himself or his family for the absence, he was not given an adequate allowance for the days spent away from home, nor was he allowed to sleep in a resthouse like the driver. It was a part of Chikondi's assignment to sleep in or by the lorry in order to guard the load against thieves.

Patel never told Chikondi how much his daily allowance was during these journeys. Patel's strategy was to give a lump sum, undisclosed to Chikondi, to the driver, who had the responsibility of sharing it with Chikondi. On their way to Nkhata Bay, the driver gave MK 120 (US$1.70) to Chikondi, saying that it was all that he was going to get. When Chikondi expressed concern over his survival for two weeks with such an allowance, the driver told him to talk to Patel once they were back in Lilongwe. For the journey to Dedza, the driver produced MK 50 (US$0.70) as Chikondi's share of the allowance, and during the Mzimba visit the driver first gave him MK 120 and, after a few days, another MK 100 (US$1.40). Chikondi's accounts indicated his reluctance to antagonize the driver, who was many years older than he, higher in the hierarchy of workers, and capable of causing considerable hardship to Chikondi as the only lorry boy on these journeys. On the other hand, he could not be sure how much money Patel had given to the driver in the first place. Chikondi and the driver had not developed the kind of close rapport in which such information might have been divulged.

Chikondi never succeeded to elicit from Patel the exact amount of allowance that he had given to the driver. Nor did the CHRR's legal officers reveal to Chikondi that they had told Patel that the allowance should have been, at minimum, MK 600 (US$8) per day.[4] Patel, for his part, simply shrugged off Chikondi's queries, telling him, according to Chikondi's account, "You should take care of money; you must eat according to your problems" *(Ndalama musamale; muzidya malinga ndi m'mene mukuvutikira).* Chikondi had also expected to receive the outstanding allowances in conjunction with his salary, only to find out that nothing was ever added to the meager MK 900 that he was supposed to receive monthly. Not even the Sundays that he was occasionally ordered to work at the store were compensated. What he received at the end of a month, moreover, was never MK 900, because he had been forced to take advances in order to survive until the next payday.

The Impossibility of Integrity

Chikondi's financial troubles, while serious enough in their own right, were only one aspect of his exploitation. His very humanity appeared to be at risk throughout his employment at Patel's enterprise, which subjected him to such treatment that a loss of personal integrity would have been inevitable had it not been forestalled by a loss of employment. Consider, for example, the difference between the driver and the lorry boy during their trips to the field. While the driver had enough allowance to eat in modest restaurants, Chikondi survived on the food he could buy from various roadside vendors. The visit to Nkhata Bay reduced him to a beggar who had to ask locals to share with him whatever food, even refuse, they had. Although the driver slept in resthouses that had mats instead of beds, his situation was incomparably better than Chikondi's. Chikondi slept, as mentioned, by the load as a measure of vigilance. While in remote areas he could sleep inside the lorry cabin, the driver ordered him to sleep outside when they parked near villages or towns. These journeys coincided with the onset of the rainy season, with Chikondi finding shelter only under the lorry, the cold bare ground as his mat.

During their stay in Mzimba, Chikondi, clothed only in a T-shirt and a pair of trousers, tore his T-shirt while sleeping on the ground. After returning to Lilongwe, Chikondi complained to Patel about the abrupt departures that prevented him from taking enough clothes with him. He brought the torn shirt to Patel and asked, "Master, look at the shirt, do you see how it has been ruined?" According to Chikondi, Patel's response was curt: "Ah, that's work."[5]

Patel's suspicions of theft in his store increased Chikondi's discomfort and heralded his dismissal. The journey to Mzimba had involved a mechanical problem in the lorry, and the driver returned to Lilongwe by bus to collect spare parts. He came back with the news that Patel had dismissed two young men who had been working in a position similar to Chikondi's. Patel had noticed an unexplained decrease in the number of switches that his store was selling. He and his manager subsequently found switches hidden in tires that the suspects were carrying in wheelbarrows. As if dismissal were not enough, Patel ordered his sons to beat up the two men. Sticks and clubs were the instruments of the battering, and the suspects, dripping in blood, were told by Patel never to come anywhere near the store again. A notice, or a payment in lieu of notice, preoccupied no one at that violent moment of dismissal.

Upon his return to Lilongwe, Chikondi was surprised to discover that Patel suspected him of complicity in the theft. Patel called him to his office and asked what he knew about it. Chikondi answered, "I do not know anything at all. How could I know, master? I was in Mzimba while the incident took place here." Patel refused to believe him, saying, "You are the one who knows."[6] Irritated, Chikondi proceeded to criticize Patel for beating the suspects and dismissing them instead of taking them to the police. If he had waited until Chikondi's return before dismissing the suspects, the police could have investigated different suspects' culpability. Now, Chikondi told Patel, the suspects were nowhere to be seen, and it was him, Chikondi, who stood accused of the theft.

This exchange, described further below, was one example of Chikondi's attempts to argue with Patel rather than accepting his pronouncements without a protest. They did not, however, exchange opinions from equal positions. The impossibility of genuine dialogue between the two became clear when Patel soon dismissed this argumentative lorry boy. Patel first asked him to find the suspects of the theft so that the case could be investigated as Chikondi had suggested. Chikondi said that he could not find the suspects because he did not know where they lived. He had been working with them only for a short period, and they had not seen each other outside work.

This exchange between Patel and Chikondi took place on the twenty-sixth day of Chikondi's third month of employment. At the end of the month, Patel called him to his office again and said, "Chikondi, leave work. Now you can work anywhere. Go and look for work elsewhere." To Chikondi's "why?" Patel's answer was, "Ah, when you have problems, you should come back." The answer made no sense to Chikondi, who exclaimed, "I work because I have problems! So you are telling me that I should go and have problems? Exactly what have I done wrong?" Patel's response was again curt: "Enough, you must go."[7] Despite being told to leave on the last day of the month, Chikondi did not receive his last salary on that day. A dispute ensued over the exact date of his dismissal and the amount of money that Patel owed him.

Crime begets crime. As was mentioned in chapter 5, protests against exploitation in Malawian labor relations seldom culminated in strikes. Unorganized labor, working under the constant shadow of summary dismissals, found more subtle forms of protest and resistance in, for example, theft, absenteeism, and laziness. Chikondi's tribulations highlight the conditions under which Patel's employees had to make their living. With salaries too low to sustain even an impoverished version of the urban lifestyle, and with arbitrary harassment almost a daily feature of their workplace, Patel's employees were practically pushed to commit crimes.[8] Yet even if workers' crimes were reprisals against Patel's crimes of exploitation, the master invariably had the last word. Suspicions of theft and other misconduct provided grounds for instant dismissal, and workers, especially those deemed to be "difficult," were ousted before their demands for more pay became too vociferous. Workers who did not last long also had little time to organize themselves into a collective force confronting the master.

Defying Dehumanization

An apparent collusion between a legal officer and Patel was not based on premeditated conspiracy. It did, however, reveal the thin line that existed between the two kinds of contempt for victimhood that Chikondi's case indicated. Legal officers held their clients in contempt to the extent that they, the officers, regarded their knowledge as exclusively their own. Chikondi's tribulations disclosed, in turn, a form of labor relations in which the worker was treated as something less than human. This tendency to perceive, if only implicitly, Malawian unskilled laborers as subhuman was also revealed to me during my conversations with Patel and certain other prominent employers in Lilongwe.[9] Malawi's vast disparities in income and opportunity were not lost on any of us, but the inequalities became more comprehensible, and more acceptable, when the poor were considered to have needs that were clearly distinct from those of the others.[10] The "less privileged," to use the notion mentioned in the introduction, appeared as a distinct species altogether, a type that simply did not need, or even want, all the commodities and services that were at others' disposal. The perspective came in both malevolent and benevolent variants. For some, including Patel, Malawian labor *deserved* to be treated with suspicion, because its failure to advance through education and its evident lack of efficiency bespoke intrinsic worthlessness. For others, the poor, while always to be kept at arm's length, were the objects of charity, in their abject misery an ever-present opportunity to demonstrate one's own high-mindedness.

Perhaps the most insidious feature of the regime at Patel's store was that workers were pitted against one another. I mentioned above how the most difficult workers were dismissed before they could disturb Patel's regime. Another strategy to curb labor unrest was to selectively assign responsibilities to certain employees. An example of this is Patel's having given a lump sum allowance to the lorry driver during Chikondi's journeys. Dismayed at the insufficient amount of money that the driver gave him, Chikondi was ultimately unable to know for sure who was cheating him, the driver or Patel. Another example is the suspicions that Patel inflicted on Chikondi after the thefts at his store. While Patel may have had other reasons for dismissing Chikondi, the accusations of complicity served to shift the focus from Patel's arbitrariness to misconduct among Chikondi's colleagues. Blame, in other words, came to be apportioned to other workers, not to the employer. Chikondi's refusal to be deceived by these machinations showed the limits of Patel's capacity to control Chikondi's understanding of the dispute. However, Chikondi's perceptions neither prevented Patel from dismissing him nor ensured a fair compensation for his exploitation.

Patel's other strategy to control his workers was, as is common in employers' patronizing attitudes in Malawi, to treat them as children. The above quotes, supported by my observations of how Patel addressed his workers, indicate that he used the second-person singular that is, in Chichewa, used for children or one's subordinates or between youngsters who know each other well. The contribution of Patel's usage to sharply hierarchical relations was evident, for example, in Chikondi's habit of addressing Patel in the second-person plural, often together with the honorific *bwana*. Chikondi's failure, in Patel's eyes, to qualify as an adult also facilitated a cavalier attitude toward his demands for better pay. When he asked Patel why he gave all the allowances to the driver, Patel replied, "You waste money" *(umaononga ndalama)*. The answer surprised Chikondi, who did not think that Patel had much knowledge of his patterns of consumption. In any case, Chikondi retorted, "When you give me money, the money I waste is my own."[11]

Chikondi's counterarguments, confirmed to me by his coworkers, show how he consistently refused to be regarded as a child or subhuman. Patel's dismissive responses and arbitrary rulings usually prompted Chikondi to offer his own view of issues, his argumentative tone probably expediting the end of his employment. An illuminating example is the way in which he presented, after his journey to Mzimba, his own understanding of the right procedure with suspected thieves. The stolen goods should have been kept separate for subsequent investigations, and the suspects should not have been beaten or dismissed before the investigation. If Patel had followed these procedures, Chikondi concluded, he could have given the case to the police. Such lecturing on Chikondi's part was rather too much for Patel to tolerate, and he spat out, "Don't teach me" (*usandiphunzitse*).

These examples of a worker's attempts to argue with his employer indicate a groping for proper and just procedures even when the worker is unaware of relevant legislation. Chikondi's understanding was that he had entered into a contract with Patel, although no written documents had been produced when he was employed. This understanding became particularly clear when Chikondi started to claim his final salary after the dismissal. The issue was complicated by his and Patel's different views on the date of dismissal. Patel insisted that Chikondi had been dismissed on the twenty-sixth day of his last month, while Chikondi thought that he had been employed the whole month. Chikondi also awaited compensation for the Sundays he had been at work as well as for the weeks he had spent in "the field." He was aware that two advances had to be deducted from the final pay. The first was MK 150 (US$2), which he had taken himself early in the month, and the second was MK 200 (US$2.80), which his wife had taken while he was in Mzimba. The wife, who had not been informed about Chikondi's journey, had taken the money when she visited the store to inquire about his whereabouts.

It was a measure of Patel's meanness with money that the few days became a matter of dispute between him and Chikondi. As mentioned, Chikondi was told about his dismissal only at the end of the month, and he claimed to have run errands for Patel even after the twenty-sixth day. In any case, Patel did not pay Chikondi on the same day that he dismissed him. For four days into a new month, when he should have been looking for another employment, Chikondi came to Patel's store to finalize the payment, but Patel simply ignored him as if he did not see him, or he chased Chikondi away, claiming that he was too busy to attend to him. When Patel finally asked Chikondi to enter his office, a shock awaited the employee. Not only did Patel insist on paying for only twenty-six days, with MK 30 as the daily salary; he also deducted from the total of MK 780 both the two advances *and* the MK 220 that had been paid to Chikondi as allowances during the journey to Mzimba. A pitiful MK 210 (US$2.90) emerged as Chikondi's final salary.

Shaken and demoralized, Chikondi staggered out of the office without taking the money. Consulting his coworkers during the lunch hour outside the store, he was told by a store manager not to accept the payment. Moreover, the manager advised him not to sign any paper that Patel was offering, because if he did so, he would be seen to agree with Patel, and the case would be closed. As a further indication of how little actual control Patel had over his employees, it was this same manager who urged Chikondi to seek legal redress, first at the governmental labor office and then at the CHRR's Legal Clinic. Despite his closeness to Patel, the manager saw little reason to defend Patel's interests in this case. In fact, despite being used by Patel to enforce discipline and order in the workplace, the manager identified with the plight of the workers. His position was ambiguous, accountable to Patel while, to some extent, dependent on other workers' consent.

Chikondi's reflections on the micropolitics of the workplace assumed a clearly racial content. During the several accounts and statements I heard him give, he emphatically defined the manager as "black" *(wokuda),* and he often began his account with the words, "I worked for an Indian" *(Ndinagwira ntchito kwa mwenye).* While one ought to deplore racism regardless of who engages in it, it is crucial here to realize how Chikondi arrived at a racial account of his tribulations.[12] Just as crimes of exploitation beget crimes committed by workers, so too does dehumanization produce an equally abhorrent counterreaction. Patel failed to crush Chikondi's self-assurance and dignity, although the treatment suited more a child or a subhuman than an adult breadwinner. After his futile attempts to reason with Patel, Chikondi's experiences became a part of the generally exploitative relations between Asian employers and Malawian workers. Chikondi had few other options than to consider Patel as a generic "Indian" *(mwenye),* a brute whose wealth was based on exploitation and violence.

Seeking Legal Redress

The dismissal had far-reaching consequences for Chikondi's family. Because he had not received the salary for the final month, he had failed to pay the rent for their house. The further delay caused by Patel's failure to pay the salary on time and Chikondi's subsequent refusal to accept it made him default on the rent for a long time. When the case was being considered at the Legal Clinic, Chikondi found his family and all their belongings outside one day, removed from the house and the house locked by the landlord. The family had to be accommodated in a house rented by a relative of Chikondi's wife in a different township. Chikondi's inability to provide for his family also led to a serious food shortage, exacerbated by his wife's lack of her own source of income because of her preoccupation with their two small children. Chikondi's unemployment continued throughout the period of some four weeks while the case was pending at the Legal Clinic. By the time the case was concluded, his destitution seemed to leave only two alternatives: crime or a return to the village.

In light of these hardships and humiliations, it is remarkable that Chikondi chose to follow the path of legal redress. Despite his bitter complaints, Chikondi never threatened to use violence. Moreover, although his final salary was overdue, his patience was not worn out by the several weeks that it took to establish what the legal redress would be. If the achievement of democracy and human rights depends as much on citizens' participation as on institutional reforms, then Chikondi's actions could only reassure those who sought to consolidate Malawi's democracy. Here was a disgruntled citizen whose experiences of exploitation revealed some of the challenges that democracy and human rights faced in the context of the impoverishment of Malawians' everyday lives. This citizen was not intimidated by the enormous gap in wealth and opportunity between his adversary and himself. Submitting his fate to the discretion of democratic institutions, Chikondi did his part in the transformation of Malawian society.

The transformation remained, however, nominal insofar as the new citizenship that Chikondi and other marginalized Malawians possessed was merely political, an invitation to exercise choice in multiparty elections. It should be clear that to focus exclusively on Chikondi's brave move would be to commit the same mistake, for example, as that of the civic educators of NICE. As previously discussed, these civic educators viewed the values, attitudes, and behavior of the grassroots as the crucial test of democracy in Malawi. Obscured in their focus were the wider relations of power and hierarchy in which citizens, including those with the best values and attitudes, attempted to envisage democracy and human rights.

Chikondi's tribulations, for instance, were far from over when he decided to seek legal redress. His encounters with institutional problems started at the governmental labor office. As in many other cases that were brought to the CHRR's Legal Clinic, the client had first sought redress through the labor office only to discover that assistance was not forthcoming. After listening to Chikondi's complaints, an officer told him to go back to Patel because "that one is simply your boss" *(amenewa ndi bwana wanu basi)*. The officer repeated several times during their conversation, "Go and discuss with him" *(Mukakambirane naye)* and "He was angry; go and discuss with him" *(Anakwiya; mukakambirane naye),* although Chikondi tried to make clear that he did not want further employment with Patel. It soon became apparent to Chikondi that the labor office was not interested in the case or able to investigate it.

The response at the labor office drew on a simplistic faith in dialogue that has a long history in Malawi. Its usefulness as a framework for settling disputes begins to unravel when it is recalled that Kamuzu Banda was the most prominent champion of "contact and dialogue" after Malawi had gained its independence. Even during the deepening political and economic crisis that culminated in the change of the system of government, Banda's sycophants claimed that he was engaged in a dialogue with his opponents. A similar effort to disarm critics by appealing to dialogue informed Malawi under Muluzi.[13] The infiltration of this discourse into labor disputes presents an excellent opportunity to expose its fallacies. Chikondi had attempted dialogue with his employer on several occasions before seeking legal aid, but every time he had failed to make Patel see his point of view. Even worse, these dialogues were frustrated by Patel's treatment of Chikondi as somebody who was not a full adult person. The two interlocutors did not enter the dialogue on equal terms. One was almost infinitely more powerful than the other, more capable of defending his interests and more brutal in deciding what the dialogues could be about.

Chikondi found, after further advice from the manager at Patel's store, more attentive officers at the CHRR's Legal Clinic. Two different officers considered his case on different occasions, each giving him an extensive opportunity to narrate his tribulations. Despite their interest in the case, which the officers privately professed to me, swearing that they "show no mercy" to abusive employers of Asian origin, they appeared careful not to indicate their inclinations to Chikondi. Throughout the five different meetings that Chikondi had at the Legal Clinic, the officers were taciturn about what Chikondi might expect from them or where their sympathies lay. The strategy was consistent with the pattern of detached professionalism discerned in chapter 5. It also provided a veil to hide the officers' own weak bargaining position with employers such as Patel.

The Erasure of Exploitation

Although the client was allowed to take his time in recounting his experiences, this recounting had the effect of making Chikondi responsible for defining the crux of his complaints. For example, when explaining how he had worked the whole of January, which was his last month of employment, the officer interrupted him with a sharp demand to be precise.

Chikondi: Yeah. I was working.

  Officer: January?

Chikondi: Yes, January, yes. I found that the boss, while I was working, could send me, he gave me money amounting to . . . apparently = [14]

  Officer: = You must say only the necessary things!

Chikondi: Yes. Ah =

  Officer: = Tell us only the necessary things.[15]

By urging Chikondi to say only the necessary things, the officer placed the burden of deciding what constituted essential information on Chikondi himself. Rather than steering the client's account to reveal information that could be used to produce a strong case against exploitation, the officers made Chikondi hesitate over what he should divulge. After Chikondi had presented his account for the first time, moreover, an officer left it to him to condense all the details into a single claim.

  Officer: Now, what is it that you want?

Chikondi: What I want, I don't want to return there to work, no.

  Officer: Mm.

Chikondi: I just want him to give me my money from the salary . . . and . . . [16]

The question "What is it that you want?" coming after an extensive account of exploitation, was remarkable for its tacit refusal to advise Chikondi on the full scope of the case that he had against Patel. Chikondi, with the labor office's advice to seek dialogue fresh in mind, was quick to emphasize that he did not want to return to Patel. The actual claim, seeking monetary compensation, reflected the immediacy of his financial problems. The true extent of abuse and exploitation did not become the focus of Chikondi's complaint, because he had little idea of the relevant legal framework to support other claims against Patel. The officers, in turn, took the case as a technical issue requiring the payment of an overdue salary and allowances. Seeking justice through legal aid was, in effect, undermined by all that the officers either ignored or took for granted in the client's account of exploitation.

Consider what was left out by focusing on the final salary. The most appalling omission was the level of the salary itself, with Chikondi's nine hundred kwacha far below the minimum wage of fifteen hundred kwacha. I could ascertain during my private conversations with the officers at the Legal Clinic that they were well aware of the legislation on minimum wage. These human rights activists ignored the issue in Chikondi's case, as they also ignored the compensation that he could have claimed for working on Sundays.[17] Nor did Chikondi's abrupt dismissal raise questions at the Legal Clinic, and his entitlement to a one-month notice or to one month's salary in lieu of notice was never explained to him.[18] Even more, the battering of the suspected thieves might have prompted an investigation of the extent to which corporal punishment was used as a disciplinary action at Patel's store.[19] In addition to all these violations of workers' rights to which legal redress could have been sought were the dehumanizing details that violated Chikondi's dignity as a family man. I consider the reasons for the officers' circumspection below, but what these omissions revealed was the officers' lack of practical commitment to workers' rights.

In view of the officers' skepticism toward many clients' accounts, Chikondi could have considered himself fortunate to have prompted any investigation at all. In his case, the officers did not demand written evidence but assured the client that they would visit Patel's store to find out more about the case. This was virtually the only indication of the officers' interest in the case that Chikondi could detect. Yet before he made the visit, an officer had attempted, as in most other cases, to make Chikondi "assist" him with a bus fare.

Officer: Please bring the transport money for me.

Chikondi: Okay.

Officer: To go to town and to return. That's all, that's our charge.

Chikondi: Thank you.

Officer: Yes. If you come with that money . . . right now we don't have money . . . and also we help in disputes without money.

Chikondi: Yes.

Officer: So we ask customers that they assist us with transport.

Chikondi: Okay.[20]

Despite his apparent agreement with the officer's request, Chikondi did not return to give money. Sensing that it would be difficult to elicit any money at all from Chikondi, the officer decided to use the CHRR's funds for his bus fare to Patel's store. He later told Chikondi and myself that he had found Patel, who had received him well.[21] After the officer explained who he was and why he had come, Patel had asked him, "What does he [Chikondi] want?" *(Kodi iyeyo akufuna chiyani?)*. The officer had focused on the nonpayment of the final month's salary, further complaining that Patel had deducted Chikondi's allowances as if they were debts. Questioned on the issue, Patel admitted that allowances were not debts, and he explained that when he sent employees to the field, he gave them a lump sum, the amount of which depended on the number of the people in the team. He evaded, however, the officer's question of how much the allowance was per person and instead asked for more time to consult his driver, who had been responsible for sharing the lump sum with Chikondi. The officer obliged, because, as he explained to Chikondi, the Legal Clinic gave defendants fourteen days to prepare a response. For fourteen days more, therefore, Chikondi, already facing food shortages and eviction from his accommodation, had to wait for redress.

Enter Mr. Patel, Exit the Laws of Malawi

Four weeks after Chikondi's first visit to the Legal Clinic, a dazzling white Mercedes Benz pulled up and parked outside it. Out stepped Hassam Patel, determined to close the case once and for all. Twelve of the fourteen days that the officer had given him had passed, and Patel preempted another visit by the officer to his store by coming himself to the Legal Clinic. This, as the officer commented to me afterward, was a means of preventing workers at his store from witnessing how he was made to compensate for abusing their former colleague. Patel came alone, dressed casually but smartly, amicable throughout the brief meeting in the officer's room. This was the first time he met me, but he did not ask questions, nor did the officer introduce me to him. We merely exchanged brief greetings before he and the officer began to discuss the case.[22]

The officer's strategy was to show respect to Patel, not to appear as a contentious advocate of socioeconomic rights. It was clear that even in the relative privacy of the officer's room, he was not going to challenge Patel on a whole range of abuses. The two men discussed a problem that appeared technical, a hitch that could be dispensed with once there was an agreement over the amount of the final payment. The officer's strategy was not predicated on entirely rational considerations, however. The desire for status distinctions also undermined a human rights activist's commitment to the empowerment of the marginalized. Slick in his manners and the owner of a luxurious car, Patel did not strike the officer as a despicable exploiter but as an embodiment of success, no doubt ruthless but, with his paraphernalia of status, someone who radiated educational achievement and business acumen. Face to face with this master, the officer seemed to forget what he had told me some weeks earlier about showing "no mercy" to the people of his kind.

My recording of the encounter provides ample evidence that the officer sought rapport with Patel rather than identification with Chikondi. If the quest for rapport had been based on entirely rational considerations, the officer would have had to concede that the conversation took place on Patel's terms. It was here that their contempt for Chikondi's situation converged. From their choice of English as the language of their interaction to their ultimate agreement, Patel and the officer appeared united in their sophistication, as two gentlemen clearly above the client, whose fate they had the power to decide. Immediately after exchanging greetings with Patel, the officer sought Patel's acceptance with the following words.

Officer: No, thanks a lot for your cooperation. I was expecting him to come here today =

Patel: = Okay =

Officer: = but he was complaining that he has got no money. So he always walks. I said, "You are a man, you must walk sometimes." (laughs)

Patel: Mm.

The officer opened the discussion by pointing out Chikondi's failure to come to the Legal Clinic, implying it was the result of his laziness. Chikondi's "failure" contrasted with Patel's "cooperation." The officer argued that, as a man, Chikondi should have walked to the Legal Clinic, never mind that it had been the officer himself who had earlier asked Chikondi to provide money for transport to investigate the case. The shocking disparity between Chikondi's inability to pay a bus fare and his former employer's access to a Mercedes Benz was also forgotten in this initial attempt at building rapport between the officer and Patel. The officer's laughter, while not breaking Patel's cautious front, was consistent with the patronizing attitude that the officer knew informed labor relations in workplaces like Patel's own. The desire to gain Patel's acceptance, and thereby forge a distinction between their status and Chikondi's, became a more serious breach of duty when the officer volunteered, while negotiating the settlement, to overlook the laws of Malawi.

Officer: Okay . . . So after looking into the whole matter, I feel that, Mr. Patel, you try to be very understanding and cooperative with me . . . in the sense that . . . if we can really try to follow the laws of Malawi, you are going to pay more than whatever we are asking now.

Patel: Okay.

Officer: In the sense that, at the moment this . . . the . . . minimum amount that can be given to an employee when he is out of station . . . is six hundred a day.

Patel: Six hundred a day.

Officer: Yeah. This means whether he is a messenger, a driver, or what have you, minimum amount is six hundred. So if someone stays outside maybe seven days . . . times six, how much is it? It is a lot of money. Regardless whatever job he is doing.

Patel: Okay.

Officer: Because there is no this that "you go together, this is the amount." Block amount, there is no that in labor laws . . . because each and everyone has to manage his own resources. You give him six hundred kwacha. It's up to the employee to give two hundred to his wife and he takes four hundred with him out . . . because when he goes out of his station, he leaves dependents behind. Now, he can eat there, he can sleep, but how can the dependents? That's why that allowance . . . is for dependents; . . . however, let's forget about that. We don't mention this to him; otherwise he would have been now creating another problem.

Patel: Okay.

Officer: So, let's put that aside . . . that's why I was still thinking that if you can still try to be considerate . . . ah . . . you can still give him something like . . . three . . .

Patel: The figure =

Officer: = Three hundred and seventeen.

Patel: The figure which I gave you =

Officer: = Yeah, three hundred and seventeen.

Patel: Yes . . .

Officer: We can accept that.

Patel: Oh?

Officer: Yeah.

Patel: Okay.

Taken at face value, the outcome of the settlement seemed unlikely to have been mediated by a human rights activist. It disregarded the client's version of the dispute that he was entitled to a whole month's salary. The officer used, instead, the employer's insistence on twenty-six days as the basis for calculation and persuaded him to deduct only the client's advances, not the money that he had received during the trip to Mzimba.[23] The officer indicated to Patel that he was requested to pay only a fraction of the amount that would have been due Chikondi if they had really tried to follow the laws of Malawi. With the phrases "let's forget about that" and "let's put that aside" the officer cleared the way for a settlement that advantaged the employer. The overall tone of the officer's submissions was again conducive to the rapport between him and Patel, as if the two men shared similar interests. It was Chikondi that appeared to be the source of problems, the one who might have *created* problems if he had known the provisions of the laws. The officer and Patel had to conspire to keep him satisfied with a minimal compensation, itself well below the minimum stipulated in the laws of Malawi.

This minimal compensation also conveniently obscured, as mentioned, the full range of exploitation and abuse at Patel's store. The emerging conclusion of the conversation between Patel and the officer was, in fact, that Patel had acted out of ignorance and was the one who actually needed help. In the above extract, the officer taught him the purpose of allowances, pointing out that employees had dependents who needed money while the breadwinner was away. The observation was banal, basically a statement that asserted the presence of relationships in every human being's life, and yet Patel was taken to be ignorant of this. Toward the end of the meeting, he seized on this role that the officer had allocated to him and explicitly pleaded for help. When the officer explained the importance of providing employees with written documents that stipulated the conditions of their employment, Patel made his neglect of such procedures seem like a consequence of his ignorance.

Patel: Okay, but do you think you could help me with the lett . . . this letter . . . format of the letter and that, if you can help me?

Officer: Yeah.

Patel: So that you can help me a little bit, you know.

Officer: Yes, I can assist you.

Patel: And I can =

Officer: = I can even give you all the laws of Malawi.

Patel: Please.

Officer: Employment laws, because those you are supposed to =

Patel: = Not now! I don't need =

Officer: = No, no, but I can furnish you all those . . . because those are not classified information.

Patel: Okay.

Officer: That information is for you as an employer.

Patel: Okay, just to help me out.

Officer: Yes, sure . . . ah, there's no problem. We can do that, and it is free of charge. That's part of our services. We don't charge anything.

The officer's assurance that Malawi's employment laws were not classified information indicated the remarkable assumption that Patel could possibly have thought they were. Patel's appeals to the officer to help him out were consistent with his role that emerged during the conversation. A case that had begun as a probe into an appalling instance of lawless exploitation ended with compassion for the exploiter. As if to make the irony complete, Patel delivered the final blow to any attempt to see in this case a systematic violation of human rights. As he produced a thick bundle of banknotes from his pocket, most of them in the five hundred kwacha denomination, he lamented the difficulties that the fundamental freedom of employment sometimes presented to the employer.

Patel: There is always a problem. When they want to leave, there is always too much problem.

Officer: Yeah, sure.

Patel: And you know, we are so busy there.

Officer: Yes, yes.

Patel: You said three hundred and seventeen?

Officer: And seventeen, yes.

Chikondi, the dehumanized object of exploitation, suddenly appeared to be the source of problems as an employee who wanted to leave, who was *free* to leave and to look for other employment, whereas the employer was "busy" to the point of being distressed. A few days later, Chikondi came to the Legal Clinic to collect his MK 317 (US$4.40), resigned to his fate. The meeting was subdued and brief, and the officer afterward filed the case as "successfully completed." When I interrogated him about the selective use of the laws of Malawi, the officer appealed to my knowledge about Malawian society. He expected me to know how difficult it was to elicit any compensation at all from employers of Asian origin. If he had insisted on the full amount of compensation, Patel would have become "uncooperative," possibly buying Chikondi off before the case could be pursued further. The officer's strategy appeared rational, as mediation that could only yield a compromise. The settlement, however, looked nothing like a compromise from Chikondi's perspective, which revealed Patel's power to decide its extent. It was, in fact, in their mutual interest that Patel and the officer co-operated. Patel secured a cheap settlement, whereas the officer could claim to have won the case. The added benefit, for the officer, was the enjoyment of a moment of status enhancement when he was able to negotiate with a sophisticated and wealthy "Indian" as if they were equals. The only casualty in this case was Yamikani Chikondi, the dehumanized "lorry boy" who had chosen to seek redress for injustice through the legal aid of a human rights NGO.

Extralegal Aid and the Freedom to Exploit

Much as this case added insult to Chikondi's injury, the critical issue is the way in which legal-aid officers chained themselves to an ultimately inconsequential position, and this applied to other cases as well. Apart from status distinctions, belief in exclusive knowledge, and clinical metaphors — all important factors in creating officers' quasi-professional identity — officers operated with an abstract notion of what constituted cases. Chikondi was individualized not as an active subject but as a simultaneously distinct and generic example of universal victimhood. His capacity as a productive moral being was obliterated by the conduct of mediation that the officers' abstract notion entailed. Rather than seeing in these cases a pattern for a specific situation of human rights, legal-aid officers sought exploiters' collusion. The officers and exploiters' shared contempt for the victim resulted in the officers' illusion of their shared equality as the basis for mediation.

The procedure bore resemblance to the judicial process, but it could evolve into extralegal aid that ignored relevant laws precisely because of the weak bargaining position into which officers had maneuvered themselves through their individualizing and abstract notions of the injured subjects. Little impact was felt on the structural inequalities that disempowered Malawi's impoverished majority. Although each case that I witnessed had its unique features, Chikondi's tribulations revealed the extent to which exploitation formed the context of labor-related grievances. Without ethnographic witnessing, much of the abuse and injustice that he experienced would have been obscured by the NGO's classification of the case as "successfully completed." Where money spoke louder than laws and where even the most enlightened human rights activists failed to transcend the historical inequalities of their society, the individualization of grievances unchained neither the exploited nor the advocates of their human rights. It merely made legal aid a tool of disempowerment.

As a measure of how commonplace Chikondi's experiences of exploitation were, his legal officers either ignored or took for granted the details involved. The employer's abusive failure to pay the minimum wage, to provide proper allowances, and to follow the procedures of dismissal were sacrificed to a cheap deal. Yet these misdeeds were only the most glaring abuses from a legal point of view. Another perspective, based on moral rather than legal considerations, informed Chikondi's own accounts of his grievances. Here the issue was dehumanization, the low pay combined with insults to the employee's dignity. He was expected to sleep outside while his colleague slept in a resthouse; he was denied the opportunity to forewarn his family of his journeys; and he had to endure hunger and face eviction from his house when the legal process failed to provide timely redress. The claims that these experiences could have prompted, revealing the abusive relationships that the freedom of labor obscured, were not allowed to emerge.

That human rights activists were instrumental in this dehumanization appears less counterintuitive if a central thesis of this book is recalled. Human rights are pursued in real-life situations, and their proponents do not cease to be embedded in contradictory realities once they clothe themselves in the refined raiment of human rights advocacy. They remain malleable by particular interests, constituted by the very inequalities that human rights discourse ostensibly challenges. The exchanges at the Legal Clinic were instances of "rights regimes converting themselves into regimes of truth" (Gledhill 2003, 213). Only a very particular form of claims was conceivable, its alternatives preempted by, among other things, the persistent habit of perceiving the poor as children or as something less than human. The officers at the Legal Clinic, like the civic educators in chapters 3 and 4, were influenced by the cultural disposition that the historical inequalities of their world fostered. Even if they were poor themselves, legal-aid officers found it irresistible to see in status distinctions a divide between adults and children. The parallel to civic educators' colonial mentality was apparent in the ease with which clients as children could assume savagelike qualities of irresponsibility (Jahoda 1999, 178–193). Chikondi had failed to come to the Legal Clinic when he was expected, he did not contribute to the officer's investigations by paying his bus fare, and he could create further problems if he was told of the provisions in Malawi's labor legislation. While not as aggressively hostile as Patel's views, these views objectified the impoverished client as a focus of contempt, as someone who could not be entrusted with the officers' knowledge.

This chapter has shown for labor relations that the status quo could prevail even when legal aid managed to arrange some compensation for the claimant. The status quo involved, under the conditions of Malawi's historical inequalities, a sharp cultural and social cleavage between employers and employees, apparent in the opportunities that their contrasting lifestyles permitted. The cleavage was based on one of the worst income discrepancies in the world, a problem of fundamental importance that few Malawian human rights activists were able to address during the first decade of democracy.[24] Instead, insofar as their advocacy of economic rights focused on the technical and piecemeal solutions offered in legal aid, they contributed to the continuing disempowerment of Malawian labor. Legal aid was an answer to some donor agencies' desire for tangible interventions, and it enhanced activists' status as professional experts. Yet it did little to lift Malawian workers from the depths of their exploitation. Indeed, by conducting mediation on employers' terms, it asserted their freedom to exploit.

The individualization of grievances supported the marginalization of trade unions, as described in the previous chapter. With its resemblance to the judicial process, legal aid also created the impression that Malawian labor disputes were solved in an orderly fashion. This impression, in turn, was crucial to the general condition that disempowerment in the guise of democracy perpetuated in Malawi: docility. Docility's history is virtually coterminous with the political history of Malawi, and Kamuzu Banda's regime etched docility on the nation's self-consciousness by declaring "discipline" and "obedience" as some of Malawi's cornerstones. Bakili Muluzi's regime made little effort to erase it, with "peace" an increasingly central preoccupation in Muluzi's speeches toward the end of his presidency. While disarming in itself, peace kept docility a national virtue. Any direct challenge to authorities was deemed "un-Malawian." One example among many was the way in which the minister of commerce and industry accused Mozambicans of causing violent clashes between land-hungry smallholders and large agricultural estates in Mulanje District in 2002. "Malawians," he was quoted, "cannot go to the extent of destroying things like these people have done. Malawians are a respectful people."[25]

To be sure, disobedience has occasionally erupted in Malawi, from anticolonial revolts to the campaigns against one-party rule and Muluzi's third term in office. As was seen, moreover, the micropolitics of Hassam Patel's store involved subversive agency among its workers. Yet the upshot of these overt and covert rebellions was not substantial improvement in the conditions of living among impoverished Malawians such as Yamikani Chikondi. Docility reigned, assisted by new democratic institutions that set their seal of legitimacy on the perpetuation of injustice. Docility did not, of course, prevent the victims of injustice from seeing *illegitimacy* in these institutions. Nor did the erasure of exploitation from human rights discourse entirely displace other kinds of claims, including ones that insisted on the reality of exploitation. The question is whether alternative claims could be discerned in a public sphere dominated by the discourse on rights as freedoms. By taking moral panic as its point of departure, the next chapter brings ethnographic witnessing to bear on popular alternatives to rights talk.

CHAPTER 7

Human Rights and Moral Panics

Listening to Popular Grievances

Toward the end of 2003, several primary schools in Lilongwe became the sites of a moral panic. Parents rushed to collect their children and take them back home, ordered them not to attend school at all, or demanded that the schools' management provide greater security. The reason was a perceived rise in the abductions and abuse of children in the capital. Strangers had been reported to wait for children outside schools to entice them away. Further rumors quickly provided a context for the scare. The abducted children were said to be killed, their body parts sold during President Bakili Muluzi's frequent trips abroad. This trade sustained Muluzi's and his cabinet ministers' infinite riches while it gave raw material to wealthy nations for their own pursuit of affluence. Human flesh was needed as a bait to attract a certain fish species in the Indian Ocean. The fish ate sand found in the bottom of the sea, and the sand transformed into gold while inside the fish. Some countries produced their unrivaled wealth through processing gold, and the leaders of poor countries secured their personal comfort through the provision of human body parts as raw material.

These rumors, easily dismissed as superstition by those who do not live under the conditions in which they emerge, open up an alternative perspective on democracy and human rights. The previous chapters have demonstrated how activists and politicians proclaimed a particular interpretation of human rights during Malawi's first decade of neoliberal democracy. The poor were asked to assume responsibility for their poverty, to embrace "participation" even if their resources remained as depleted as ever, and to face their exploitative employers as mere individuals seeking legal redress. Docility, as the previous chapter indicated, was often an obvious feature of this human rights regime. Yet perhaps it was too obvious, masking the many contentious discourses and subversive practices that actually informed the everyday experiences of being poor. The entrenched habits of elitism ensured orderly crowds during civic-education sessions and submissive clients seeking legal aid, only exceptionally replaced with direct challenges to activists' chosen framework of human rights. Collective outbursts of anger inevitably seemed, to activists and authorities alike, equally exceptional diversions from the real project of consolidating democracy. No NGO was prepared to analyze these outbursts in the context of inconsequential civic education or ineffective legal aid. Neoliberal governance, despite NGOs' best efforts, secured only a very uneasy peace.

This chapter examines the above-mentioned rumors and the circumstances around their emergence in order to highlight some of the channels for expressing popular discontent in democratic Malawi. Although the diversity of views among the populace presents a problematic standpoint for studying popular discontent, a moral panic reveals commonly felt frustrations, a predicament that can be juxtaposed with the preoccupations of human rights activists analyzed in the previous chapters. The moral panic of 2003 directs our attention to impoverished parents' desire to provide their children with quality education, it forces us to consider the moral and material conditions of these parents' livelihoods, and it brings into focus popular ideas of Malawi's place in the world. An examination of these circumstances can lead to an enriched understanding of the kinds of claims that Malawians made in spite of human rights activists' best efforts to inculcate neoliberal values and attitudes. The predominance of individual freedoms, asserted in the human rights discourse of activists and politicians, risked eclipsing the actual diversity of claims and concerns. Ethnographic witnessing uncovers in popular concerns intellectual resources, "modes of thinking which help us think" (Strathern 2004, 203). Crucially, the aim of this chapter is less to give a voice to the voiceless than to lend ears to the earless. The Malawian poor were just as opinionated as their civic educators, sometimes to the point of being vociferous. Their problem was not a lack of voice; the problem was that so few listened to them.

The bulk of my observations in this chapter comes from several years of fieldwork in the capital's Chinsapo Township. By the end of the 1990s, the township hosted some thirty thousand residents, the vast majority of whom were migrants from rural areas (see Englund 2002d). An "un-planned" area built on the land of old Chewa villages, Chinsapo had grown to become the largest residential area in Lilongwe. Plots in its congested neighborhoods, allocated by local chiefs, lacked basic amenities, such as running water, and while access to electricity greatly improved during the late 1990s, the majority of households were still unable to afford it in 2003. Located some five kilometers from the capital's commercial center in Old Town, Chinsapo was the home of small-scale traders and vendors, low-ranking civil servants, self-employed service providers, and semiskilled laborers. Their involvement in the moral panic of 2003 was, however, more than a simple reaction to their miseries. A remarkable emphasis on civil virtues coexisted with harrowing impoverishment. Just as Yamikani Chikondi sought to observe proper procedures in the administration of justice, so too did Chinsapo residents pursue their livelihoods in the context of moral considerations. They were not abstract subjects whose victimhood would have justified human rights activists' interventions and intellectual leadership. By the same token, the intellectual challenge also applies to the ethnographic description of Chinsapo residents' situation. While the injustices of their situation were obvious enough, how does the ethnographer find a descriptive language that is not a version of the human rights discourse it interrogates, including its particular idea of freedom?

Bombs of the Poor

"Moral panic" refers, in widespread academic usage, to extraordinary collective actions that seek to counter perceived threats to fundamental values (La Fontaine 1998, 19–21). Mass hysteria or psychosis is not at issue, because the subjects of a moral panic are able to analyze the causes of their distress and are adamant about the values they seek to defend. The class position of those who are gripped by a moral panic is not constant. Whereas the moral panic of 2003 in Malawi tormented the urban poor, South Africa has provided examples of middle-class citizens' moral panic over crime and disorder (see Samara 2005).

The challenge to ethnographic description becomes apparent, as in a host of recent studies from Africa (see especially J. Comaroff and J. L. Comaroff 1999 and Geschiere 1997),[1] when beliefs in witchcraft and the occult are observed as recurring expressions of moral panic. The perceived rise in witchcraft accusations has been related, in this cited literature, to the unevenly distributed profits of neoliberalism, seen as "occult economies," in which some seem capable of gathering inexplicable wealth with the smallest effort. When the chances of the Malawian poor to initiate public debates about their exploitation were preempted by their official status as "partners" in development, few secular or recognizably rational counterdiscourses were at their disposal. However, the academic focus on witchcraft discourses, while welcome as an effort to reach beyond official rhetorics, can create its own virtual reality in which, as studies of the occult multiply, generalizations begin to gloss over the actual range of situations. Not only can beliefs in witchcraft and the occult appear as the most potent, if not the only, popular modes of critique and subversion, but also the variable significance and scope of these beliefs in moral panic may be overlooked. The moral panic of 2003 in Lilongwe arose from entirely rational concerns over the safety and success of schoolchildren. Beliefs in the occult appeared to be of secondary importance, expressed as fears over Satanism among prominent entrepreneurs.[2]

Residents in Lilongwe had long believed that certain entrepreneurs and politicians in the city engaged in Satanic rituals involving the consumption of human body parts. Popular reflections often referred to a particular building in the low-density Area 3, where the most prominent Satanic worshippers were thought to gather. The building was white and windowless, and it had been used by the Freemasons during the colonial era.[3] Ministerial vehicles, along with the cars of Lilongwe's business class of Asian origin, were rumored to have brought people to the building even before the democratic transition. Initiation into the group was thought to involve murder, and a major activity inside the building was said to be the comparison and sale of human body parts. A principal source of these rumors was born-again Christians, even among those who did not belong to Christian churches.[4] In 1999, for example, a letter signed by Lucifer Satan was intercepted by pentecostal pastors in Lilongwe. It contained a reminder to Satanists of forthcoming meetings in the General Assembly Headquarters, understood as the building in Area 3. However, even though such rumors were long-standing and widespread in the city, one would too hastily conclude that the moral panic of 2003 was about Satanism as such. Lilongwe residents understood some abductors and suppliers of body parts to be mere criminals taking orders from high-level authorities, who in turn participated in transnational trade. Insofar as Satanism and the occult appeared in popular discourses during this moral panic, they were related to the new constitutional provision that granted Malawians the freedom of worship (*ufulu wachipem-*

bedzo). This freedom, residents in Chinsapo Township told me, had facilitated Satanism and expanded its networks.

Parents' concerns during this moral panic were less about witchcraft than about trade in human body parts. The concerns appeared to resonate with widespread fear over bodies becoming commodities, items that could be bought and sold in a transnational market (see Sharp 2000; Scheper-Hughes and Wacquant 2002). Studies of these scares elsewhere have demonstrated that illicit trade in human body parts does take place and that, in its particularly insidious form, the organs of healthy poor people in the South have been exported to the North, appropriated to enhance the condition of ailing millionaires. On the other hand, in Malawi as elsewhere in the region, human body parts, particularly the genitals and eyes, have long been thought to provide potent items to witches. Scares over organ thefts can, therefore, draw on a variety of issues, and they need not arise from similar cosmologies of the body. What the rumors in Lilongwe appeared to emphasize was, again, not so much witchcraft as a transnational division of labor. I discuss this view of transnationalism toward the end of this chapter, but it is already worth mentioning that the rumor about the use of Malawians' flesh in rich countries' production of wealth evoked Malawi's historical role as a labor reserve. When the large-scale export of male labor to mines and plantations in southern Africa ended in the 1980s, it had lasted for several decades, making a profound impact on the social life of many areas of Malawi. The highly unequal exchange that underlay this labor migration occasionally raised Malawian concerns over, for example, the theft of their blood.[5] For the participants in the moral panic of 2003, many of whom were too young to have personal experience of labor migration, the rumors expressed the continuing subservient status of Malawi in the world.

The historical resonances of scares over trade in body parts indicate, therefore, that these scares can be more than simple responses to neoliberal injustices. In point of fact, historians and anthropologists have traced the origins of such scares and associated beliefs in the occult much further in history, from extractive labor regimes under late colonialism (White 2000) to the transcontinental slave trade (Shaw 2002). Exact chronologies remain a moot point, established with great difficulty, if at all, because rumors take on new meanings and forms as they travel through history. An illuminating example is the fault that Maia Green (2003) has found with Luise White's account of white Catholic priests and blood stealing in colonial Zambia (White 2000, 175–207). "The origins of tales of blood stealing for sale," Green writes, "lie in the legacy of the slave trade rather than Catholic ritual, hence the widespread association of blood thieves with 'Arabs' as stereotypical representatives of the trade in people" (2003, 73).

The precise history of the rumors inciting the 2003 moral panic is beyond the scope of this book. More pertinent here are two other issues: one, that generally such scares are indeed historical and, two, the ways in which they gripped the imagination of impoverished township dwellers. White's comment that the "generic qualities" of rumors assume efficacy only when they are "locally credible" goes to the heart of the matter (2000, 6, 83). Rumors must be adjusted to particular landscapes and relationships in order to appear plausible. Moreover, once credibility is achieved, rumors cease to inspire contemplation but find their force in the lived experience of those who believe in them. As such, although unscrupulous opposition politicians may manipulate popular discontent by launching such rumors, much more than the mere gullibility of the populace is at issue. Subjective experience under harrowing conditions determined the veracity of these rumors, and authorities found themselves compelled to comment on them. As a "poor man's bomb" (Mbembe 2001), rumor contested official discourses and had the potential of affecting the conduct of those who wielded political, economic, and spiritual power (see Ellis 1993; Ellis and ter Haar 2004).

In Malawi at the turn of the millennium, the thefts of body parts and human blood appeared to occur with alarming frequency. The reaction of the United Democratic Front was to deny ruling politicians' involvement in this trade and to issue warnings through the state media that anyone found spreading such rumors would be arrested. As in White's study of colonial Africa, "published denunciations of rumor were often thought to prove its truth" (2000, 57). Far from extinguishing the flames of popular discontent, the official denunciations, especially when broadcast on the national radio, only served to circulate elements of the rumors to even wider audiences. Human rights NGOs, in turn, demonstrated their detachment from popular concerns either by failing to consider the cases at all or by condemning the outbursts of violence as "mob justice." While also keen to condemn mob justice, the mass media were somewhat more attuned to popular discourses. Articles about the abuse of children by witches in both Malawi and other African countries were published by *The Nation,* Malawi's biggest daily, when the moral panic rocked Lilongwe.[6] The same period also witnessed letters to the editor demanding a "witchcraft law," which would assist in prosecuting witches rather than merely proscribing witchcraft accusations.[7] Although the vast majority of residents in Chinsapo Township could not afford to buy newspapers, their stories were widely known and discussed. Many township dwellers visited the city every day and came back with accounts of what the newspapers had said.

The events and rumors that culminated in the moral panic of 2003 were preceded by several incidents that, while not directly linked to the predicament of schoolchildren in Lilongwe, influenced their parents' sense of impending tragedies. Toward the end of the 1990s, Chiradzulu, a rural district in southern Malawi, was the scene for brutal attacks on women. At least twenty women were killed, their corpses — usually without genitals, eyes, breasts — found near roads, flimsily hidden in the bush. Popular rumors in Lilongwe claimed that Gwanda Chakuamba, then the leader of the Malawi Congress Party, had implicated the UDF in these hideous crimes, promptly countered by Muluzi's visit to the area and his efforts to console the bereaved at the Sanjika Palace. UDF officials became the targets of direct assaults soon afterward, when the famine of 2001–2 devastated many areas in the country. The government was believed to receive relief maize in return for its citizens' blood. Victims emerged to tell terrifying tales of nocturnal attacks by unknown blood suckers, and local leaders of the UDF were beaten in some areas. This crisis occasioned the official denouncements mentioned above.

These dramatic incidents were only the most high-profile disturbances in a series of events. Locally known entrepreneurs who owned refrigerators became particularly vulnerable to popular suspicions and rumors. A number of related rumors in Malawi's urban centers suggested that fridges were used to store human body parts. In one case in Blantyre, for example, the house of a businessman and his family was attacked by angry residents in the city's Zingwangwa Township. Rumors claimed that he was in possession of seven human heads and other body parts and that he was personally responsible for killing people, particularly children, in order to sell their organs. When the angry crowd started to pelt stones at the house, swearing to kill the businessman if found, the police arrived to protect his house and property. Two aspects of the police's behavior were reported to have intensified the crowd's fury.[8] First, the businessman was thought to have been arrested earlier, but the police had released him on bail. How could, members of the crowd asked the reporters, a murderer be allowed to return home? Second, the crowd's observations would have seemed sarcastic if they had not touched on the very core of insecurity and injustice in the township. Whenever the poor majority had reported cases of theft and other crimes to the police, people in the crowd said, the police had explained their inertia as a result of their lack of vehicles. Now that a prominent businessman came under attack, the police suddenly appeared with vehicles and in force.

Distrust of the police was also common in Lilongwe, and the owner-ship of refrigerators was also a key issue in the rumors there. One notable case implicated the founder of the Miracle Church of God, a pentecostal preacher who had also gained some popularity as a singer. This man of God shocked the capital by becoming embroiled in a scandal in which human body parts were said to have been stored in his fridge. When he emerged to protest his innocence on the national radio, popular opinion began to entertain the possibility that the real culprit was the preacher's second-in-command, who had taken advantage of his leader's fridge. In the meantime, incidents involving schoolchildren appeared to multiply. A ten-year-old girl, who had been on her way to the Assemblies of God church in her neighborhood in a high-density area in Lilongwe, disap-peared, her abused corpse subsequently found in Lilongwe River. An-other girl also disappeared from her residential area and was later found in a different area several miles away. Crying and confused, the girl refused to talk about her ordeal. A common explanation suggested that her abductors had pitied her and decided to abandon her. Even schools were seen to be unsafe when, at the end of September 2003, a large tree sud-denly fell and crushed the young primary school pupils studying under it. This fatal accident prompted popular reflections on the government's fail-ure to construct enough school buildings, leaving children to learn out-doors. The impending moral panic gained momentum from this per-ceived lack of order and safety in schools, with children coming under threat not only from old trees but also from abductors.

The Conditions of a Moral Panic

Mphekesera, the Chichewa word for "rumors" or unverified stories, did not appear in Chinsapo residents' reflections on the above-mentioned incidents. The incidents were considered news *(nkhani),* something that had happened *(zimene zidachitika),* amply verified by eyewitness testi-mony, even if heard through second- or thirdhand sources. After all, women actually had been found mutilated and killed in Chiradzulu, and the abused corpse of a schoolgirl had been sighted in Lilongwe River. The other stories contributed to a popular understanding of a pattern, to a gradual realization of the horrifying circumstances of poor people in general coming under attack. The stories were more than mere stories — they condensed aspects of commonly felt threats and crises. It is, therefore, essential to reach beyond the stories to the conditions that made them appear compelling to many Chinsapo residents. Understanding those conditions brings us one step closer to understanding the limited relevance of Malawi's human rights discourse.

The township offers a wide range of schools, but most of them are privately owned, following liberalization in Muluzi's Malawi. As elsewhere in Malawi, it soon became apparent that insufficient mechanisms were in place to monitor the quality of education in these private institutions, many operating without an official license and overcharging for their teaching. Some private schools did have a policy of recruiting teachers with diplomas or degrees, thus contributing to the lack of qualified teaching staff in government schools. The prospect of having a five- to tenfold increase in salary was irresistible to teachers in government primary schools, who earned well under two thousand kwacha (twenty U.S. dollars) per month in 2003.[9] Teachers' public image was not improved by the scandals and rumors that implicated them, which involved incidents ranging from teachers having written exams on behalf of students for a fee to sexual misconduct, as publicized in, among other venues, the popular news program *Nkhani za m'maboma* (News from the Districts) on the national radio.

Such incidents and the rumors they helped to stimulate did little justice to the many committed teachers who continued to pursue their vocation under difficult circumstances. Government schools were virtual megaschools in Chinsapo, in which the majority of children came from families unable to pay for private education. The largest primary school in the township was a source of pride to both its political and its "traditional" leaders. Funded by the World Bank, the United Nations Children's Fund had supervised the construction of several buildings equipped with electricity and enclosed by a brick wall. It would have been a triumph of development, an oasis of education amid searing poverty, if the school had not been rendered inadequate as soon as it was completed. Some seven thousand pupils studied there at the turn of the millennium, their number far exceeding what some sixty teachers could possibly manage. The number of teachers had been almost halved, through deaths and resignations, since the new premises were inaugurated in 1998. Yet the number of classes continued to grow, because in the following year the school assumed the status of a full primary school offering eight grades, known as standards in Malawi. During the first standards, one lone teacher would face a class of some three hundred pupils. Worse still, despite the imposing new buildings, only a minority of classes could be accommodated in them. All pupils from the first through the sixth standards studied outside, sitting on the ground under trees or, if all shaded space had been taken, under the scorching sun. Whether the children remained seated was, of course, often beyond any teacher's control. The school, praised by UDF politicians when they held their meetings there on the weekends, was reduced to a scene of pandemonium during the school hours.

It was painfully clear to most parents that their children appeared to learn nothing in a school like Chinsapo Full Primary School. Many parents complained to me that children "only played" *(amangosewera)* at school and failed to read and write properly even after several years of schooling. Added to these frustrations over academic performance — and to the crushed expectations of personal advancement through education — was the popular understanding of the township's schools as sites of criminal activities. Not only were many private schools established by dubious entrepreneurs, operating without an official permission, but also government schools were deprived of their scarce resources by thefts, sometimes perpetrated by their own members of staff. The new primary school lost large amounts of donated exercise books and other learning materials when its teachers allegedly sold them to private schools. The new buildings also attracted armed burglars, who either overpowered the school's unarmed guards or, as rumors suggested, were actively assisted by them. More learning materials were thereby lost, together with other items that could be removed, including the main switch for electricity. Despite the efforts of some church-based and humanitarian well-wishers to replace these lost items, burglars kept coming back to steal the main switch, leaving the school without electricity for long periods of time.

These dismal material conditions and illegitimate activities had created the conditions for a moral panic when rumors suggested the arrival of more insidious criminals. One remarkable feature of these rumors was that they consistently focused on the low-income, high-density areas of the capital, with parents, pupils, and teachers in Kawale, Chilinde, Mchesi, Area 24, Area 23, and Area 22 becoming gripped by fears similar to those of their counterparts in Chinsapo. In Area 24, pupils fled their school in panic when the word spread that strangers had entered the school to abduct children.[10] Their parents were quick to come on the scene, and they searched the school for remaining children. In Chinsapo as in many other areas, the moral panic involved confrontations between parents and the school management. When the rumors of abductions were at their height, a group of parents stormed into a headmaster's office in Chinsapo. They demanded greater security at school, achieved, among other measures, through a policy of releasing children only to those whom they recognized as their parents or guardians. Pupils were also expected to be escorted by these parents and guardians between home and school.

I observed that teachers were often quite as distraught as parents when the rumors about abductions and the sale of human body parts circulated in the capital. The focus of these rumors on the schools could only increase teachers' personal sense of failure. Not only had the conditions for academic achievement been ruined, but also teachers were powerless when their students' lives came to be at risk. As a consequence, some parents withdrew their children from school. I also witnessed parents in Chinsapo instructing their children to shun strangers, particularly those who attempted to persuade children to go into their cars. Chinsapo parents often pointed out that, because they did not know anyone who had a car, their children should not trust such strangers.

It was, in the end, these private instructions that appeared more efficient than the measures the school management could devise in collaboration with parents' representatives and local leaders in school committees. The resolutions at these meetings ranged from the provision of escort services to the recruitment of additional guards to the issuing of identity cards, all rather substantial initiatives beyond the actual means of government schools. Local UDF leaders and Chinsapo's headmen were eager to represent the threat of abductions as an isolated and passing danger, probably committed by an ill-defined gang of marijuana (*chamba*) smokers. Yet they could not distract the popular attention from the lived reality of primary education, offered free of charge by the Muluzi administration but woefully inadequate to equip children with knowledge and skills. It was as if the rumors about life-threatening abductions gave a form to grievances, which had intensified over the years since the democratic transition.

From Injustice to Mob Justice

The moral panic in 2003 inevitably extended the popular attention from the management of schools to the conduct of other authorities. Although

Chinsapo's headmen settled disputes involving both "those who were born" *(obadwa)* and "those who had arrived" *(obwera)* in the township, their jurisdiction did not encompass criminal offenses. The rumors about trade in human body parts brought into focus what the police did in response to them. As was seen above in the case of popular uproar in Blantyre's Zingwangwa Township, the alleged atrocities by an evil businessman created a context for remembering how inaction by the police had often obstructed the pursuit of justice in the township. The arrival of police officers to protect the house and property of this businessman appeared to confirm their complicity in crime. The crowd resorted to direct action in order to punish the businessman, a mode of intervention condemned by the police, the media, and human rights NGOs alike as "mob justice."

The incidents of violence against wealthy and powerful individuals unleashed by otherwise docile subjects raise the question of the full extent of grievances that this moral panic evoked. Chinsapo residents also had ample reason to doubt the integrity of the police force when the rumors about abducted schoolchildren and trade in body parts provoked their moral panic. Again, eyewitness testimony and personal experience played a part in launching rumors. A major incident in Chinsapo involved the realization that a prominent shopkeeper appeared to be a participant in the trade in human body parts. He was one of those few individuals who had been able to make full use of electricity by buying a refrigerator for his store. When township residents were becoming increasingly alarmed by child abductors, burglars broke into his store at night. They wanted to take the fridge, but it was too heavy to be carried very far. Assuming that the fridge was full of beer, the burglars opened it to remove the drinks, only to be shocked to find it packed with human body parts. Horrified by their finding, the burglars forgot their own criminal pursuit and rushed to the police. The police came to inspect the fridge at dawn, the township already bustling with life. Their vehicle attracted considerable attention, and a large crowd witnessed the police driving away with the fridge and its owner. Both returned the next day, with the police issuing a warning against "mob justice." Anyone found inciting hatred against the shopkeeper, the police proclaimed, would be arrested — the man was innocent.

Because the information offered by the police was as implausible as it was minimal, rumors quickly answered the popular demand for explanations. According to rumor, the reason the police denied that anything criminal had taken place, not only in this case but in *every* case, was that the highest political authorities in the country were implicated. Rumor explained that when abductors and traders in human body parts had been taken to a police station, they had pointed out that they were not working alone. After the suspects named the cabinet ministers for whom they had acquired human body parts, the police had allegedly called these ministers to ascertain the veracity of the claims. The cabinet ministers, in turn, had explained that they themselves had received orders from their *bwana*, President Muluzi. The ministers had directed the police to release the detainees and to issue denials that anything criminal was at issue.

The plausibility of such rumors derived from the reality of township dwellers' situation. The frustrations and fears over schools were the immediate reasons for the speed with which rumors about high-profile perpetrators of trade in body parts assumed currency in the township. Yet, so too had township dwellers' trust in the police evaporated over a long period of time. The police force, one of the clenched fists of the one-party state, had gained little popular credibility after the democratic transition. Township dwellers considered both the police and the army corrupt, and both were seen to collaborate with criminals. Armed criminals acquired their guns from these apparent custodians of law and order, the deal stipulating that the owners of the weapons were entitled to a share in the loot. Thieves who had not struck a deal with the police could buy their way back to freedom by giving them the money they had stolen. Such rumors were consistent with what some township dwellers were able to witness in the city. Roaming the streets as hawkers, they had ample opportunity to observe how uniformed police officers collected bribes from known criminals in backstreets. The most distressing, if not absurd, practice was familiar to any township dweller who had attempted to deliver a thief to a police station. If they wanted the culprit to stay for investigation, the police had told them, they had to provide food. There could hardly be a more potent example of the injustice of the formal justice system from the point of view of impoverished township dwellers. What was the purpose of catching a thief, I was often asked, if one was obliged to forget food shortages in one's own house and give the thief a bag of maize?

Under these circumstances, the notion of mob justice would seem to obscure impoverished Malawians' grievances. The police, journalists, and human rights NGOs deployed the notion with little regard to the actual conditions in which people were expected to trust the police. The condemnations of mob justice viewed the poor through the usual elitist lenses as ignorant and impulsive masses, all too eager to commit murders if not restrained by civic education. Not only did such views bypass the question of why poor Malawians distrusted the police; they also assumed that popular modes of delivering justice were brutal and, in a word, unjustified. Excessive violence was certainly the fate of many captured thieves and other criminals in the townships and villages of Malawi, but vigilante groups in many villages and townships were overseen by locally elected committees. In Chinsapo as in many other locations, such a group was known as Inkatha, its name evoking the ferocious warriorhood of South African Zulus. Armed with clubs, the men representing Inkatha patrolled the township especially at night, interrogating those who were found outdoors at unusual hours. Like other vigilantes, Inkatha trod a tightrope in seeking to keep violence against potentially violent offenders to a minimum. The task was to bring these offenders before a committee of elders, often led by a headman, who decided on the punishment. Rather than permitting violence, Inkatha committees often made offenders perform work for those who had been their victims. Crop thefts, for example, were compensated by work in the victim's garden.[11]

The recommendations proposed in the media and the civic-education materials of NGOs, by contrast, began from the assumption that the police and formal courts delivered justice. An editorial commenting on the above-mentioned incident in Blantyre's Zingwangwa Township reprimanded people for damaging the house of the accused.[12] While admitting that murder and trade in body parts were serious offenses that made people's anger understandable, the editorial insisted that the police were not to be faulted: "The problem is not the police, they are following the laws of this country" *(Vuto si la apolisi koma nawo akutsatira malamulo a dziko lino)*. The police had, the editorial pointed out, released the suspect on bail because of a law that granted this provision, and it reminded the readers that passing judgment was the task of neither Zingwangwa residents nor newspapers but of a court of law. Yet the author of the editorial was only too pleased to present the case from a particular point of view. The very reason for popular uproar was questioned when the editorial expressed doubt that enough evidence existed to prove that anyone had actually gone missing in the township. In language that was likely to sound offensive to Zingwangwa residents, the editorial referred to the issue as *mphekesera* (rumor, hearsay) and *nkhambakamwa* (chatter).

The editorial is only one example of the way in which journalists and human rights activists were unable to distinguish between different modes and rationales of so-called mob justice. The Centre for Human Rights and Rehabilitation, a provider of legal aid, was at the forefront of spreading civic education that demanded the public's compliance with the orders of the police. Its audio tape made with the popular comedians Izeki and Jacob, for example, included an episode entitled "Ufulu wokhala ndi moyo" (Freedom to Be Alive).[13] In the episode, two men who had participated in burning a thief were rebuked by a better-informed citizen. She condemned the men's action and stressed that such cases should be determined "only in a court of law" *(pokhapokha pabwalo la khoti).* She presented the procedure of taking a criminal to the court as a straightforward matter of "simply catching him or her and going with him or her to the police" *(kungomugwira ndi kupita naye kupolisi).* In a similar vein, the CHRR's leaflet on mob justice, entitled *Kulanga kwa mchigulu* (To Punish through a Mob), insisted that only courts had the right to deliver justice.[14] Those who took the law into their own hands must themselves be deposited at the police. "The police make sure that such people are taken to the court quickly so that they are tried and given a punishment if they are found guilty" *(Apolisi awonetsetsa kuti anthu amenewa atengeredwe kukhoti mwansangansanga kuti akaweruzidwe ndi kupatsidwa chilango ngati atapezeka olakwa).*

The gap between such messages of civic education and the reality of the situation described earlier does not stem from dissimilar ideas of justice. Taking someone's life is always a serious matter among Malawians who despise the world of crime. The moral panic over human body parts would hardly have sparked widespread anxiety if murder were not considered an atrocity. The discrepancy between activists' civic education and popular views was, rather, *produced* by the former's refusal to take the actual circumstances of impoverishment and disempowerment as a point of departure. The discrepancy was paradoxical insofar as human rights NGOs, including the CHRR, had criticized the police for their partisan approach in investigating cases of political violence. Toward the end of Muluzi's regime, the police looked the other way on several occasions when the UDF's youth wing, the Young Democrats, had descended on Muluzi's critics, such as the clergy and supporters of the opposition (see Englund 2002c). The executive officers of the CHRR were invariably outspoken in their condemnation of political bias among the police, and they were among the most prominent activists demanding the resignation of the inspector general of the police after the 2004 general elections. Yet it was precisely this focus on high-profile political cases that made activists deaf to the actual expressions of insecurity among the rural and urban poor. Much as the CHRR contributed to democracy by publicly condemning the police for turning a blind eye to the violence of the UDF's Young Democrats, its civic education represented the police as the unproblematic custodians of law and order.

In other words, while activists were fully aware of problems in the police force, their civic education proceeded from the assumption that the police could be entrusted with the investigation of the cases in which poor Malawians had been the victims. Witnesses to the bias of the police toward the rich and the powerful, who sometimes doubled as the masterminds behind crime, ordinary Malawians had learned to expect little justice from the institutions promoted by civic educators. Crippled, in turn, by their elitist assumption that the poor were prone to violence and easily excitable, civic educators were unable to listen properly to popular grievances. As such, those grievances were likely to be given little attention in the reform of justice delivery in Malawi.[15]

Trust in an Immoral Economy

Human rights activism is hardly an obvious instrument in policing the poor. By sharing the same discourse on mob justice with the police, however, some human rights activists in democratic Malawi became agents of the neoliberal order, one of the media through which popular grievances were actually erased from public discourse. It is plausible to assume that moral panics are at least partly provoked by this lack of recognition for the lived experience in actual situations. Yet a focus on moral panics may also obscure that very experience by representing extraordinary events as typical instances of people's tribulations. Distrust of the police, political leaders, and some entrepreneurs was certainly palpable during Chinsapo residents' moral panic in 2003, but distrust could not be their only reality. Along with distrust existed trust, a necessary feature of their precarious livelihoods. If the notion of trust acquires meaning only in relation to risk (see Gambetta 1988), then Chinsapo residents' daily pursuits of money and food provide perfect illustrations of this general condition. Small-scale traders and vendors, making up some 50 percent of Chinsapo's adult population (see Englund 2002d), were particularly vulnerable to fluctuations in incomes and obliged to offer goods on credit in order to cultivate their essential relationships with customers. Under such circumstances, the civil virtues of trust, courtesy, and patience were constitutive of successful entrepreneurship. It is against the background of such civil virtues that the eruptions of so-called mob justice must be understood, occasioned by an economy that, despite all the trust it appeared to demand of its participants, was never quite as moral as those virtues seemed to promise.

The moral panic of 2003 resonated not only with Malawians' historical experiences of selling their labor to companies in other countries, as mentioned, but also with contemporary changes in their livelihoods. The liberalization of the economy flooded the streets of urban centers with vendors and hawkers selling imported or smuggled goods and local foodstuffs. It was only appropriate that nightmarish rumors drew on the idioms of vending. The primary suppliers of human body parts were said to receive "orders" from more prominent entrepreneurs in this sinister commerce, "order" spoken of with the same term, *odala,* used in all vending. Vendors "ordered" their goods from wholesalers, and just as the trade in body parts involved entrepreneurs with highly disparate means, so too was street vending embedded in strikingly unequal economic relations. Secondhand clothes, for example, arrived in Malawi in large shipments, which were sold in bales to traders of various means.[16] The sizes of the bales decreased from bundles of hundreds of clothes, often acquired by entrepreneurs of Asian origin, to half a dozen items that the poorest vendors were able to "order" at any one time. Instead of being entitled even to enter the stores of Asian entrepreneurs, most vendors from Chinsapo had to deal with Malawian middlemen, who had bought bales of clothes and acted as wholesalers in their own right. The larger the initial capital, the greater the profits, with better-off vendors having the privilege to choose items from bales before their poorer peers could. The cycle of poverty thus continued, the poorest vendors selling the cheapest and least desirable clothes.

The issue of credit discloses in a particularly vivid fashion the vicissitudes of trust in an immoral economy. As was seen in chapter 4, microcredits were as generously promised by politicians in democratic Malawi as they were desired by the poor. They became, however, accessible on a much smaller scale than what the neoliberal rhetoric of private entrepreneurship had led many to expect. The vast majority of vendors and hawkers who lived in Chinsapo at the turn of the millennium had never obtained credit from formal financial institutions. At the same time, credit or "debt" *(ngongole)* was critical to the relations of trust underlying their livelihoods. At one extreme were the above-mentioned wholesalers who would not enter into debt relations with vendors who were short of money. Anyone who wished to purchase items from wholesalers had to pay cash. Vendors' access to goods reflected, therefore, the lack of trust they inspired among wholesalers, whether Malawians or Asians. At another extreme, vendors were forced to accommodate considerable uncertainty in their business because of customers who defaulted on agreed credit. Among the dozen vendors I came to know particularly well in

Chinsapo, about half of their monthly income derived from payments on credit that their customers had requested, often several weeks earlier. Especially toward the end of the month before salaries were paid in civil service, the largest employer in Malawi, cash transactions were exceptional.

Considerable time in vendors' work, in other words, went into efforts to persuade their debtors to pay back their loans. Different goods entailed, of course, different kinds of relationships, with the vendors of foodstuffs, particularly those who delivered their goods to customers' homes, often developing rapport with their customers. The capacity to make conversation, "to chat" *(kucheza)*, was virtually more important than the consistency in the supply and quality of goods. The vendor had little choice but to appear cheerful even when his or her customer defaulted on credit. For their part, some of these "customers" *(makastomala)* — a specific status that was earned through loyal cooperation with the same vendor — complained to me that they had to tolerate occasional poor quality in order to enjoy the privileges this status provided. Not only could they count on receiving items on credit, an unthinkable option in the city's largest stores, but also they were often treated to discounts or small amounts of free goods, known as *price* that the vendor added after an agreement on a purchase had been reached.

Trust thus joined persons with very different standings in the overall economy. Work in the office, associated with appropriate status symbols as described previously, could not completely alienate the salaried class from the poorest echelons of the neoliberal economy. Civil servants' salaries, although paid fairly regularly, were often too low to last until the end of the month, and credit arrangements had to be negotiated with vendors, service providers, and more affluent relatives and friends. The relationships of trust varied in the extent to which people of different economic means contributed to one another's lives. Many vendors retained some influence over their regular customers by granting them credit, patiently maintaining a façade of compassion when the payment of a debt was delayed. When some vendors discovered that their customers were their ethnic compatriots or members of the same church, for example, the relationship could begin to cater to other aspects of their mutual welfare. In such cases, it was not uncommon for the customer to assist the vendor when a funeral or illness occurred in the latter's household. These gestures were usually the customer's prerogative, however, which bespoke an entrenched discrepancy even in the most trusted relationships. Much as a vendor could apply moral pressure to make a customer stay loyal to him or her, in the end it was the customer who was understood by both parties to have access to regular income and the benefits it entailed. Seemingly trivial incidents in the customer's personal finances, such as unforeseen expenditures or even a simple failure to withdraw money from the bank on a particular day, could seriously affect the vendor's livelihood. I witnessed cases in which vendors awaited the payment of debts until they had depleted both their food supplies at home and their capital to start another cycle of vending. It was usually futile for a vendor to plead with his or her customer under such circumstances. A penniless customer was rarely prepared to take on another debt to settle his or her accounts with a vendor.

It may be assumed that food vendors were particularly vulnerable to the whims of their customers. As vendors of perishable goods, they had to dispose of their merchandise even when prompt payments were not forthcoming. Yet the vending of goods such as secondhand clothes was no less detached from the vicissitudes of trust. While some vendors could enter into credit arrangements with customers they met in the streets, many had to look actively for customers in offices and companies where salaried people worked. Access to the markets that these sites represented involved intricate negotiations. Vendors' first challenge was often to find their way past the security guards that most offices and companies in the city deployed at their gates and their front doors. Whether an outright bribe, a discount on goods, or a simple friendly greeting was needed varied enormously. Another hurdle awaited inside these institutions, with low-ranking office personnel often jealously guarding their own access to those with higher status and better purchasing power. In many cases, vendors had to enter into agreements whereby someone in the office took the responsibility for the actual trade. Hospitals, for example, were highly desired locations for vending, because the potential clientele included not only the administrative and medical personnel but also patients and their guardians. Nurses or low-ranking administrators who sold goods on vendors' behalf required a share of the money these goods generated and the privilege to buy them at a lower price than what vendors demanded from others. Just as the relationship between a food vendor and a customer could involve expressions of concern for their mutual welfare, so too was it possible for relationships between vendors and office workers to produce long-term rapport, with vendors addressed as "brothers" *(achimwene)* by their business partners. Yet crises revealed, once again, the precarious position that vendors occupied in the economy. Their salaried partners could violate the agreed principles without vendors having a proper channel to settle the disputes, or their partners could abruptly lose interest in trading or be warned by their superiors against engaging in such practices. It was invariably the vendor who stood the greatest risk of losing his income.

Lest this predicament be seen as a "good-faith economy," which, according to Pierre Bourdieu, is one that devotes "as much time to concealing the reality of economic acts as it expends in carrying them out" (1977, 172), it is important to emphasize the imperatives of trust. Although money was often as scarce as it was needed, credit arrangements indicated that the monetary side of trust did not exhaust the moral considerations involved. Rather than seeking to conceal their self-interest, participants in this economy came to develop the quality of their relationship as the very foundation of their economic transactions. Jane Guyer (2004, 92) has usefully pointed out that the quality of goods also needs to be trusted when credit is negotiated. As my account has suggested, however, vendors were not always in control of the quality of the goods they obtained from wholesalers or local food producers, and their customers sometimes needed to endure considerable variation in quality. In this instance, quality inhered in relationships rather than in goods, with various appeals to moral considerations keeping the transaction alive despite obvious deficiencies both in goods and in customers' credit worthiness. More broadly, vendors and customers did not approach their transactions as mutually independent individuals. Both had something to gain from a relationship that evoked, among other things, kinship, ethnic, or religious affiliations and at the same time provided money and goods. As Marcel Mauss (1954) observed long ago, it is only under particular conditions that the distinction between interested and disinterested action becomes absolute. Contemporary Malawians are among the vast majority who cannot afford to alienate themselves from the moral considerations that relationships entail.

The significance of trust and debt indicates the sense of freedom under these circumstances. Subjects' potential to exercise freedom was predicated on a range of deliberate dependencies. Rather than being a necessary evil in this economy, debt was actively desired. After all, debt signified trust for both sides of the transaction, a continuing relationship in an economy of ever-present uncertainties and sudden personal bankruptcies. The contrast to the human rights discourse preferred by Malawian activists is clear. Persons sought to make their mutual dependence explicit as the ground on which transactions were built. They did not claim their dues as rights or *individual* freedoms, as if their transactions could be sustained by mutual strangers. Instead, debt generated relationships in which people owed one another not only money and goods but also the morally binding pledge to stay loyal to the relationship. The situations of conflict mentioned above emerged not so much from self-interest as from the economy remaining profoundly unequal. Too constrained to create wealth among the majority, whether salaried or self-employed, the Malawian economy constantly pushed its subjects to encounter the limits of their moral considerations. Trust was a precarious achievement, and petty traders were often the first casualties when it vanished.

Popular Perspectives on Transnational Governance

The moral dimensions of Chinsapo residents' livelihoods serve to remind us of the discursive resources in which rumors about trade in body parts came to capture their imagination. Seeking to cultivate civil virtues against considerable odds, township dwellers were horrified by the total inversion of their trading practices. "Mob justice" was, therefore, a sign of a moral panic, a consequence of a perceived assault on fundamental values. Yet the moral panic of 2003 resonated not only with the predicaments of petty trade but also with the popular understandings of Malawi's place in the world. As mentioned, rumors about blood thieves during the 2001–2 famine had suggested that the Malawi government received relief maize in exchange for its citizens' blood. The moral panic of 2003 indicated similar concerns with transnational exchange that exploited ordinary Malawians. It provided not only an explanation for the infinite riches of Muluzi and his cronies and the searing poverty of their subjects — the body parts of the poor, sold by Muluzi, were the raw material for rich countries' production of wealth — but also a basis for understanding the breathtaking affluence of "Indians" (amwenye) and "whites" (azungu), though this affluence was hardly made more acceptable.

The notion of transnational governance, in other words, finds some equivalence among popular Malawian discourses on the unequal world. Moreover, just as the rumor about trade in body parts evoked far-reaching historical and contemporary parallels, so too was its perspective on unequal transnational exchange merely an extreme version of other popular discourses on the subject. After the transition in the early 1990s, Muluzi's Muslim identity aroused suspicions, particularly among Christians. Although only about 12 percent of Malawians were Muslims, usually associated with the Yao ethnic identity, rumors about Muluzi's desire to turn Malawi into an Islamic state had emerged soon after his ascension to power. They became particularly intense during the run-up to the 1999 parliamentary and presidential elections. The fears these rumors caused were manipulated by opposition politicians, who insisted on the need to have a Christian president in a country where the majority was Christian. The 2004 elections, in which Muluzi's chosen heir was a Catholic, were also preceded by similar arguments, fueled by a common belief that Muluzi would continue to rule the country behind the scenes. His choice of Cassim Chilumpha, an apparently devout Muslim, as the vice president only seemed to lend credence to the rumors about Islamization.

Muluzi usually played down his religious affiliation in public life, preferring greed to creed, but Malawians found evidence for impending Islamization in the arrival of new entrepreneurs from the Middle East and North Africa, in the building of new mosques across the country, and in Muluzi's fraternization with the Libyan leader Colonel Muammar Gaddafi. These developments, coupled with the arrival of Islamic charities handing out food and goods and the urban-based businesses of Lebanese entrepreneurs, often as exploitative as those of Indian and Pakistani merchants who had begun to arrive in Malawi during the colonial period, were taken to be signs of profound changes in Malawi's religious, political, and economic landscape. Perhaps the most disconcerting rumor was the one that circulated before the 1999 elections. Muluzi had allegedly sold Malawi for nine hundred million kwacha to Gaddafi, who would build oil rigs in Lake Malawi after the elections and close churches in order to build mosques in their stead. In 2002, Malawians witnessed a spectacle of Gaddafi's power. In response to his visit to Malawi, Muluzi vacated the official presidential residence in Lilongwe and moved to a hotel; the presidential residence was taken over by Gaddafi and his entourage. A more poignant example of Malawi's subservient role in world politics and economy was barely imaginable.

Whites *(azungu)*, Malawi's more traditional donors, were shown equal deference by Muluzi and his cabinet ministers. Although Muluzi would occasionally assert the independent status of Malawi in a thinly veiled reference to some donor representatives' criticism, he eagerly seized on any remark or report that could be interpreted as an endorsement of his government by the *azungu*. An analysis of Malawi's forthcoming elections published in *The Economist* in 2003 predicted victory for the UDF. Muluzi made the UDF's publicity secretary read aloud an extract from the analysis at a political rally.[17] Muluzi then asked the crowd, in a triumphant voice, to tell everyone that "whites in England" *(azungu a ku Mangalande)* were saying that the UDF would win the elections. For the disillusioned majority in Chinsapo Township, such declarations could only deepen the suspicions of complicity between their national leaders and foreign agencies. If the *azungu* already knew that the UDF was going to win the elections, I heard Chinsapo residents discussing, did it not indicate their vested interests in the regime? Access to money was the long and the short of it, Chinsapo residents thought, sharing some of ruling politicians' ambivalence over foreign power. The wealth of the *azungu* was understood to be spectacular enough to attract anyone to them, including the poorest Christian congregations in Chinsapo (see Englund 2001b). Yet Chinsapo residents also understood themselves to be doomed to witness the *azungu* from a distance, separated by language, lifestyle, and virtually inconceivable disparities in opportunity. Employment as the domestic servants of *azungu* rarely bridged the gap and, on the contrary, often gave the poor only more imaginative resources to make it even wider. Only those who ran the government could enjoy unmitigated access to the *azungu*, sometimes acting as their partners in sinister businesses.

Popular perspectives on transnational governance provide yet another example of how implausible the discourse of human rights activists could be from the viewpoint of impoverished Malawians. Activists' exhortations of participation located, as discussed in chapter 4, the subjects of development and democracy in individual persons or in the immediate communities where they lived. The freedoms and responsibilities of the new era were primarily attributes of individuals, the poorest of whom were deemed by activists to need civic education in order to harness the new potentials. During the first ten years of democracy in Malawi, activists' high-profile interventions in the media were not more attuned to realities beyond Malawi. Despite their own location in various transnational networks, activists portrayed the Malawi government as an independent actor, surely accountable to foreign donors but nevertheless a sovereign entity. In line with their general indifference toward economic issues, activists seldom paused to reflect on the extent to which problems in Malawi's democracy had to be understood from a transnational perspective. In this regard, the popular perspectives described in this chapter were somewhat more enlightened, despite the moral panic that their most extreme forms incited. The alternative sense of freedom that also emerged in this chapter may likewise be more compatible with Chinsapo residents' situation of human rights than with the abstractions informing activists' interventions. When the potential to exercise freedom is understood to depend on relationships with others, the objectification of the poor as ignorant masses, their redemption prompted by tacit contempt, becomes much less plausible.

CHAPTER 8

Redeeming Freedom

Cultural relativism has long hampered intellectual and political engagement with human rights discourse. At best a delightfully iconoclastic pursuit, cultural relativism all too often subverts not only its own justification but also the authority of those in whose name it ostensibly speaks. If everything is culturally relative, then the various cultural others have little else to offer than passing instants of bewilderment and thrill, the stuff that the connoisseurs of cultures can build their prowess on.[1] This book has shown, by contrast, how human rights discourse compels careful consideration of who has the authority to participate in it. The idea of cultural discreteness appears insidious when it obscures, among other things, the transnational economic and political processes by which African activists and their foreign donors agree on a particular definition of human rights. For critics, the issue should not be a simple inversion of dominant rights talk, as if a coherent counterdiscourse awaited its discovery by the heroic ethnographer. The issue is to devise ways in which negotiation and contest can be made explicit and inclusive.

Translation, as seen in chapter 2, is a troubling example of what can happen if the power to define human rights is exclusive, inimical to a recognition of multiple interests in the situations in which the rights are evoked. Left to grapple with a narrow and ultimately meaningless notion of human rights, Malawians found other outlets for their grievances. The perceived attacks on fundamental values, as described in chapter 7, provoked a moral panic, its associated incidents of "mob justice" blinding human rights activists and authorities to the popular civil virtues that underlay the outrage in the first place. The reason for their blindness was historical, the ease with which elitist dispositions had contributed to the objectification of the impoverished majority. Even when asked to consider themselves as individuals in a neoliberal political and economic order, the poor could appear only as particular kinds of individuals, the generic representatives of ignorant and irresponsible masses.

Under these circumstances, a struggle, uncertain in its direction, will continue on both intellectual and political fronts. By itself, human rights discourse will not deliver substantive democracy, if only because its universalism may conceal highly particular interests. Vociferous and bold, activists kept politicians on their toes and independent journalists preoccupied during the first decade of neoliberal democracy, all the while circumscribing the scope of what could actually be expressed through rights talk. Yet if the expectations of democracy were not fulfilled, the teleology of these expectations must also caution us against seeing Malawi as a failure. The idiom of failure plays into the hands of self-proclaimed democrats, such as President Bakili Muluzi, who found in every shortcoming an opportunity to remind the world of Malawi's inexperience in democratization, to be compensated by a flow of foreign aid, preferably of the monetary kind. Talk about failure is also factually incorrect insofar as the Malawi government and its foreign sponsors sought to establish a democracy suited to the neoliberal order. Multipartyism, regular elections, a new constitution, civil society, free press, privatization — all these were achieved in Malawi during the first ten years of democratization. They define the institutional and procedural essence of neoliberal democracy, and because hitches occur everywhere, Malawi could hardly be argued to have fared much worse than more established democracies. Within the institutional parameters of neoliberal democracy, Malawi was a success, not a failure.

This achievement of democracy appears in an intriguing light when it allows for continuities from an earlier era. Institutional perspectives are insufficient to uncover the subjective and historical dimensions of democratization. Kamuzu Banda, the diminutive dictator of the first republic, is the most potent symbol for the mode of rule that neoliberal democracy only superficially replaced. Yet the shadow he cast over Malawi's democratic experiment was too long to be his own. Since the indirect rule under colonialism, Malawi's prospects for substantive democracy had been dimmed by the shadow of elitism. This book has shown how even those human rights advocates who despised Ngwazi[2] generally harbored, within their own modest means, elitist aspirations. Their penchant for titles and professional markers, their reverence for the English language, their habit of regarding the poor as "the grassroots" — all were instances of a mode of rule that showed no sign of abating in Malawi. It took Thandika Mkandawire, a Geneva-based international civil servant, to tell a Malawian audience of activists and donors in 2003 that "many of [your] NGOs are replicas of the old MCP with their own little *Ngwazis*" (2003, 17). The observation left activists startled and yet unable to analyze their own habits. In the absence of more reflective activists, analysis risked becoming the prerogative of populist and partisan critics, hardly a hopeful prospect for intellectual engagement.

Even more lamentable is activists' inability to reflect on their own assumptions, which also kept them prisoners of individual freedoms, their prime definition of human rights. Writing at the onset of the new democracy movement in Africa, Claude Ake predicted that popular cravings for "material betterment, equal opportunity and cultural upliftment, and concrete rights" would eventually displace the initial emphasis on neoliberal reform (2000, 137). The evidence in this book, gathered a decade after the democratic transition, suggests that human rights NGOs and projects may not be at the forefront of articulating such aspirations. They subscribe to what Richard Falk (2000, 89) has identified for many Western human rights NGOs — the view that gives priority to political and civil rights at the expense of social and economic rights.

The task of this book is less to imagine alternative democracies than to demonstrate why such alternatives are necessary in the first place — and where the intellectual resources for their imagining might be found. I have shunned perspectives that lay all the blame for disempowerment on the national elite. Rita Abrahamsen is undoubtedly correct in observing that "what is acceptable to . . . elites frequently provides the boundaries of democratic politics" (2000, 78). Yet the conclusion that emerges here demands more attention to the ways in which the nonelite mimic the elite in their encounters with those who have been relegated to the status of the grassroots. Substantive democracy, patently, requires far more than controlling or even abolishing elites. It also has very little to do with utopias of absolute equality. Much as the impediments in Malawi have appeared to be historically entrenched inequalities, their critique must be kept separate from the question of equality itself. Yamikani Chikondi's case, in chapter 6, presented a harrowing instance of a failure to defend even the bare minimum of decent living. Utopias may have to be suspended as long as progressive legislation fails to command practice.

How Donors Disempower

The shift of focus from elites to the more intractable disposition of elitism opens up fresh problems in understanding democracy in a country like Malawi. These problems are not best envisaged as results of a conspiracy or a class-based agenda to disempower the poor. The critical question is how human rights activists regulated themselves as certain kinds of subjects, whatever their participatory rhetoric may have otherwise told them. At the same time, elitism as a cultural disposition did not exist in a political and economic vacuum. It served particular interests, even if those who succumbed to it — such as volunteers working for a civic education project — rarely reaped any substantial rewards from doing so. The disposition and the notion of rights it sustains were integral to a mode of governance that was transnational.

The interest of foreign aid donors and creditors in democracy and human rights is fairly recent in Africa. During the period of the Cold War, World Bank documents, for example, usually made no mention at all of politics (Ferguson 1990, 68). The new attention would deserve to be applauded if it were to present a genuine opportunity for open debate about government policies and various human rights. More often than not, however, the most powerful donors and creditors, with the International Monetary Fund at the helm, preempted such a debate during the 1990s. They did so by imposing a highly specific scheme of governance and economic development on recipient countries based on a neoliberal approach (see, e.g., Ferguson 1995; Neocosmos 2001; Olukoshi 1998; Williams and Young 1994; Young 1995). It remains the case that, virtually across Africa, "the key macroeconomic policies which a state undertakes are not open for democratic discussion within a country" (Harrison 2002, 100). Even the so-called civil society was modeled on priorities and objectives that may have resonated more with the conditions of donor countries than with the concerns of the poor in recipient countries (Howell 2000; Kasfir 1998). The leading donor agencies, such as the European Union and many bilateral donors, proved to be highly rigid in envisaging the forms that their engagement with democratization could take. Various indigenous practices, in particular, remained unthinkable as targets of external funding (Kelsall 2003, 198).

Neoliberal economic reform and a particular brand of democracy are more than compatible. The freedoms of the latter appear to provide the appropriate institutional and ideological framework for the former. The complicity of a donor agency, even when it claimed to promote democracy and human rights, has been amply demonstrated in the practices of the European Union–funded National Initiative for Civic Education. Rather than representing a simple imposition of inappropriate priorities on its Malawian recipients, the project deserves particular attention for the way in which it articulated with entrenched inequalities in Malawi. NICE contributed to the transnational governance of a poor African country by defusing the threat that disillusioned youths could pose to the neoliberal order. It improved young people's wounded self-esteem by giving them the status of human rights experts who were able to enlighten ignorant masses. The status resonated with the elitist assumption of a great divide between the educated and the uneducated, between those who were capable of leading and those who were led. The little sense that the actual messages on democracy and human rights made to their recipients was not noticed. Both the donor and its Malawian partners regarded their approach as natural.

As self-regulating subjects, civic educators imagined, in their patterns of consumption, hygiene, and language use, the grounds for their cultural and intellectual supremacy, all vital subjective enhancements of their self-esteem in the context of an educational and economic crisis. Their contempt for the fact that human rights could assume meaning only in concrete situations is common in a humanitarian regime that builds its approach on a concept of abstract and universal humanity (Badiou 2001). Yet civic educators were not mere dupes of "neoliberal governmentality." While their quasi-professional status involved "a consciously contrived style of conduct" (Burchell 1996, 24), they were quite as much embedded in complex social relationships as those whom they deemed to belong to the grassroots. Outside the context of civic education, they felt the burdens and rewards of obligations as resourceful persons in extended families and neighborhoods, at once compelled to confine abstractions to the narrow domain of human rights professionalism.

Civic education on democracy and human rights ceased to be merely irrelevant when it implicitly made the poor responsible for their poverty, an assignation achieved through the exhortations of "participation" (Bornstein 2003; Cooke and Kothari 2001). Here was neoliberalism at its most destructive, at its most insidious — erasing from discussion the actual power relations underlying poverty. It is important to note, however, that these tenets coexist with more radical notions even in some major donor agencies. The British Department for International Development (DFID), for example, pursues a "rights-based approach to development," seeking to promote rights as "concrete entitlements" that poor people can claim (see DFID 2000). This approach was expected to be spearheaded in Malawi by a project entitled Transform, whose explicit aim was to promote social and economic rights. The project was going to manage funds that were intended to assist marginalized Malawians to organize themselves into collective forces that would assert their rights.

The realities of democratic Malawi became chillingly obvious when the official launching of the project failed in 2002, followed by the closure of its office in 2003. A cabinet minister had taken exception to the notion that there were *marginalized* Malawians. The British High Commission foresaw a diplomatic quarrel and had the project terminated before it was properly launched, advising Malawian NGOs to "work together with the government."[3] Diplomatic convenience took precedence over both the official policy of the DFID and the rights of poor Malawians.

The ill-fated Transform project demonstrated the formidable power that the Malawian state, especially in collusion with its donors and creditors, could exercise over the supposedly independent civil society. Another example of donors' involvement in disempowerment comes directly from my own research. The expatriate manager of NICE, as mentioned in the introduction, was angered by the early results of my fieldwork. He came to learn about them at an international conference held in Lilongwe to assess Malawi's ten years of democracy. The democratic nature of the conference did not seem to impress the project manager when he pulled me aside, minutes before my session was due to begin, and tried to bully me into withdrawing every mention of NICE from my presentation. Nervous about the presence of Malawi's presidential adviser on NGOs and civil society at the conference, he feared that my analysis could imperil the future of NICE.

The sleepy presidential adviser was not perturbed by my presentation, which I had proceeded to make, and NICE's expatriate manager was visibly relieved afterward. Yet the discussion it provoked at the conference indicated that high-ranking officials of Malawian human rights organizations were willing to reflect on problems in the current approaches to civic education. The representative of the Malawi Human Rights Commission admitted that NGOs often sent young people to conduct civic education without adequately monitoring their performance, a problem that had led to the public's frequent complaints to the commission. The representative of the Centre for Human Rights and Rehabilitation observed that a major shortcoming in Malawian civic education was its failure to involve beneficiaries in planning its contents and objectives. The representative of the Public Affairs Committee asked the audience to consider how civic education could assist people in claiming their rights and thereby incorporate advocacy as one of its components.

These responses could have inaugurated a new era in Malawian civic education on human rights had not NICE, which was one of the main sponsors of the conference, steered the discussion back to the status quo. At the start of the session, the expatriate manager took a seat next to the deputy project manager, a Malawian. The expatriate manager placed his mouth near his deputy's ear, and for a good part of the session, his lips were seen to be moving. After the above-mentioned officials had made their comments, the deputy manager asked for the floor. He stated that a distinction between information delivery and advocacy should be maintained in civic education. Beneficiaries, he argued, had to process the information themselves according to their own needs. NICE's influence was also considerable in a subsequent working group that deliberated on the problems and prospects of civic education in Malawi. The deputy manager's report to the rest of the conference emphasized issues that were more relevant to donors than to Malawians. He lamented the preoccupation of local-level civic educators with allowances and called for a greater sense of "self-help" among Malawians in general.

The NICE managers' interventions were consistent with what has already been described for this project. With its unrivaled funds and its nationwide network, NICE wielded considerable influence over the direction of civic education in Malawi. The above account of its managers' interventions at a conference is particularly revealing of its role as an instrument of transnational governance. The emerging self-critique among Malawian human rights activists came to an abrupt end, cut short by a tacit need to defer to politically appointed state officials. The survival of the project seemed to override the problems of survival among poor Malawians. The deputy manager's position indicated Malawian activists' predicament in a heavily donor-dependent context. The expatriate manager used him as his proxy, aware that a black man's intervention looked better than a white man's. Whatever the deputy manager might have thought, on the basis of his experience as a Malawian, of letting poor people process information on their own without anyone to advocate their rights, his own relatively comfortable employment was at stake. Democracy and human rights thus trivialized, the status quo prevailed.

After Freedom — Another Freedom?

The status quo within human rights organizations themselves may be a fragile achievement. No teleology needs to be associated with the assumption that tensions may arise as activists become impatient with their narrowly defined concept of human rights. The reasons for their impatience can derive from various sources, including critical interventions by scholars and the persistence of the very injustices that most of them feel strongly about. Since I conducted my fieldwork, the two organizations that have been the focus of this book seem to have begun to examine their priorities. A board member of the CHRR, while directing his words to the media, expressed concern in 2005 that too much attention had been given to politics despite its often limited relevance to the lives of poor people.[4] During one of their in-house workshops in 2004, NICE officers discussed, among other things, their preoccupation with these workshops that seemed to divert them from the substance of their work.[5] They also considered how "signposting," the practice of referring people to other organizations, could be made more consequential. Particularly promising were the efforts to address officers' elitist disposition, evident in their tendency to associate more with other officials in district capitals than with villagers. Their master-servant relationships with office personnel and the continuing paucity of female officers were also criticized.

Without sustained observation, it is impossible to assess whether these deliberations amounted to anything other than routine procedures of self-examination in an apparently "transparent" organization, carried out on an annual basis. At any rate, the expatriate project manager's change of status to a technical adviser in 2005 was said to anticipate a more comprehensive Malawian responsibility for NICE, a move that could have made donors' influence somewhat less obvious. However, the task of this book, as mentioned, is not to appraise particular organizations or individuals but to offer intellectual resources for thinking beyond the particular human rights discourse that has captured the imagination of Malawian activists and their foreign donors. In this regard, if tensions *are* emerging in activists' understandings of their work, what can a critique of human rights discourse offer them? How, in particular, can their preoccupation with the idea of freedom be harnessed to address issues that may have some bearing on the status quo in Malawi and beyond?

Sticking to the idea of freedom is more than a mere concession to the realpolitik of neoliberalism. The need is to reclaim freedom from its abuse in neoliberal projects, which carry, in many parts of Africa, uncanny similarities to the late-colonial orders of exclusion and exploitation. If freedom is not, as I have argued, a permanent condition to be achieved but is, rather, discontinuous and precarious, then the crucial question is how persons can exercise it in their situations. This book has offered observations on the preconditions of freedom that is not reducible to the exercise of individual choice. Chapter 7, for example, showed how small-scale traders actively sought debt relationships in order to expand their room to maneuver under stultifying economic conditions. The abused worker in chapter 6, moreover, evoked a range of moral considerations to support his case, which legal-aid officers were inclined to see as a one-to-one confrontation with an employer. The import of these observations is not in their apparent compatibility with an emphasis on "community," a notion, as has been seen, that has too often obscured the national and transnational underpinnings of seemingly local and community-based interventions. The idea of freedom is stimulating precisely because the problematic notions of individuals and communities are not necessarily its corollaries at all. The exercise of choice in situations is an attribute of subjects who are neither autonomous individuals nor abstract communities. Debt, obligation, and entitlements are some of the social facts that give freedom — situated and intermittent — its parameters and meaning.

Citizenship is an issue that engages these considerations with current concerns in democratization. As was discussed in chapter 1, a major difficulty in recent African experiments with democracy has been a one-dimensional view of citizenship, attached to individuals who are envisaged, in the main, as bearers of political rights. The freedoms to vote, associate, and express opinions that these rights entail, while essential to democracy, represent a fraction of what freedom might involve among the African poor. Citizenship has to include more dimensions than one, composed of a mixture of liberties and subjections (Nyamnjoh 2005, 17). Thus expanded, citizenship becomes a site of struggles to transform the status quo, with the actual conditions of membership in political society the focus of so-called participatory projects (Hickey and Mohan 2005). A certain radicalization of these projects seems inevitable, in both intellectual and practical senses, because rethought human rights compel a confrontation with marginalization and impoverishment.

Radicalization can, of course, lead critics and activists in contradictory directions, some violent, others conciliatory. The conclusion to this study attempts to unchain the minds of those who became the prisoners of a specific kind of freedom, while retaining the idea of freedom for alternative projects of socioeconomic transformation. The commitment to freedom also indicates reluctance to cut the connection to liberalism entirely. The injustices of neoliberalism provide a weak alibi to dismiss liberalism, particularly those strands of liberal political philosophy that have defended the ideas of social justice and equality against utilitarianism

(Kelly 2005). Even when liberalism is seen, as many followers of Foucault do, as a mode of rule rather than a set of reflections on rule, its susceptibility to radical political projects is by no means precluded by its current association with neoliberalism. If it is possible to read Foucault as a critic of a "zero-sum conception of power" (Bell 1996, 83), as an advocate of situational possibilities rather than totalizing perspectives that limit our political vision, then cynicism about the potentials of freedom may also have to be suspended.

The link to liberalism, at least in the argument of this book, is a certain redemptive momentum triggered by the evocation of freedom. As Asad has observed in his critique of liberalism (2003, 61–62), secular redemptive politics has often failed to envisage a condition in which redeemers *themselves* submit to suffering in order to redeem others. An illustration might be all those officious human rights activists who, imagining themselves as the already redeemed vanguard, disengaged from the situations in which others suffered. The fact that redeeming freedom through more evenly distributed suffering constitutes another mode of rule is neither here nor there. Democracy, whatever the epithet we may wish to attach to it (liberal, socialist, global), *is* a mode of rule.

Democracy and Its Futures

"I don't think our message is very complicated. We want more democracy, we want more human rights, we want to take care of the planet." A European activist thought he was stating the obvious when the BBC interviewed him during a protest march organized on the occasion of the United Nations World Summit on Sustainable Development in 2002. The popular trust in the capacity of international organizations to promote peace and democracy has waned in the post–Cold War era. "Antiglobalization" and "global justice" have become the most common labels for an internally highly diverse movement. Bringing Northern and Southern activists together, it urges us all to "take care of the planet" and make "another world possible." Apart from the noisy and well-publicized protests that now accompany many high-powered international summits, the movement seeks to produce coherent plans of action at the meetings of the World Social Forum (see Fisher and Ponniah 2003; Klein 2002).

The movement, despite its internal diversity, has had a positive impact on the struggles for democratization across the world. It has, among other things, directed the attention of those who follow the international mass media to competing definitions of democracy. While authoritative accounts of the world's "new democracies" continue to confine the meaning of democracy to a prescriptive neoliberalism (see, e.g., Diamond and Plattner 2001), alternative voices question the very notion of "old democracies." Voter apathy, widespread ignorance and indifference about the public life, corruption, and wars without popular consent are glaring characteristics of the decline of democracy in Europe and North America. This decline makes possible the expedience with which donor agencies, as has been seen, contribute to the disempowerment of Africans. Citizens in donor countries generally do not know and do not care about what takes place in remote recipient countries. The disarming rhetoric of democratization is usually enough to counter any lingering doubts about foreign aid. The relatively small costs of civic education, for example, also ensure that aid for democratization does not put rich countries' resources at risk.

Much as some contemporary currents facilitate the imagining of democratic alternatives, many aspects of those alternatives remain ill understood. The evidence in this book calls for considerable caution when the various critical elements seek to identify their partners. Civil society, in particular, presents itself far too readily for collaborative pursuits. As has been seen, not only are the local agents of civil society embedded in entrenched inequalities and daily struggles for survival, but also the networks and resources that sustain civil society in Africa often make it an instrument of transnational governance. The most consequential associations of people seeking justice, often focusing on specific issues such as access to land (see Kanyongolo 2005), can evade the attention of potential collaborators who arrive on the scene with rigid ideas of NGOs in mind. As long as human rights NGOs fail to engage in contingent collaborations with existing ways of mobilizing the poor and to consider local poverty and transnational governance in an integrated framework, the prospects for democratic alternatives remain limited (Ferguson and Gupta 2002; Paley 2004). Without such a framework, the right to vote and to participate addresses the populist concerns of neoliberalism rather than the concerns of the populace.

The critic's quandary is not simply the practical one of canvassing strategies for democratic renewal. It is also, inextricably, intellectual. With relativism discredited and discarded, universalism must continue to give us pause. As a preliminary step, critics and activists would do well to examine what they consider to represent the universal and the particular in the current predicaments. In Malawi, activists have too often imagined themselves as the agents of the universal and "the grassroots" as the captives of the particular. The procedure has precluded the discovery of general import in particular claims, no less than the identification of particular interests in activists' universalism — hence the need to see intellectual resources in the actual variety of claims that people make. "It would be a pity," Marilyn Strathern writes, "to lose possible ways of thinking about the manner in which people make claims on others simply because vernaculars seem local and strange" (2004, 203; see also Strathern 2001). There is nothing noble or democratic in suspicions that incite attacks on innocent people. Yet even a moral panic can offer insights into the conditions of moral being *anywhere*. Just as ethnography once challenged European ignorance of African magic, so too can it still employ universal categories to question "the right of the ruling community to a monopoly of moral judgement" (James 1973, 46).

While in culture talk there can be nothing that is truly universal, one message of this study is to reconsider the grounds for making general claims. The particularity of the viewpoints of the activists and politicians encountered during my fieldwork has been amply demonstrated. They subscribed to a notion of human rights that, far from being universally or globally relevant, emphasized freedoms that bore the greatest relevance, in Malawi, to their own subject positions. In contrast with that, women in villages visited by NICE, claimants seeking legal aid, and the urban poor caught in the midst of a moral panic consistently voiced concerns that were of general import. They demanded attention to the necessity to inform any realization of human rights with an understanding of the situations in which people live. Their claims help us, in effect, to recover not only freedom but also universalism from the morass in which the neoliberal moment has buried them.

Notes

Introduction

1. "Microsoft Helps China to Censor Bloggers," *Guardian Weekly*, June 24–30, 2005. An analysis of China's efforts to police the internet is available at www.opennetinitiative.net/studies/china.

2. Radio address by President George W. Bush to the nation, May 21, 2005, transcript distributed by Bureau of International Information Programs, U.S. Department of State.

3. For arguments in political philosophy on the meaning and scope of freedom and on the history of the idea, see, e.g., Raz 1986 and Skinner 1998.

4. President Bakili Muluzi addressing a rally in Chiradzulu West constituency, March 20, 2002. Muluzi deployed his usual mix of languages: *"Pamene ndikunena pano aUnited States akhala zaka* under *demokalase* for over two hundred years. *Ife tangoyamba kumene kumanga demokalase, kumanga nyumba ya demokalase."*

5. In an insightful essay, Stephen Ellis (2002) criticizes the conventions whereby African history is divided into periods, often prefixed with "pre-" or "post-" and assuming formal independence as a decisive watershed. Ellis emphasizes the oil crisis and related events during the 1970s as more consequential to the fortunes of African states. He also notes how, regardless of academic fashions, expectations of modernization and development in Africa continue to be expressed by reference to criteria that were current forty years ago, themselves rooted in the centuries-old Euro-American belief that history has a direction. In this sense, the current expectations of democracy have a very long pedigree indeed. For a further critique of teleology in the social and historical study of Africa, see Ferguson 1999. For a case of changing themes in African historiography, see Ranger 2004.

6. Lest I am suspected of mischief in quoting Zeleza and Mbembe so close to one another, I must acknowledge that differences exist between the two influ-

ential scholars. Zeleza has been the more vociferous side in this dispute, bemoaning Mbembe's "verbose and overexcited postmodernist fulminations" and his "gratuitous" stress on "Africa's pathological exceptionalism" (Zeleza 2003, 282). However, the fact that both admit uncertainty about African democratization suggests that the issue need not be seen as an argument about postmodernism. Nor should my references to Mbembe be seen as an uncritical adoption of his ideas. I am mindful of other critiques of Mbembe's work, including Gikandi 2002; Karlström 2003; Quayson 2001; and Weate 2003.

7. Rather than qualifying the terms "democracy" and "democratic" with quotation marks every time they appear in this book, I expect that their nature as contested concepts will be evident in the context of my argument. The same applies to the notion of "the grassroots" in subsequent chapters.

8. Francis Nyamnjoh (2002, 2004, 2005) has produced compelling critiques of this assumption.

9. Werbner's contrast is between Zimbabwe and Botswana, between maximal and minimal state theatrics — between a huge presidential motorcade and a modest entourage (2004, 189–190).

10. For critiques of Afropessimism, see Zeleza 2003 and Werbner 2004.

11. Muluzi developed the habit of carrying large amounts of cash and handing them out during his public appearances. He would also distribute free maize on these occasions. He dismissed the criticism of such gestures by emphasizing his own compassion through slogans such as "the president without cruelty" (pulezidenti wopanda nkhanza), an obvious reference to Banda's mean ways.

12. In 2003, Muluzi invited Hetherwick Ntaba, a top official in the main opposition party, MCP, and a doctor who had not practiced medicine for several years, to escort his mother to a hospital in South Africa. Ntaba's acceptance of this invitation caused considerable uproar in the MCP and led to his resignation from the party. There can be no doubt that Muluzi used his old mother to create rifts in the opposition.

13. In 2003, about a year before the next general and presidential elections in 2004, Muluzi announced that Bingu Wa Mutharika, then the deputy governor of the Reserve Bank of Malawi, was to be his successor. Muluzi, virtually the sole financier of the UDF, had both its National Executive and National Convention accept his choice. After winning the elections in 2004, Mutharika launched a new anticorruption campaign and resigned from the UDF.

14. Some politicians undoubtedly wanted to defend the principles of democracy. Many others, in both opposition and government, were less upright. John Tembo, then the leader of opposition who enjoyed Muluzi's patronage (see Englund 2002c), voted for the open-term bill. It was only after the bill had been defeated that he paid attention to the popular opinion. Aleke Banda and Harry Thomson, two of the senior ministers who clashed with Muluzi, remained quiet throughout the mounting pressure against the constitutional amendment. It was only after Muluzi had announced his choice of a successor that they expressed concern over democratic procedures.

15. Kenneth Ross (2004) has, however, raised doubts over the extent to which human rights NGOs actually spearheaded the campaign against the third

term, pointing out the central role of the clergy in providing both leadership and infrastructure.

16. As will become clear in the subsequent chapters, my work builds, of course, on more than two previous studies of Malawi's democratization. The other studies include, above all: Kishindo 2000, on translation; Kasambara 1998 and Tengatenga 1998, on civic education; Dzimbiri 2002, on labor relations; and Kanyongolo 1998, 2004, 2005, on legalism.

17. Quoted in "Government Asked to Finance Civil Society," *Daily Times,* March 6, 2002.

18. "How Much Foreign Influence to Tolerate?" (the D. D. Phiri column), *The Nation,* June 25, 2002.

19. See "Human Rights Consultative Committee (HRCC) Communique," *The Nation,* December 24, 2003; "NGOs Snub Their Board," *Malawi News,* January 3–9, 2004; "NGO Law Restrictive, Says Lawyer Mhango," *The Nation,* December 19, 2003; "No Thanks — HRCC," *The Nation,* December 22, 2003. An editorial criticized the NGOs, however, for "crying for water which is already under the bridge"; see "NGOs Should Have Known, Consulted," *The Nation,* December 19, 2003.

20. See "NGOs Snub Their Board," *Malawi News,* January 3–9, 2004.

21. For a selection of overviews and case studies of various faith-based and "developmental" NGOs, see, e.g., Barrow and Jennings 2002; Bornstein 2003; Dorman 2002; Fisher 1997; Howell and Pearce 2001; and Tvedt 1998.

22. My findings have made it necessary not to mention the districts where I carried out fieldwork, because the district officers in question could be easily traced. As will become clear, the focus of my study is on patterns and habits of discourse and practice, not on the individuals who engage in them.

1. The Situation of Human Rights

1. Ishay's (2004) sense of history is also remarkably teleological, stressing progressive and cumulative historical movement toward the realization of human rights.

2. The notion of a generation of rights, of course, properly refers to the temporal sequence of international human rights instruments and declarations. The impression that economic, social, and cultural rights are "younger" than political and civil rights may be used to explain why legal provisions for the former lag behind the latter (Hunt 1999). It should be clear that the argument advanced here is different, stressing the mutual implication of rights and the possibility that claims can be couched in discourses other than rights talk.

3. The idea of entitlement has been present in theories of rights, including liberal political philosophy, for virtually as long as the idea of individual freedoms. The debate on entitlements was reinvigorated by Sen's 1981 study of poverty and famines, which questioned the validity of natural and individualistic explanations.

4. Giorgio Agamben refers to the increasing abstraction of human rights from

the contexts of citizenship in his influential argument about "bare life" and politics (1998, 132–133). The separation between humanitarianism and politics that this abstraction entails is, in his argument, more apparent than real, because both come to consider human life in its imagined bare essence. This affinity between humanitarianism and politics appears particularly disquieting when Agamben argues that the protection of authentic life has historically been only the flip side of annihilating a life lacking any political value. I return to this argument below.

5. One exception in Africa is Botswana, whose experiments with liberal democracy extend unusually far in the history of African independence. Public debate on the relation between political legitimacy and ethnic, regional, and local belonging has flourished there in a way that has been impossible in, for example, Malawi (see Werbner 2004). The regionalism that characterized Malawian politics during the first ten years of multiparty democracy was considered pathological by many Malawians and foreign observers alike (see Chirwa 1998).

6. However, group or collective rights, as I have argued elsewhere (Englund 2004b), cannot be seen as true alternatives to individual rights, if the groups they posit are themselves imagined as corporate bodies, abstracted from a relational field of identity politics.

7. As a definition, the statement that "every situation, inasmuch as it is, is a multiple composed of an infinity of elements, each one of which is itself a multiple" (Badiou 2001, 25) carries few insights of immediate relevance to those human rights activists who might be persuaded to contemplate the intricacies of situations. Yet the statement does indicate deeper *political* problems than can be addressed in this book. For example, it involves a rejection of Aristotle's ontological view that the world is composed of distinct entities and substances that belong to a totality that is itself a unity. The idea that there are multiplicities that do not obey any primordial unity opens up a radical critique of power, especially when Badiou makes it clear that it is not linguistic idealism, such as the reduction of situations to language games, that underlies his philosophy (2003, 133). For further discussion on aspects of Badiou's critique of human rights and ethics, see Hallward 2000 and Noys 2003. Situational analysis has its own pedigree in anthropology, where it has challenged conventional juxtapositions between micro- and macropolitics (see Gluckman 1940; Turner 1957; Englund 2002b). In this book, chapter 6 comes closest to providing this sort of situational analysis.

8. Throughout the book, I attempt to qualify this conclusion by giving due attention to some human rights NGOs' successful campaigns for political rights. The limits of their engagement in the Malawian case prevent me, however, from providing the kind of upbeat analysis that Tsing is capable of in her account of a community-managed forest in Indonesia (2005, 245–268).

9. "The poor" as a category have been central to the nightmares of the privileged in European history too. In Victorian Britain, for example, evolutionary gradualism allayed the dominant classes' fear of mass democracy, because it was believed to prove to the working classes that progress had to come slowly (Stocking 1987, 232).

10. The notion of transnational processes has the benefit of directing attention to scale instead of to abstract levels of analysis, such as the juxtaposition between global and local in influential imaginings of globalization. As Yael Navaro-Yashin has noted, the global-local dichotomy also bears resemblance to the universalism-relativism debate, which "has kept anthropologists from more radically analyzing the discourses and politics of modern legal systems" (2003, 90).

11. In this regard, Agamben's (2001) more recent example of how state security and terrorism may come to form a single system seems more poignant than his account of the concentration camp as a "biopolitical paradigm" (see Agamben 1998, 119–188).

12. As such, the Malawian poor were subjected to a different rhetoric than, for example, Aborigines in multicultural Australia, where a confining indigenous identity made them "melancholic subjects" (Povinelli 2003, 56).

13. A resurgence of independent newspapers accompanied Malawi's transition to multipartyism in the early 1990s, in tandem with a quickening of other forms of cultural production (see Chimombo and Chimombo 1996). The focus of the new media was on the political process, and they also published articles in a wider range of Malawian languages than was the case toward the end of the 1990s. By the early twenty-first century, the independent press had been reduced in numbers to a handful of established outlets, with *The Chronicle,* based in Lilongwe, perhaps the most vocal of all. Apart from its regular features on HIV/AIDS issues, it pursued a focus on political personalities and constitutional freedoms, often using activists in human rights NGOs for interviews and contributions. *Daily Times,* Malawi's oldest newspaper, and *The Nation,* the biggest daily, have been more ambivalent about the so-called civil society organizations, as can be seen in some of the references in this book (see also Englund 2002c). Their criticisms have rarely indicated a desire to expand the themes discussed under the topic of human rights. However, in a country where newspapers have a highly irregular distribution outside urban areas and publish most of their stories in English, a language not properly understood by the vast majority of citizens, radio is the most significant medium. The state radio remained under the tight control of the ruling party after the democratic transition, offering little scope for independent debate. Independent radio stations had a far more limited reach, but at least three of them gained considerable popularity with their independent news and debate programs. The most influential station, reaching several rural areas in Central and Southern Malawi and broadcasting in Chichewa, was Radio Maria, sponsored by the Catholic Church. Its alleged castigation of Muluzi almost persuaded the Malawi Regulatory Authority to withdraw its broadcasting license in 2004. Interestingly, one of Muluzi's first acts after stepping down as state president in 2004 was to launch his own private radio station, known as Joy Radio.

14. An important forum for these disputes has been press releases published in major newspapers. For an example of the UDF's rhetoric seeking to discredit human rights NGOs, among other critics, see, e.g., "Is Democracy Really Eroded in Malawi?" *The Nation,* June 17, 2002.

15. Another contrast was the attempted support of the critical analysis of economic issues by some church-based organizations in Zimbabwe. However, NGOs' "subculture" and "professionalization," evident in the emergence of a quasi-professional class of non-governmental technocrats, undermined these organizations' advocacy of economic rights (Dorman 2002, 85). See also a critique of human rights NGOs in Nigeria that points out "a 'disconnect' between the programmatic focus of these NGOs and the priorities of most ordinary Nigerians" and the fact that "the NGO community in Nigeria is in general both elitist and urban-centred" (Okafor 2004, 48).

16. Many opposition politicians were persuaded to support the unconstitutional bid, such as John Tembo, the MCP's long-standing strongman. As a result, the National Assembly's vote on the so-called open-term bill in 2002 was only three votes short of the two-thirds majority required for an amendment to the Constitution.

2. Rights as Freedoms

1. See Lwanda 2002 for an account of how an inappropriate translation fueled misconceptions about HIV/AIDS in Malawi.

2. *Mwayi wokhala momasuka, mokondwa ndi mopanda mantha.*

3. Chinyanja has the status of mother tongue (or first language) and lingua franca mainly in Eastern Province and Lusaka, the capital city of Zambia. It is also the language of the Zambian police and armed forces. Between 1966 and 1992 English was the medium of instruction throughout the Zambian school system (Kashoki 1994, 7). The government made a decision in 1992 to use seven "major local languages" as the media of instruction for the first four years of primary school.

4. The language is also commonly considered an important aspect of national identity in Malawi. See, for example, "Chichewa Gives Malawians Identity," *The Nation,* April 5, 2002. This article reprimanded some private schools for failing to offer Chichewa/Chinyanja as a subject.

5. By contrast, Chinyanja gets twenty-one hours of broadcasting time per week on Radio One of the Zambian National Broadcasting Corporation. For the MBC, the programs in other Malawian languages are mainly news bulletins, with only Chitumbuka and Chiyao also having separate social programs.

6. Another variation is *zomuyenereza za munthu,* based on the verb *kuyenereza,* which is explained by the monolingual Chinyanja dictionary as "to be with things that make a thing or a person what it or he/she should be" *(kukhala ndi zinthu zochititsa chinthu kapena munthu kukhala woyenera)* (Centre for Language Studies 2000, 363).

7. In many respects Zambia has undergone, before Malawi, some of the challenges to multiparty democracy (see Burnell 2001; Gould 2001). Not only did Zambia institute multipartyism before Malawi, it was also the first to go through a dispute over the possibility of the new president to stand for a third

term in office. This possibility, which was not provided for in the new constitutions of the two countries, was rejected in both Zambia and Malawi, but only after intense debates. The debates served to heighten civil society organizations' sensitivity to the importance of safeguarding political and civil freedoms even after the transition to multipartyism. While clearly necessary and worthwhile, the debates did little to broaden the perspectives on human rights. Alternatives to the emphasis on freedoms were virtually as limited in Zambia as in Malawi, despite Zambia's longer history of industrialization, its first president Kenneth Kaunda's "humanism," and its second president Frederick Chiluba's background in the trade union movement.

8. Linguistic relativism — the thesis that languages determine their speakers' world-views — appears acceptable in current scholarship as a contextual rather than as a grammatical or lexical structuring of meaning (see Gumperz and Levinson 2000, 8–9). In other words, the understanding of meaning in different languages requires as much contextual as grammatical and lexical knowledge. The problem with linguistically and culturally insensitive translations is their inappropriate sense of context and conceivability (Brennan 2001; Povinelli 2001).

9. The Curriculum Development Centre is a governmental institution in Zambia that, among other things, develops learning materials.

10. Poor standardization also hampers the development of other Zambian languages. In Bemba, for example, the spelling of nominals varies considerably (see Mann [1977] 1999, 13).

11. The title of the leaflet reads *Zi dziwiso Za Osankha Azisogoleli Pa Nthawi Yama Sankho,* itself presenting an idiosyncratic mode of dividing words. The Zambian Civic Education Association is an NGO that was established in 1993. Most of the documents produced by NGOs do not give a date of publication.

12. The additional *n* conveys incorrect phonological information, the correct spelling being *kupenyetsetsa.*

13. The title of the text is *Cifupikitso ca malamulo khumi (10) oyenera kutsatiridwa ndi anchito a malamulo.*

14. Consider how the title of the Universal Declaration has been translated. The Zambian version is entitled *Chibvomerezo ca lamulo losamalira khalidwe la munthu pa dziko lonse la pansi* (literally, "agreement of a law to look after the person's conduct everywhere in the world"), while the Malawian version is entitled *Ufulu wachibadwidwe wokhazikitsidwa ndi maiko* (literally, "the freedom one is born with as established by the countries").

15. This observation is based on an understanding of what it means to be a moral person, a complex topic that cannot be fully addressed here. For accounts of "relational persons" in Malawi, see Englund 1999 and 2002b, and for accounts of the interface between relationships, subjectivity, and individuality elsewhere in Africa, see Riesman 1986 and Werbner 2002.

16. Lest I am suspected of doing injustice to this Chinyanja version, a few explanations are needed. The standard spelling of *nchito* is *ntchito.* I translate *nchito za cisangalalo ca moyo wace* as "improving his/her life," although *cisangalalo,*

as can be seen later in the text, properly means "entertainment" or "happiness." *Nchito za cisangalalo,* while without an established meaning, clearly refers to something positive. *Ayenera kuzindikira* becomes "he/she should understand" in my translation to underline the meaning of the verb "to realize," *kuzindikira,* in Chinyanja. In other words, the Chinyanja translator has sought an equivalent to "realization" without considering what its corresponding verb means in the language. The rest of the text, beginning with the word "thing," is as incomprehensible as my free translation attempts to indicate.

17. It is, of course, heartening that progressive legislation, particularly in the field of labor relations, exists at all. However, chapters 5 and 6 describe how a leading human rights NGO effectively ignored this legislation in its provision of legal aid.

18. This Civil Liberties Committee's leaflet is entitled *Ndondomeko ofotokoza za Ufulu wachibadwidwe m'Malawi* and was published by the CILIC with support from the Inter-ministerial Committee on Human Rights and Democracy.

19. As Lindholt observes, the charter also has a number of clauses that defuse any serious challenge to national laws and the autonomy of states (2001, 135–136). As such, the charter has enjoyed a very high level of ratification among African states.

20. One variant of the notion that emphasizes children's intrinsic worth is the idealistic claim, used particularly in charity work, that they embody "pure" humanity, untainted by politics and intrigue (see, e.g., Bornstein 2003, 67–95; Malkki and Martin 2003).

21. This translation was commissioned by the National Democratic Institute and published and distributed by the Public Affairs Committee with funding from the United States Agency for International Development (USAID). The title of the translation is *Malamulo oyendetsera dziko la Malawi* (the laws to conduct Malawi).

22. For example, the second subsection of section 30 is translated as *boma lidzipereke kuti ufulu wopititsa mtsogolo chitukuko udzioneka kuti ulipodi. Ndipo pa mfundo zothandiza pa ntchitoyi pakhalenso kuonetsetsa kuti onse mosakondera ali ndi mwayi wopezera chuma, maphunziro, chithandizo pa umoyo wabwino, chakudya, pogona pabwino, mwayi wokhala pa ntchito, komanso zithandizo zina monga misika, madzi ndi misewu.*

23. *Funso langa ndi lokhudzana ndi maphunziro, masekondari amene bomu lakhazikitsa, masukulu amene amatchedwa ma* Community Day Secondary School. *Amapezeka masekondari ngati amene aja amene muli mateachers oti ena sali* qualified *kwenikweni pamene masekondari ngati ifeyo tili ndi aziphunzitsi* almost all *ali ndi madegree kapena madiploma. Apapa sitinganene kuti anzathu aja a ma* community *anawaphwanyira ufulu wawo wa maphunziro okwanira?*

24. These details come from *Presidential Inquiry into Malawi School Certificate of Education (MSCE) Examination Results, Final Report, November 2000.*

25. Her words were *aphunzitsi a boma sakuphunzitsani ... angobwera* headmaster *wachisawawa,* headmistress *wachisawawa, muli ndi ufulu ...* The uproar lasted for eighteen seconds, with the speaker smiling in embarrassment and discarding the topic once she had the chance to be heard again.

26. Quoted in "Drink Mars Schools' Day," *The Nation,* July 20, 2001.

27. Quoted in "CHRR Blames Govt. for Low Educational Standards," *The Chronicle,* April 22–28, 2002.

28. Quoted in "Osavala Zothina — Chitalo," *Tamvani,* April 19–20, 2003.

29. For a more comprehensive account of this story, see Englund 2001a.

30. "On Violence" (the D. D. Phiri column), *The Nation,* July 8, 2003.

31. Quoted in "Youth NGOs Group," *The Nation,* March 5, 2002.

3. The Hidden Lessons of Civic Education

1. Kamuzu Banda, for example, repeatedly warned that multipartyism would usher the country into chaos.

2. A rare comment to a similar effect in Malawi can be found in Tina Chimombo's article (1999, 52–53), which suggests that priests, lawyers, and students may also be in need of civic education on the meanings of democracy.

3. The Danish government announced that corruption and human rights violations had prompted it to withdraw its aid, a criticism keenly taken up by the Malawian opposition and independent newspapers (for an analysis, see Englund 2002c, 15–17). The rise to power of a populist right-wing coalition in Denmark received little attention in Malawi.

4. *National Initiative for Civic Education: Making Democracy Work — Take Part in Public Life* (a leaflet, no date of publication).

5. For its second phase of operation, extending from 2000 until 2004, NICE was granted EUR 7.4 million by the European Union. Although its district offices did not generally have vehicles and their access to computers was limited, they did not face problems with unpaid bills and salaries that frequently impaired the functioning of government departments. The lack of vehicles in NICE district offices was eased by the capacity of these offices to hire transport for visits to distant places, and salaries and daily allowances paid at workshops provided officers with income many times higher than it would have been with their similar qualifications in government.

6. In 2002, civic education officers' monthly salaries varied between MK 22,000 and 25,000 (about US$300 and 330). It should be noted that salaries excluded daily allowances, which were paid for attending workshops and could as much as double an officer's monthly income.

7. Daily allowances are important to Malawian professionals in both NGOs and civil service. For an account of the role they play in Malawian civil service, see Anders 2002.

8. *Thangata* was a system whereby European and Asian landlords exploited African labor on tea and tobacco estates during the early twentieth century. The idiom of "assistance" masked the little option African tenants had but to pay their rent through labor.

9. As mentioned, a German expatriate was the project manager during my fieldwork. In 2005, he became the project's technical adviser, and a Malawian became the project manager.

10. President Muluzi banned all demonstrations on the issue, effectively giving the state media the chance to campaign for the third term without opposition.

11. The dramatic decline in the standards of primary and secondary education was a direct consequence of the Muluzi administration's populist policies. The Educational Statistics for 1997, released by the Ministry of Education, Science, and Technology, revealed, for example, that three million pupils attended Malawi's four thousand primary schools. In Community Day Secondary Schools (CDSS), which catered to those who did not qualify for conventional schools, qualified teachers made up just 1 percent of the teaching staff. In 2000, a presidential commission of inquiry into the crisis in secondary education found that the proportion of candidates writing the Malawi School Certificate of Education ("O" levels) in CDSS had increased from 1 percent in 1990 to 51.3 percent in 1999. As mentioned in the previous chapter, in 1999 the pass rate in conventional schools was 27.5 percent; and in CDSS, 3.6 percent.

12. In fact, the monolingual Chichewa/Chinyanja dictionary does not even list formal "politics" as one of the meanings of *ndale* (see Centre for Language Studies 2000, 251). Both meanings that it gives refer to deceit that one person practices in relation to another, whether in physical or verbal contest.

13. Werbner's case from Botswana involves the "big men" of the city becoming "small boys" in the village, dressing modestly and running errands for rural dignitaries (2004, 140). Although most officers in Malawi did not wear suits or elaborate dresses in their home villages, as they did during their sessions of civic education, their conduct did indicate a distinction between their status and that of home villagers. In contrast, officers and village dignitaries showed mutual respect and embodied authority that was complementary rather than oppositional.

14. The content of civic education messages was the subject of different workshops, sometimes led by foreign experts on democracy and human rights. These workshops were usually open to full-time officers only, while volunteers learned the messages from the manual *Gwira Mpini Kwacha* (Grab the hoe handle, it's morning) (see Cairns and Dambula 1999). Published by the Public Affairs Committee, it was commonly used among organizations that conducted civic education on democracy and human rights. It was only in 2005 that NICE produced its own manual for civic education.

15. I stress similarity, because in both cases extraversion brings resources to individuals and organizations to engage in various local and national projects. I have elsewhere discussed the need to analyze further the different strategies of extraversion, pointing out how in some religious communities the boundaries between the external and the internal become blurred (see Englund 2003).

16. Incoherence here is a feature of the original utterance. Three dots in reported dialogue represent micropauses of more than two seconds. They do not represent omitted words.

17. See Simpson 2003 for examples from Zambia on the uses of "jack-up" in local English. A further example of the distinctions between civic educators and the grassroots was that this kind of language featured more in civic educators' internal workshops than during their sessions in villages and townships.

18. A case in point is Malawi's parliament, where English has been the only

language all along, despite many parliamentarians' evident difficulties in expressing themselves in it. Many Malawians, including parliamentarians, have recently become more positive about a bilingual or multilingual language policy for the Parliament (see Matiki 2003). However, a counteropinion claims that a parliamentarian's inability to speak English means that he or she "has not been to school" and is therefore incompetent (see, e.g., "Aphungu asamalankhule Chichewa," *Tamvani*, June 7–8, 2003).

19. Another well-known aspect of Banda's contradictory character was his respect for Chewa ethnicity and language (see Vail and White 1989). It is worth mentioning that this respect was largely nostalgic, even if it contributed to consolidating his power in the Chewa heartlands of Central Malawi. Banda saw that the proper place of the Chichewa language was in the villages, embedded in timeless traditions, while advancement through the science and education of the modern world was possible only through English. Malawi's historical links with Scotland rather than with England (see, e.g., McCracken 1977) have had little impact on the popular idiom of Mangalande, which depicts England as the original home of white people.

20. This audio tape is titled *Dziwani Malamulo a Dziko Lanu* (Know the laws of your country) and was produced by the Centre for Human Rights and Rehabilitation, with funding from the GTZ-Democracy project, no date.

4. Watchdogs Unleashed?

1. The value of ethnographic fieldwork in reaching beyond appearances and rhetorics is evident here. While the jargon in English summons up "discussion" and "facilitation," the concept of "teacher" *(mphunzitsi)* often endures in the practice of NICE's civic education. While a Chichewa term for "facilitator," such as *wothandiza* (the one who assists), could easily be identified, I have never witnessed civic educators using any such alternative to *mphunzitsi.*

2. NICE's concept of goat culture, described in chapter 3, delegated to the community the responsibility of feeding and hosting its civic education officers.

3. According to NICE's jargon, "edutainment" combined entertainment with the actual delivery of civic education. It contrasted with an effort to investigate the issues that people expressed in their own cultural productions (see Tengatenga 1998).

4. *Zikomo kwambiri. Ndilongosole tanthauzo la demokalase mwachidule. Demokalase imatanthauza boma lomwe limayendetsedwa ndi anthu.*

5. *Alipo amene ali ndi funso, amene sanamvetsetse bwinobwino?*

6. Some NICE sessions went as far as staging competitions in which the participants received gifts, such as soap or sugar, for right answers. While there are, of course, correct answers to questions about, for example, specific laws or constitutional rights, the element of patronage that NICE introduced into its civic education strategies is striking.

7. *Kodi tikanena boma loyendera mphamvu za anthu tikutanthauza chiyani? Tikutanthauza kuti boma lomwe limayendetsedwa ndi anthu, anthu ake ndi ifeyo*

anthu a kumidzi. Ngati boma limeneli ndi loyendetsedwa ndi anthu, tikutanthauza chiyani? Chifukwa choti atsogoleri aja timasankha ifeyo, anthu a kumidzi. Ndiye anthu amene aja ntchito ili yonse imene amachita imakhala yochokera kwa ndani, kwa ife anthu. Ndiye demokalase tanthauzo lake ndi boma lovomerezeka ndi anthu onse, chifukwa choti anthu ndi amene amasankha atsogoleri.

8. I choose not to reveal the name of the agency mentioned in the song.

9. *Chifukwa chiyani anthu ambiri amanena kuti "ah, mwayesa ndi thangata imeneyi?" Eti? Timatero, za ulere zinapita; nthawi yogwira ntchito ya ulere inapita ndi Kamuzu, eti? Masiku ano ntchito yake ndi yotani, yolipiridwa. Koma taiwala kuti ntchito imene timagwira ife, kwenikweni za chitukuko, timakhala kuthandiza ife tomwe.*

10. *Pali mabungwe ena amene amachita kusankhana, amachita kulembana. Titenge bwanji mbali ngati sitinasankhidwe?*

11. *Mudzi uno ndi waukulu, koma chipatala kulibe.*

12. *Mwina mawu amenewa apite ku X.*

13. *Ana samvera makolo awo, mwano, akazi amavala akabudula, kusamvera madandaulo a ife anthu a kumidzi, kusalandira chithandizo cha ngongole, kusowa kwa ndalama.*

14. It should be noted that critical remarks on women's new modes of dressing were voiced as much by women as by men in these villages. The issue has become highly controversial in Malawi. Kamuzu Banda's regime imposed a dress code that prohibited skirts that it deemed too short. The new regime removed the dress code, but many Malawians continued to expect old-fashioned modes of dress among women. The relation of such expectations to women's broader emancipation has also been debated elsewhere in southern Africa (see, e.g., Hansen 2000).

15. *Pamenepa ndisankhapo kuchita mwano, kusamvera makolo ndi kusokoneza kwa chitetezo.*

16. Civic education officer: *Komano ife tili pano lero, tadziwa tanthauzo la demokalase, eti? . . . Tadziwanso mfundo za demokalase, m'mene zinthu zimayenera kukhalira m'boma loti muli demokalase. Sitinganene kuti (zovuta) zimachitika chifukwa cha demokalase, eti? . . . Simuyankha ndi mphamvu. . . .*

Literacy class instructor: *Ayi, m'mene ndamverera maphunziro a lero, mwina sizikuchitika chifukwa cha demokalase.*

17. *Ufulu wolankhula, ufulu wophunzira, ufulu wovala modzilemekeza, ufulu wopewa mwamuna ndi mkazi, tikuthokoza Bakili.*

18. Officer: *Kodi nanga ufulu umenewu unayamba liti? Kuti munthu akhale ndi ufulu, ufulu umenewu umayamba liti?*

Woman 1: *Unayamba 1994.*

Officer: *1994. Tikumva mayiyo, eti? 1994. Nanga achemwali kumbuyoko? Ufulu wanu unayamba liti?*

Woman 2: *Chimodzimodzi.*

Officer: *Chimodzimodzi, eti? 1994. Apa achemwali?*

Woman 3: *'94.*

Officer: *'94. Tikatha kuzindikira maufulu amenewa amayambira pamene munthu uja ngakhale asanabadwe.*

19. *Ufulu umayamba munthu asanabadwe, pamene mayi ali ndi thunzi la mwa-nayo. . . . Tsopano mwana uja akabadwa ndi pamene amangopitiriza maufulu ena.*

20. *Ndanena kuti ufulu uja umayamba ngakhale munthu asanabadwe, akabad-wa umangopitiriza, eti?*

21. *Ndikukhulupirira kuti akuluakulu ali apawa adzatiganiziranso ulendo wina kuti tidzangobweretsa maphunziro okhaokha oti m'mene mungayendetsere mabizine-si ang'onoang'ono. Akabweranso opatsa ndalama aja, musasokere ndi ndalama zija.*

22. This policy enabled FINCA officials to detach themselves from the wide-spread confiscation of property that the nonpayment of loans occasioned. It was the women themselves, FINCA chiefs maintained, who did the confiscation. See "Mbiri ya bungwe la FINCA: FINCA silanda katundu, amalandana okha-okha," *Tamvani,* December 7–8, 2002. Similar policies informed lending insti-tutions beyond Africa (see, e.g., Lazar 2004, 306).

23. *Anzanga akunena kuti a bungwe amene akunenawa, ndalama imakhala yochepa, chifukwa ukhoza kukongoza ndalama zija 3,000. Kodi 3,000 muyambitsa geni yanji?* At the time of research, three thousand kwacha were equivalent to about forty U.S. dollars.

24. *Ndiponso okongoza ndalama ndife amphawi, koma usanakongoze ndalama kubungwe kuja, amanena kuti amene akufuna kutenga ndalama, aliyense apereke kaya 300, mwina 200, ena 400. Tikufuna ndalama; tiperekenso 200 kuti tipeze ndalama?*

25. Television Malawi News, September 9, 2003.

26. Rafiq Hajat, then a member of the UDF's Executive Committee, quoted in "Interview with Democracy Activist, Rafiq Hajat," UN Integrated Regional Information Networks, posted on www.allAfrica.com on November 19, 2001.

27. Emmie Chanika, executive director of CILIC, quoted in "Muluzi Accused of Buying Chiefs," *Daily Times,* May 17, 2002. Chanika was reacting to the news that President Muluzi had increased chiefs' monthly stipends by 25 percent.

28. Accurate statistics on the rate of illiteracy are difficult to maintain, but the government and its donors regard the figure of 42 percent as the official illit-eracy rate in the country (UNDP 2001, 29). This percentage improved very lit-tle during the 1990s.

29. An advertisement by Bambino Private Schools in, e.g., *Tamvani,* Octo-ber 5–6, 2002.

30. The song, entitled "Amadikira" (They wait), is on the audio cassette *Chidiso Mumtolomo,* by Charles Sinetre (2002).

5. Legal Aid for Abused Labor

1. "Ombudsman Lets Go Disputes," *The Nation,* February 14, 2002.

2. See rule 24 in *Industrial Relations Court (Procedure) Rules,* published in the *Malawi Gazette Supplement,* April 30, 1999.

3. During its first five years, Malawi CARER considered over two thousand cases (Chirwa 2000b, 35). This high figure is explained by its having offices not only in the commercial capital, Blantyre, but also in three other districts. CHRR, on the other hand, had an office only in Lilongwe.

4. Unlike in courts, where the official language was English and interpretation services were offered, the vast majority of cases I heard during my fieldwork were expressed and discussed in Chichewa. English was used very rarely.

5. See section 11(3c) of the Labor Relations Act.

6. See the sections 29 and 30 of the Employment Act.

7. Quoted in "Veep Opens Sadc Ministers Meet," *Daily Times,* August 7, 2001.

8. See also "Companies Abusing K50 Minimum Wage," *Malawi News,* November 2–8, 2002.

9. For an account of how Malawian civil servants use their formal employment as a basis for personal businesses, see Anders 2002.

10. Quoted in "Strike Looms Large at LL Water Board," *The Chronicle,* October 1–7, 2001.

11. "Asians Exploiting Malawians," *MCTU Newsletter,* no. 1, August 1999.

12. See "Companies Abusing K50 Minimum Wage," *Malawi News,* November 2–8, 2002.

13. "Workers in Problems," *The Nation,* July 9, 2003.

14. "Complainant Dishonest," *The Nation,* July 14, 2003.

15. The issue of attending funerals, mentioned in the above correspondence, is a frequent source of conflict in labor relations in Malawi and many other African countries. It should be noted that most funerals in Malawi take place in the deceased's village of origin, which may be far away from the workplace. Yet attending the funerals of one's kin is hardly optional, placing a considerable burden on the working population.

16. It was, for example, active in organizing a protest against the unconstitutional aim to allow the president to stand for a third term.

17. Office of the Ombudsman, *1st Annual Report (January 1995 to March 1996).*

18. "Lay Magistrates, Be Gentlemen, Not Bullies in Settling Your Disputes," *Daily Times,* June 26, 2003.

19. Quoted in "Ministry Spends K1.5m on Coffins," *Daily Times,* December 12, 2002.

20. Quoted in "'You Are Ignorant of Criminal Procedure,'" *Daily Times,* March 11, 2002.

21. Since I did not discern major differences in lawyers' and paralegal officers' approaches to their clients, I refer to both categories as legal officers. All the recordings, transcriptions, and translations of conversations at the Legal Clinic were done by myself. For a more detailed sociolinguistic analysis of this data, see Englund 2004c.

22. Officer: *Kumakhala ngati kuchipatala, eti?*
Client: *Ee.*
Officer: *Ndinenanso, eti? Mukhoza kupita pachipatala ku dokotala, "ine ndikudwala maso," koma dokotala mwapeza si wa maso. Amakupangani opareshoni ya maso ngati?*
Client: *Sizitheka.*

23. Compare these remarks by Richard Wilson on human rights reporting in Guatemala: "The language in which most cases are presented is generally realist and legalist, and it engages in a decontextualisation of events. Accounts of

human rights violations are characterised by a literalism and minimalism which strip events of their subjective meanings in a pursuit of objective legal facts" (1997, 134).

24. Officer: *Inuyo, mukufuna* notice pay *ya masiku angati? Chimene ndikufunsa ineyo.*

Client: *Bwana ndapanga* claim notice pay *ya* one month.

Officer: *Chifukwa chiyani* one month? *Mwayesa ndanena choncho?*

Client: No, Sir.

Officer: *Ndiye* one month *yachokera kuti? Mwangoilota?*

25. Officer: *Kuno munabwera ngati ku* Legal Office.

Client: *Ee.*

Officer: *Sitifuna za mawu ayi.*

Client: *Ee.*

Officer: *Tikufuna* information, material *kuti izi zili pati, zili apa.*

Client: *Koma* =

Officer: =We can't just act on a thing, *koma kuti palibe chiyani—umboni wa ifeyo. Inuyo ngati muchoka kwanu kubwera kudzadandaula muli ndi umboni wokwanira, si choncho?*

The sign "=" indicates overlapping speech.

26. Officer: *Munthu akafuna kusiya ntchito kapena amuchotsa ntchito, amapereka* notice *ya masiku angati?*

Client: *Monga mwachitsanzo m'mene anaperekera dalaiva amene* =

Officer: = *Inuyo ndikufunsa za inuyo osati anzanu ayi.*

27. Officer: *Sanakupatseni* overtime?

Client: *Ayi, sitimapatsidwa.*

Officer: *Bwanji simunadandaule musanachoke?*

Client: *Ah, bwana, kunalibe chifukwa choti ndidandaule, ndimayembekezera yoti* =

Officer: = *Ndiye tsopano zigwira bwanji pamene munagwira* overtime *ija, munthu akagwira* overtime *mwezi uno,* next month *ukupitirirabe, sakupatsa* overtime. *Ukugwirabe, ukugwirabe, ukugwirabe. Tsopano achita kukuchotsa, "ndifuna* overtime *yanga yambuyo ya* eleven months." *Zimveke ngati?*

28. *Ino ndi* organization *yopanda ndalama. Si ya boma moti mwina mwake ambiri amaganiza kuti mwina mwake boma limapatsa ndalama kuti tithandize anthu koma ayi. Kuthandiza chabe ngati mavolunteers. Koma chili kwa munthu wobwera ndi madandaulo apeze njira yoti ife titani, timuthandize. Ndi malipiro ake basi. Poti "ndi mlandu wanu, patseni* one thousand," *ayi sitipanga zimenezo, koma ifeyo ngati pali foni kaya pali maemvulopu tikalemba makalata, kaguleni emvulopu, patseni.*

6. Crimes of Exploitation

1. The names are pseudonyms.

2. Many areas in Lilongwe are known by numbers rather than names.

3. Since the early 1990s, the urban markets of southern and eastern Africa have witnessed considerable changes. New entrepreneurs, often young men, are highly visible as street vendors and hawkers. For more details on the develop-

ments in Malawi, see Englund 2002d and Jimu 2003. On Zambia, see, e.g., Hansen 2000.

4. In fact, there was no legal provision in regard to daily allowances in the private sector. However, the minimum allowance for government employees was, in 2002, MK 960 per day.

5. Chikondi: *Bwana, taonani malaya, mukuona m'mene malaya anathera?*
Patel: *Ayi, imeneyi ndi ntchito.*

6. Chikondi: *Sindikudziwa kena kalikonse. Ine ndingadziwe bwanji bwana, ndinali ku Mzimba, nkhani yachitikira kuno.*
Patel: *Iweyo ndi amene akudziwa.*

7. Patel: *Chikondi, basi ntchito usiye. Mpakadali pano ukhoza kugwira ntchito kwina kulikonse. Ukafunefune kwina ntchito.*
Chikondi: *Chifukwa chiyani?*
Patel: *Ayi, ukadzavutika udzabwere.*
Chikondi: *Ndimagwira ntchito chifukwa cha mavuto! Ndiye mukundiuza ndikavutike? Kwenikweni ndalakwa chiyani?*
Patel: *Ayi, basi, uzipita.*

8. As far as I could ascertain, Chikondi was not involved in thefts at Patel's store. He and the suspects had not established enough rapport to embark on such clandestine activities. Whatever the case, however, the issue here is how some workers may *become* criminals under the conditions of their employment.

9. I began these conversations in 1996, when I was considering fieldwork among the so-called Indian community in Lilongwe. I have also detected similar perspectives among expatriate employers.

10. Views about disparate needs have been intrinsic to exploitative regimes. The most blatant examples in modern times included the apartheid ideology in South Africa, where different categories of people were thought to need different forms of education and employment, among other things.

11. *Mukandipatsa ndalama zimene ndaononga ndi zanga.*

12. Recall the correspondence between Worried Malawian and Worried Expatriate that was described in chapter 5. The expatriate may have been right in criticizing the Malawian's use of the term "Boer," but the criticism begged the bigger question of why racist terminology should remain widespread in Malawi.

13. Examples include the numerous audiences — some publicized, others secretive — that Muluzi granted at his various residences. It appears that these instances of "dialogue" were regularly accompanied by donations from the state president, whether in cash or in kind. The exhortations that his critics, such as NGOs and certain members of the clergy, should "work together with the government" belonged to the same rhetoric that begged the question of who had the power to determine the conditions of cooperation and dialogue.

14. Three dots in these extracts represent a micropause of more than two seconds. They do not indicate omitted words. Again, the sign "=" indicates overlapping speech.

15. Chikondi: *Ee. Ndinali kugwira ntchito.*
Officer: *Januwale?*

Chikondi: *Ee, Januwale, ee. Ndapeza abwana aja, ndinkagwira ntchito ija, amatha kundituma ineyo, wandipatsa ndalama yokwana . . . khangati . . .*

Officer: *Muzilankhula zofunika zokhazokha!*

Chikondi: *Ee. Ah . . .*

Officer: *Tauzeni zofunika zokhazokha.*

16. Officer: *Tsopano chimene mukufuna inuyo ndi chiyani?*

Chikondi: *Chimene ndikufuna ine, sindikufuna yoti ndikabwerere uko kuntchito ayi.*

Officer: *Mm.*

Chikondi: *Ndikungofuna andipatse ndalama zanga za malipiro . . . ndi . . .*

17. Saturday was a working day at Patel's store. Section 36(4) of the Employment Act stipulates that "no employer shall require or permit an employee to work for more than six consecutive days without a period of rest, comprising at least twenty-four consecutive hours." Section 39 stipulates the level of compensation for working overtime.

18. Section 29(1a) of the Employment Act stipulates that the minimum period of notice is one month when wages are paid at a monthly rate. Section 30(2) stipulates that the payment in lieu of notice is equal to the remuneration that would have been received during the period of notice.

19. The Employment Act recognizes, under Section 56(2), only the following forms of disciplinary action: a written warning, suspension, and demotion.

20. Officer: *Mubweretse* transport *ya ineyo.*

Chikondi: Okay.

Officer: *Kupita kutawuni nkubwerera. Basi, ndi chaji yathu.*

Chikondi: *Zikomo.*

Officer: *Ee. Kaya mubwera ndi ndalamayo . . . mpakati pano ndalama tilibe . . . ndiponso timathandiza pa milandu popanda ndalama.*

Chikondi: *Ee.*

Officer: *Ndiye timafunsa makastomala kuti atithandize* transport.

Chikondi: Okay.

21. I decided not to accompany the officer on this first visit to Patel so that my presence would not influence the encounter. The subsequent events and investigations gave no reason to doubt the validity of the officer's account.

22. It is difficult to assess whether my presence in the room influenced Patel's behavior. It may have influenced the choice of English as the language of the meeting, because Patel did not know that I could speak Chichewa. On the other hand, the use of English was also a means of establishing a certain rapport between him and the officer against the uneducated client. The officer's account of his earlier meeting with Patel also indicated that Patel had always been polite to him. It was only after the case had been completed that I visited Patel's store, where he received me with some reserve but did not prevent me from talking to his workers.

23. How the officer arrived at the exact figure of MK 317 remains a mystery to me. When I asked him to explain it after Patel had left the office, he could only list the advances that had been deducted without clarifying how this par-

ticular figure was established. I was left to assume that such a figure, in contrast to round figures, was designed to defuse Chikondi's suspicions of an arbitrary ruling.

24. As mentioned, political and civil liberties have remained the preoccupation of Malawian human rights NGOs and watchdogs. Organizations monitoring the country's economy exist, such as the Malawi Economic Justice Network, but they often find it difficult to reach beyond the media's populist interests in ruling politicians' expenditure of public resources. Before the 2004 general elections, for example, the UDF government declared its commitment to "pro-poor economic growth." How economic growth would benefit the poor without reforms in the structures of income distribution did not attract critical public analysis.

25. *Amalawi sangafike poononga ngati momwe achitira anthu amenewa. Amalawi ndi anthu a ulemu.* Quoted in "Anthuwa si aMalawi," *Tikambe Supplement to Malawi News,* December 21–27, 2002.

7. Human Rights and Moral Panics

1. For an excellent review of the new and earlier anthropology of African witchcraft, see Moore and Sanders 2001.

2. By seeking to highlight the rationality of this moral panic, at least as far as its initial troubles were concerned, I do not mean to dismiss witchcraft as irrational. The rationality and irrationality of witchcraft beliefs have preoccupied anthropologists and philosophers since E. E. Evans-Pritchard's 1937 classic work. Posed as questions of relativist and universal reason, however, philosophical inquiries have often been circumscribed by a certain "elitism of doubt" (Fields 2001, 310). An ethnographic approach, by contrast, may take us beyond the problems of reason altogether, because it shows how beliefs are embedded in practical activities (see Kapferer 2002).

3. Although Freemasonry seems to have disappeared from Malawi during the postcolonial era, it is noteworthy that Kamuzu Banda took part in it during his many years abroad (Short 1974). During Banda's regime, the freedom of worship extended only to those denominations and individuals who did not voice criticism of the regime. Jehovah's Witnesses faced particularly severe persecution because of their lack of allegiance to the state. Banda's relation to Freemasonry and its status in postcolonial Malawi were among the many issues that could not be discussed openly during his rule. It appears that Lilongwe residents found ways of breaking the silence by associating the Freemasons' building with Satanism. Compare also President Bongo in Gabon, who is reported to have been initiated into Freemasonry in the city and into an occult cult in the village (Geschiere 1997, 254).

4. For born-again Christians in Africa, particularly those who worship in various pentecostal and charismatic churches, the figure of Satan is virtually as important as Christ and God (see, e.g., Englund 2004a and Meyer 1999).

5. Many elderly men, former labor migrants to South Africa, have described

to me their suspicions when authorities in the mines forced them to donate blood. The issue of blood tests also contributed to the Malawi government's decision to stop large-scale labor migration, because South African authorities were seen to make unreasonable demands in testing Malawians' blood for HIV.

6. See, for example, "Church Saves Children from Witchcraft Practice," *The Nation,* October 17, 2003; and "Witchcraft Rocking Societies as Children Are Targetted," *The Nation,* October 21, 2003. A story obtained from the news agency Reuters had an atypical headline: "Superstition Fuels Reports of Child Witches," *The Nation,* November 3, 2003.

7. See, for example, "Witchcraft Law Needed," *The Nation,* October 3, 2003; "In Support of Law on Witchcraft," *The Nation,* October 17, 2003. For a sympathetic, if essentialist, attempt to reconcile "African witchcraft" and "Western law," see Hund 2004.

8. See "Mitu ya anthu akufa iyambitsa phokoso," *Tikambe Supplement to Malawi News,* December 6–12, 2003.

9. The exchange rate became increasingly unfavorable to Malawi kwacha during 2001–4. Hence the difference between these values and those reported in the previous chapter.

10. The incident was reported in the biggest daily along with the disappearance of one of the above-mentioned schoolgirls: "The Story of Josephine," *The Nation,* October 22, 2003.

11. Chinsapo's Inkatha was in the domain of headmen and avoided direct influence from political parties and the state. For a study of relations between vigilantism and the state, see Abrahams 1998.

12. "Zonsezi ndi chifukwa cha malamulo athu," *Tikambe Supplement to Malawi News,* December 6–12, 2003.

13. *Dziwani malamulo a dziko lanu,* an audio tape released by the Centre for Human Rights and Rehabilitation (no date).

14. *Kulanga kwa mchigulu,* a leaflet published by the Centre for Human Rights and Rehabilitation in a series entitled Dziwani ufulu wanu (no date).

15. For a discussion of Malawi's posttransition reform program for the police, see Dzonzi 2003. The CHRR embarked in 2001 on a program that sought to promote security in local communities. The program, together with the NGO's involvement in controlling access to small arms, was undoubtedly beneficial to the populace. Popular grievances against the police, however, remained underresearched.

16. For a study that carefully traces the origins and destinations of secondhand clothes in Zambia, see Hansen 2000.

17. The rally occurred on December 21, 2003, in Machinga District.

8. Redeeming Freedom

1. The image of the uninhibited connoisseur of cultures has come under criticism in recent attempts to provide historically and politically nuanced accounts

of cosmopolitanism. See, for example, Englund 2004a; Ferguson 1999; and Robbins 1998.

2. *Ngwazi* is the Chichewa term for a heroic warrior, which Banda adopted as one of his honorific titles.

3. My information on the fate of the Transform project is based on discussions with several individuals, including project and NGO personnel and academics. See also "Govt. Stops UK Project," *Daily Times,* May 31, 2002; and "Govt. Blocks British Aid," *The Chronicle,* June 9–15, 2003.

4. "CHRR Urges Media to Open Debate on Rights," *The Nation,* August 24, 2005.

5. NICE: National Planning and Training Workshop, December 8–11, 2004, report prepared by Jeff Kabondo.

References

Abrahams, Ray. 1998. *Vigilant Citizens: Vigilantism and the State.* Cambridge: Polity Press.

Abrahamsen, Rita. 2000. *Disciplining Democracy: Development Discourse and Good Governance in Africa.* London: Zed Books.

Africa Watch. 1990. *Where Silence Rules: The Suppression of Dissent in Malawi.* London: Human Rights Watch.

Agamben, Giorgio. 1998. *Homo Sacer: Sovereign Power and Bare Life.* Stanford: Stanford University Press.

———. 2001. On Security and Terror. http://info.interactivist.net.

Ake, Claude. 2000. *The Feasibility of Democracy in Africa.* Dakar: Council for the Development of Social Science Research in Africa (CODESRIA).

Alence, Rod. 2004. Political Institutions and Developmental Governance in Sub-Saharan Africa. *Journal of Modern African Studies* 42: 163–187.

Amin, Samir. 1976. *Unequal Development: An Essay on the Social Formations of Peripheral Capitalism.* New York: Monthly Review Press.

Anders, Gerhard. 2002. Freedom and Insecurity: Civil Servants between Support Networks, the Free Market and the Civil Service Reform. In H. Englund, ed., *A Democracy of Chameleons: Politics and Culture in the New Malawi.* Uppsala: Nordic Africa Institute and Blantyre: Christian Literature Association in Malawi (CLAIM).

Anderson, Benedict. 1983. *Imagined Communities: Reflections on the Origin and Spread of Nationalism.* New York: Verso.

Archibald, Steven, and Paul Richards. 2002. Converts to Human Rights? Popular Debate about War and Justice in Rural Central Sierra Leone. *Africa* 72: 339–367.

Asad, Talal. 1986. The Concept of Cultural Translation in British Social Anthropology. In J. Clifford and G. E. Marcus, eds., *Writing Culture: The Poetics and Politics of Ethnography.* Berkeley: University of California Press.

——. 2003. *Formations of the Secular: Christianity, Islam, Modernity*. Stanford: Stanford University Press.

Ashforth, Adam. 2005. *Witchcraft, Violence, and Democracy in South Africa*. Chicago: University of Chicago Press.

Badiou, Alain. 2001. *Ethics: An Essay on the Understanding of Evil*. London: Verso.

——. 2003. *Infinite Thought: Truth and the Return to Philosophy*. London: Continuum.

Baker, Colin. 2001. *Revolt of the Ministers: The Malawi Cabinet Crisis, 1964–1965*. London: I. B. Tauris.

Bamgbose, Ayo. 2000. *Language and Exclusion: The Consequences of Language Policies in Africa*. Hamburg: Lit Verlag Muster.

Banda, Ellias E. Ngalande, Flora S. Nankhuni, and Ephraim W. Chirwa. 1998. Economy and Democracy: Background, Current Situation and Future Prospects. In K. M. Phiri and K. R. Ross, eds., *Democratization in Malawi: A Stocktaking*. Blantyre: Christian Literature Association in Malawi (CLAIM).

Banda, Gracian Zibelu. 1995. "A Raging Calm?" The Impact of Labour Relations on Politics in Malawi. In M. S. Nzunda and K. R. Ross, eds., *Church, Law and Political Transition in Malawi 1992–1994*. Gweru: Mambo Press.

Barrett, Michael. 2004. *Paths to Adulthood: Freedom, Belonging and Temporalities in Mbunda Biographies from Western Zambia*. Uppsala: Acta Universitatis Upsaliensis.

Barrow, Ondine, and Michael Jennings, eds. 2002. *The Charitable Impulse: NGOs and Development in East and North-East Africa*. Oxford: James Currey.

Bassnett, Susan. (1980) 2002. *Translation Studies*. London: Routledge.

Bayart, Jean-François. 1993. *The State in Africa: The Politics of the Belly*. London: Longman.

——. 2000. Africa in the World: A History of Extraversion. *African Affairs* 99: 217–267.

Bayart, Jean-François, Achille Mbembe, and Christian Toulabor. 1992. *Le politique par le bas en Afrique noire: Contributions á une problematique de la démocratie*. Paris: Karthala.

Bell, Vikki. 1996. The Promise of Liberalism and the Performance of Freedom. In A. Barry, T. Osborne, and N. Rose, eds., *Foucault and Political Reason: Liberalism, Neoliberalism and Rationalities of Government*. New York: Routledge.

Berman, Bruce, Peter Eyoh, and Will Kymlicka, eds. 2004. *Ethnicity and Democracy in Africa*. Oxford: James Currey.

Blommaert, Jan. 2001. Investigating Narrative Inequality: African Asylum Seekers' Stories in Belgium. *Discourse & Society* 12: 413–449.

——. 2002. Writing in the Margins: Notes on a Sociolinguistics of Globalization. Lecture presented at Cardiff University.

Bond, Patrick. 2000. *Elite Transition: From Apartheid to Neoliberalism in South Africa*. London: Pluto Press.

Bornstein, Erica. 2003. *The Spirit of Development: Protestant NGOs, Morality, and Economics in Zimbabwe*. New York: Routledge.

Bourdieu, Pierre. 1977. *Outline of a Theory of Practice*. Cambridge: Cambridge University Press.

————. 1998. *Acts of Resistance: Against the Tyranny of the Market*. New York: New Press.

Brennan, Timothy. 1997. *At Home in the World: Cosmopolitanism Now*. Cambridge, MA: Harvard University Press.

————. 2001. The Cuts of Language: The East/West of North/South. *Public Culture* 13: 39–63.

Burchell, Graham. 1991. Peculiar Interests: Civil Society and Governing "the System of Natural Liberty." In G. Burchell, C. Gordon, and P. Miller, eds., *The Foucault Effect: Studies in Governmentality*. London: Harvester Wheatsheaf.

————. 1996. Liberal Government and Techniques of the Self. In A. Barry, T. Osborne, and N. Rose, eds., *Foucault and Political Reason: Liberalism, Neoliberalism and Rationalities of Government*. New York: Routledge.

Burke, Timothy. 1996. *Lifebuoy Men, Lux Women: Commodification, Consumption, and Cleanliness in Modern Zimbabwe*. Durham, NC: Duke University Press.

Burnell, Peter. 2001. The Party System and Party Politics in Zambia: Continuities Past, Present and Future. *African Affairs* 100: 239–263.

Butler, Judith. 2000. Restaging the Universal. In J. Butler, E. Laclau, and S. Žižek, eds., *Contingency, Hegemony, Universality: Contemporary Dialogues from the Left*. London: Verso.

Bwanali, Alick K. 2001. Developing Chichewa into a Cross-Border Lingua Franca: Prospects and Challenges. In J. F. Pfaffe, ed., *Cross-Border Languages within the Context of Mother Tongue Education*. Zomba: Centre for Language Studies.

Cairns, James L., and George S. Dambula. 1999. *Gwira Mpini Kwacha: Maphunziro a demokalase ya m'maboma aang'ono*. Lilongwe: Public Affairs Committee.

Caldeira, Teresa P. R., and James Holston. 1999. Democracy and Violence in Brazil. *Comparative Studies in Society and History* 41: 691–729.

Calhoun, Craig, ed. 1992. *Habermas and the Public Sphere*. Cambridge, MA: MIT Press.

Centre for Language Studies. 2000. *Mtanthauziramawu wa Chinyanja*. Blantyre: Dzuka.

Chambers, Robert. 1983. *Rural Development: Putting the Last First*. Harlow: Longman.

————. 1994. The Origins and Practice of Participatory Rural Appraisal. *World Development* 22: 953–969.

————. 1997. *Whose Reality Counts: Putting the Last First*. London: Intermediate Technology Publications.

Chanda, Alfred. 1999. *Informal Education on Human Rights in Zambia*. Harare: Southern African Political Economy Series (SAPES).

Chanock, Martin. 2000. "Culture" and Human Rights: Orientalising, Occidentalising and Authenticity. In M. Mamdani, ed., *Beyond Rights Talk and Cul-*

ture Talk: Comparative Essays on the Politics of Rights and Culture. Cape Town: David Philip.

Chichewa Board. 1990. *Chichewa Orthography Rules*. Blantyre: Chichewa Board.

Chilora, H. G., and R. E. M. Kathewera. 2000. *Chinyanja: Buku la Ophunzira a Fomu 1*. Blantyre: Dzuka.

Chimombo, Steven, and Moira Chimombo. 1996. *The Culture of Democracy: Language, Literature, the Arts, and Politics in Malawi, 1992–1994*. Zomba: WASI.

Chimombo, Tina D. 1999. Transition to Democracy?: Civic Education before and after the First Democratic Elections in Malawi. In M. Chimombo, ed., *Lessons in Hope: Education for Democracy in Malawi, Past, Present, Future*. Zomba: Chancellor College Publications.

Chinsinga, Blessings. 2002. The Politics of Poverty Alleviation in Malawi: A Critical Review. In H. Englund, ed., *A Democracy of Chameleons: Politics and Culture in the New Malawi*. Uppsala: Nordic Africa Institute and Blantyre: Christian Literature Association in Malawi (CLAIM).

Chirwa, Wiseman C. 1996. The Malawi Government and the South African Labour Recruiters, 1974–1992. *Journal of Modern African Studies* 34: 623–642.

———. 1998. Democracy, Ethnicity, and Regionalism: The Malawian Experience, 1992–1996. In K. M. Phiri and K. R. Ross, eds., *Democratization in Malawi: A Stocktaking*. Blantyre: Christian Literature Association in Malawi (CLAIM).

———. 2000a. Civil Society in Malawi's Democratic Transition. In M. Ott, K. M. Phiri, and N. Patel, eds., *Malawi's Second Democratic Elections: Process, Problems and Prospects*. Blantyre: Christian Literature Association in Malawi (CLAIM).

———. 2000b. Malawi CARER: Civic Education, Paralegal and Legal Assistance Programs. Evaluation report.

Chisoni, Experencia M. 2001. Developing Malawi-Zambia Cinyanja: A Focus on Teaching and Learning Materials. In J. F. Pfaffe, ed., *Cross-Border Languages within the Context of Mother Tongue Education*. Zomba: Centre for Language Studies.

Chiume, M. W. Kanyama. 1975. *Kwacha: An Autobiography*. Nairobi: East African Publishing House.

Chomsky, Noam. 1998. Free Trade and Free Market: Pretense and Practice. In F. Jameson and M. Miyoshi, eds., *The Cultures of Globalization*. Durham, NC: Duke University Press.

———. 1999. *The Umbrella of US Power: The Universal Declaration of Human Rights and the Contradictions of US Policy*. New York: Seven Stories Press.

Christiansen, Robert E., and Jonathan Kydd. 1983. The Return of Malawian Labour from South Africa and Zimbabwe. *Journal of Modern African Studies* 21: 311–326.

CHRR (Centre for Human Rights and Rehabilitation). 2003. Interim Report for the Period 1st January to 31st December 2003. Lilongwe: CHRR.

Ciekawy, Diane. 2000. Mijikenda Perspectives on Freedom, Culture and Human "Rights." In C. B. Mwaria, S. Federici, and J. McLaren, eds., *African Visions: Literary Images, Political Change, and Social Struggle in Contemporary Africa*. Westport, CT: Greenwood Press.

Collins, James. 1995. Literacy and Literacies. *Annual Review of Anthropology* 24: 75–93.

Comaroff, Jean, and John L. Comaroff. 1999. Occult Economies and the Violence of Abstraction: Notes from the South African Postcolony. *American Ethnologist* 26: 279–303.

Comaroff, John L. 2002. Governmentality, Materiality, Legality, Modernity: On the Colonial State in Africa. In J. G. Deutsch, P. Probst and H. Schmidt, eds., *African Modernities: Entangled Meanings in Current Debate*. Oxford: James Currey.

Comaroff, John L., and Jean Comaroff. 1997. *Of Revelation and Revolution*. Vol. 2: *The Dialectics of Modernity on an African Frontier*. Chicago: University of Chicago Press.

———. 1999. Introduction. In J. L. Comaroff and J. Comaroff, eds., *Civil Society and the Political Imagination in Africa: Critical Perspectives*. Chicago: University of Chicago Press.

———. 2004. Criminal Justice, Cultural Justice: The Limits of Liberalism and the Pragmatics of Difference in the New South Africa. *American Ethnologist* 31: 188–204.

Conley, John M., and William M. O'Barr. 1990. *Rules versus Relationships: The Ethnography of Legal Discourse*. Chicago: University of Chicago Press.

Cooke, Bill, and Uma Kothari, eds. 2001. *Participation: The New Tyranny?* London: Zed Books.

Cowan, Jane K., Marie-Bénédicte Dembour, and Richard A. Wilson. 2001. Introduction. In J. K. Cowan, M.-B. Dembour, and R. A. Wilson, eds., *Culture and Rights: Anthropological Perspectives*. Cambridge: Cambridge University Press.

Dean, Mitchell. 1999. *Governmentality: Power and Rule in Modern Society*. London: Sage.

de Man, Paul. 1986. Conclusions: Walter Benjamin's "The Task of the Translator." In P. de Man, ed., *The Resistance to Theory*. Minneapolis: University of Minnesota Press.

DFID (Department for International Development). 2000. *Realising Human Rights for Poor People*. London: DFID.

Diamond, Larry, and Marc F. Plattner, eds. 2001. *The Global Divergence of Democracy*. Baltimore, MD: Johns Hopkins University Press.

Diamond, Larry, Marc F. Plattner, Yun-han Chu, and Hung-mao Tien, eds. 1997. *Consolidating the Third Wave Democracies: Regional Challenges*. Baltimore, MD: Johns Hopkins University Press.

Dirks, Nicholas B. 1992. Introduction: Colonialism and Culture. In N. B. Dirks, ed., *Colonialism and Culture*. Ann Arbor: University of Michigan Press.

Donham, Donald L. 1990. *History, Power, Ideology: Central Issues in Marxism and Anthropology.* Cambridge: Cambridge University Press.

Dorman, Sarah Rich. 2002. "Rocking the Boat?" Church NGOs and Democratization in Zimbabwe. *African Affairs* 101: 75–92.

———. 2003. NGOs and the Constitutional Debate in Zimbabwe: From Inclusion to Exclusion. *Journal of Southern African Studies* 29: 845–863.

Dorwald, Andrew, and Jonathan Kydd. 2004. The Malawi 2002 Food Crisis: The Rural Development Challenge. *Journal of Modern African Studies* 42: 343–361.

Duffield, Mark. 2001. *Global Governance and the New Wars: The Merging of Development and Security.* London: Zed Books.

Durham, Deborah. 2004. Disappearing Youth: Youth as a Social Shifter in Botswana. *American Ethnologist* 31: 589–605.

Dzimbiri, Lewis B. 2002. Industrial Relations, the State and Strike Activity in Malawi. Ph.D. thesis, Keele University, UK.

Dzonzi, Lot Thauzeni Pansipandana. 2003. The Malawi Police Reform and Human Rights. In B. Immink, S. Lembani, M. Ott, and C. Peters-Berries, eds., *From Freedom to Empowerment: Ten Years of Democratisation in Malawi.* Lilongwe: Forum for Dialogue and Peace.

Ellis, Stephen. 1993. Rumour and Power in Togo. *Africa* 63: 462–475.

———. 1999. *The Mask of Anarchy: The Destruction of Liberia and the Religious Dimension of an African Civil War.* London: Hurst & Co.

———. 2002. Writing Histories of Contemporary Africa. *Journal of African History* 43: 1–26.

Ellis, Stephen, and Gerrie ter Haar. 2004. *Worlds of Power: Religious Thought and Political Practice in Africa.* London: Hurst & Co.

Engelbronner-Kolff, Marina. 1998. *The Provision of Non-formal Education for Human Rights in Zimbabwe.* Harare: Southern African Political Economy Series (SAPES).

Englund, Harri. 1996. Between God and Kamuzu: The Transition to Multiparty Politics in Central Malawi. In R. Werbner and T. Ranger, eds., *Postcolonial Identities in Africa.* London: Zed Books.

———. 1999. The Self in Self-Interest: Land, Labour and Temporalities in Malawi's Agrarian Change. *Africa* 69: 139–159.

———. 2000. The Dead Hand of Human Rights: Contrasting Christianities in Post-transition Malawi. *Journal of Modern African Studies* 38: 579–603.

———. 2001a. Chinyanja and the Language of Rights. *Nordic Journal of African Studies* 10: 299–319.

———. 2001b. The Quest for Missionaries: Transnationalism and Township Pentecostalism in Malawi. In A. Corten and R. Marshall-Fratani, eds., *Between Babel and Pentecost: Transnational Pentecostalism in Africa and Latin America.* London: Hurst & Co.

———. 2001c. Winning Elections, Losing Legitimacy: Multipartyism and the Neopatrimonial State in Malawi. In M. Cowen and L. Laakso, eds., *Multiparty Elections in Africa.* Oxford: James Currey.

———. 2002a. Ethnography after Globalism: Migration and Emplacement in Malawi. *American Ethnologist* 29: 261–286.

———. 2002b. *From War to Peace on the Mozambique-Malawi Borderland.* Edinburgh: Edinburgh University Press for the International African Institute.

———. 2002c. Introduction: The Culture of Chameleon Politics. In H. Englund, ed., *A Democracy of Chameleons: Politics and Culture in the New Malawi.* Uppsala: Nordic Africa Institute and Blantyre: Christian Literature Association in Malawi (CLAIM).

———. 2002d. The Village in the City, the City in the Village: Migrants in Lilongwe. *Journal of Southern African Studies* 28: 137–154.

———. 2003. Christian Independency and Global Membership: Pentecostal Extraversions in Malawi. *Journal of Religion in Africa* 33: 83–111.

———. 2004a. Cosmopolitanism and the Devil in Malawi. *Ethnos* 69: 293–316.

———. 2004b. Introduction: Recognizing Identities, Imagining Alternatives. In H. Englund and F. B. Nyamnjoh, eds., *Rights and the Politics of Recognition in Africa.* London: Zed Books.

———. 2004c. Towards a Critique of Rights Talk in New Democracies: The Case of Legal Aid in Malawi. *Discourse & Society* 15: 55–79.

Englund, Harri, and Francis B. Nyamnjoh, eds. 2004. *Rights and the Politics of Recognition in Africa.* London: Zed Books.

Escobar, Arturo. 1995. *Encountering Development: The Making and Unmaking of the Third World.* Princeton, NJ: Princeton University Press.

Evans-Pitchard, E. E. 1937. *Witchcraft, Oracles and Magic among the Azande.* Oxford: Clarendon Press.

Fabian, Johannes. 1998. *Moments of Freedom: Anthropology and Popular Culture.* Charlottesville: University Press of Virginia.

Falk, Richard A. 2000. *Human Rights Horizons: The Pursuit of Justice in a Globalizing World.* New York: Routledge.

Ferguson, James. 1990. *The Anti-politics Machine: "Development," Depoliticization and Bureaucratic Power in Lesotho.* Cambridge: Cambridge University Press.

———. 1995. From African Socialism to Scientific Capitalism: Reflections on the Legitimation Crisis in IMF-Ruled Africa. In D. B. Moore and G. J. Schmitz, eds., *Debating Development Discourse: Institutional and Popular Perspectives.* New York: St Martin's Press.

———. 1999. *Expectations of Modernity: Myths and Meanings of Urban Life on the Zambian Copperbelt.* Berkeley: University of California Press.

———. 2002. Of Mimicry and Membership: Africans and the "New World Society." *Cultural Anthropology* 17: 551–569.

Ferguson, James, and Akhil Gupta. 2002. Spatializing States: Toward an Ethnography of Neoliberal Governmentality. *American Ethnologist* 29: 981–1002.

Fields, Karen E. 2001. Witchcraft and Racecraft: Invisible Ontology in Its Sensible Manifestations. In G. C. Bond and D. M. Ciekawy, eds., *Witchcraft Dialogues: Anthropological and Philosophical Exchanges.* Athens: Ohio University Press.

Fisher, William F. 1997. Doing Good? The Politics and Antipolitics of NGO Practices. *Annual Review of Anthropology* 26: 439–464.

Fisher, William F., and Thomas Ponniah, eds. 2003. *Another World Is Possible: Popular Alternatives to Globalization at the World Social Forum.* London: Zed Books.

Fog Olwig, Karen, and Kirsten Hastrup, eds. 1997. *Siting Culture: The Shifting Anthropological Object.* London: Routledge.

Fortes, Meyer. 1984. Age, Generation, and Social Structure. In D. I. Kertzer and J. Keith, eds., *Age and Anthropological Theory.* Ithaca, NY: Cornell University Press.

Foucault, Michel. 1972. *The Archaeology of Knowledge.* London: Tavistock.

——. 1977. *Discipline and Punish: The Birth of the Prison.* London: Allen Lane.

——. 1991. Governmentality. In G. Burchell, C. Gordon, and P. Miller, eds., *The Foucault Effect: Studies in Governmentality.* London: Harvester Wheatsheaf.

Frank, Andre Gunder. 1969. *Latin America: Underdevelopment and Revolution.* New York: Monthly Review Press.

Freire, Paolo. 1970. *Pedagogy of the Oppressed.* New York: Herder and Herder.

Fukuyama, Francis. 2004. *State Building: Governance and World Order in the 21st Century.* New York: Profile Books.

Gambetta, Diego, ed. 1988. *Trust: Making and Breaking Co-operative Relations.* Oxford: Blackwell.

Garland, Elizabeth. 1999. Developing Bushmen: Building Civil(ized) Society in the Kalahari and Beyond. In J. L. Comaroff and J. Comaroff, eds., *Civil Society and the Political Imagination in Africa: Critical Perspectives.* Chicago: University of Chicago Press.

Geertz, Clifford. 1973. *The Interpretation of Cultures.* New York: Basic Books.

——. 1988. *Works and Lives: Anthropologist as an Author.* Chicago: University of Chicago Press.

Geschiere, Peter. 1997. *The Modernity of Witchcraft: Politics and the Occult in Postcolonial Africa.* Charlottesville: University Press of Virginia.

——. 2004. Ecology, Belonging and Xenophobia: The 1994 Forest Law in Cameroon and the Issue of "Community." In H. Englund and F. B. Nyamnjoh, eds., *Rights and the Politics of Recognition in Africa.* London: Zed Books.

Gikandi, Simon. 2002. Reason, Modernity and the African Crisis. In J.-G. Deutsch, P. Probst, and H. Schmidt, eds., *African Modernities: Entangled Meanings in Current Debate.* Oxford: James Currey.

Gledhill, John. 1994. *Power and Its Disguises.* London: Pluto Press.

——. 2003. Rights and the Poor. In R. A. Wilson and J. P. Mitchell, eds., *Human Rights in Global Perspective: Anthropological Studies of Rights, Claims and Entitlements.* London: Routledge.

Gluckman, Max. 1940. Analysis of a Social Situation in Modern Zululand. *Bantu Studies* 14: 1–30 and 147–174.

Goebel, Allison. 1998. Process, Perception and Power: Notes from "Participatory" Research in a Zimbabwean Resettlement Area. *Development and Change* 29: 277–305.

Good, Kenneth. 2002. *The Liberal Model and Africa: Elites against Democracy.* New York: Palgrave Macmillan.

Goodwin, Charles. 1994. Professional Vision. *American Anthropologist* 96: 606–633.

Gould, Jeremy. 2001. Contesting Democracy: The 1996 Elections in Zambia. In M. Cowen and L. Laakso, eds., *Multiparty Elections in Africa.* Oxford: James Currey.

Green, Maia. 2000. Participatory Development and the Appropriation of Agency in Southern Tanzania. *Critique of Anthropology* 20: 67–89.

———. 2003. *Priests, Witches and Power: Popular Christianity after Mission in Southern Tanzania.* Cambridge: Cambridge University Press.

Gumperz, John J., and Stephen C. Levinson. 2000. Introduction: Linguistic Relativity Re-examined. In J. J. Gumperz and S. C. Levinson, eds., *Rethinking Linguistic Relativity.* Cambridge: Cambridge University Press.

Gupta, Akhil, and James Ferguson, eds. 1997. *Anthropological Locations: Boundaries and Grounds of a Field Science.* Berkeley: University of California Press.

Guyer, Jane I. 1994. The Spatial Dimensions of Civil Society in Africa: An Anthropologist Looks at Nigeria. In J. W. Harbeson, D. Rothchild, and N. Chazan, eds., *Civil Society and the State in Africa.* Boulder, CO: Lynne Rienner.

———. 2004. *Marginal Gains: Monetary Transactions in Atlantic Africa.* Chicago: University of Chicago Press.

Gwengwe, J. W. (1965) 1998 . *Sikusinja ndi Gwenembe.* Blantyre: Macmillan.

Hallward, Peter. 2000. Ethics without Others: A Reply to Critchley on Badiou's Ethics. *Radical Philosophy* 102: 27–30.

Hansen, Karen Tranberg. 2000. *Salaula: The World of Second-Hand Clothing and Zambia.* Chicago: University of Chicago Press.

Harrison, Graham. 2002. *Issues in the Contemporary Politics of Sub-Saharan Africa: The Dynamics of Struggle and Resistance.* New York: Palgrave Macmillan.

Hastrup, Kirsten, ed. 2001a. *Human Rights on Common Grounds: The Quest for Universality.* The Hague: Kluwer Law International.

———. 2001b. To Follow a Rule: Rights and Responsibilities Revisited. In K. Hastrup, ed., *Human Rights on Common Grounds: The Quest for Universality.* The Hague: Kluwer Law International.

Hickey, Sam, and Giles Mohan. 2005. Relocating Participation within a Radical Politics of Development. *Development and Change* 36: 237–262.

Hilhorst, Dorothea. 2004. *The Real World of NGOs: Discourses, Diversity and Development.* London: Zed Books.

Hodgson, Dorothy L. 2002. Precarious Alliances: The Cultural Politics and Structural Predicaments of the Indigenous Rights Movement in Tanzania. *American Anthropologist* 104: 1086–1097.

Howell, Jude. 2000. Making Civil Society from the Outside: Challenges for the Donors. *European Journal of Development Research* 12: 3–22.

Howell, Jude, and Jenny Pearce. 2001. *Civil Society and Development: A Critical Exploration.* Boulder, CO: Lynne Rienner.

HRRC (Human Rights Resource Centre/Danish Centre for Human Rights). 1999. *Human Rights Needs Assessment Survey in Malawi.* Lilongwe: HRRC.

Hund, John. 2004. African Witchcraft and Western Law: Psychological and Cultural Issues. *Journal of Contemporary Religion* 19: 67–84.

Hunt, Paul. 1999. Social Rights: Building a Legal Tradition. In R. G. Patman, ed., *Universal Human Rights?* London: Macmillan.

Huntington, Samuel. 1991. *The Third Wave: Democratization in the Late Twentieth Century.* Norman: University of Oklahoma Press.

Iliffe, John. 2005. *Honour in African History.* Cambridge: Cambridge University Press.

Ingold, Tim. 1993. The Art of Translation in a Continuous World. In G. Pálsson, ed., *Beyond Boundaries: Understanding, Translation and Anthropological Discourse.* Oxford: Berg.

Ishay, Micheline R. 2004. *The History of Human Rights: From Ancient Times to the Globalization Era.* Berkeley: University of California Press.

Jahoda, Gustav. 1999. *Images of Savages: Ancient Roots of Modern Prejudice in Western Culture.* London: Routledge.

James, Wendy. 1973. The Anthropologist as Reluctant Imperialist. In T. Asad, ed., *Anthropology and the Colonial Encounter.* London: Ithaca Press.

Jenkins, Robert. 2001. Mistaking "Governance" for "Politics": Foreign Aid, Democracy and the Construction of Civil Society. In S. Kaviraj and S. Khilnani, eds., *Civil Society: History and Possibilities.* Cambridge: Cambridge University Press.

Jimu, Ignasio Malizani. 2003. Appropriation and Mediation of Urban Spaces: Growth, Dynamics and Politics of Street Vending in Blantyre, Malawi. M.A. dissertation, University of Botswana.

Kalonde, Ken. 2000. *Okongola Sanyada.* Lilongwe: Sunrise Publications.

Kandawire, J. K. 1979. *Thangata: Forced Labour or Reciprocal Assistance?* Zomba: University of Malawi.

Kanyongolo, Fidelis Edge. 1998. The Limits of Liberal Democratic Constitutionalism in Malawi. In K. M. Phiri and K. R. Ross, eds., *Democratization in Malawi: A Stocktaking.* Blantyre: Christian Literature Association in Malawi (CLAIM).

———. 2004. The Rhetoric of Human Rights in Malawi: Individualization and Judicialization. In H. Englund and F. B. Nyamnjoh, eds., *Rights and the Politics of Recognition in Africa.* London: Zed Books.

———. 2005. Land Occupations in Malawi: Challenging the Neoliberal Legal Order. In S. Moyo and P. Yeros, eds., *Reclaiming the Land: The Resurgence of Rural Movements in Africa, Asia and Latin America.* London: Zed Books.

Kapferer, Bruce. 2002. Outside All Reason: Magic, Sorcery and Epistemology in Anthropology. *Social Analysis* 46: 1–30.

Karlström, Mikael. 1996. Imagining Democracy: Political Culture and Democratisation in Buganda. *Africa* 66: 485–505.

———. 2003. On the Aesthetics and Dialogics of Power in the Postcolony. *Africa* 73: 57–76.

Kasambara, Ralph. 1998. Civic Education in Malawi Since 1992: An Appraisal. In K. M. Phiri and K. R. Ross, eds., *Democratization in Malawi: A Stocktaking*. Blantyre: Christian Literature Association in Malawi (CLAIM).

Kasfir, Nelson. 1998. The Conventional Notion of Civil Society: A Critique. In N. Kasfir, ed., *Civil Society and Democracy in Africa: Critical Perspectives*. London: Frank Cass.

Kashoki, Mubanga E. 1972. Town Bemba: A Sketch of Its Main Characteristics. *African Social Research* 13: 161–186.

———. 1994. *Loanwords in Silozi, Cinyanja and Citonga*. Lusaka: Institute of Economic and Social Research.

Kayambazinthu, Edrinnie. 1998. "I Just Mix": Code-Switching and Code-Mixing among Bilingual Malawians. *Journal of Humanities* 12: 19–43.

Kayambazinthu, Edrinnie, and Fulata Moyo. 2002. Hate Speech in the New Malawi. In H. Englund, ed., *A Democracy of Chameleons: Politics and Culture in the New Malawi*. Uppsala: Nordic Africa Institute and Blantyre: Christian Literature Association in Malawi (CLAIM).

Kelly, Paul. 2005. *Liberalism*. Cambridge: Polity Press.

Kelsall, Tim. 2002. Shop Windows and Smoke-Filled Rooms: Governance and the Re-politicisation of Tanzania. *Journal of Modern African Studies* 40: 597–619.

———. 2003. Rituals of Verification: Indigenous and Imported Accountability in Northern Tanzania. *Africa* 73: 174–201.

Kishindo, Pascal J. 1994. The Impact of a National Language on Minority Languages: The Case of Malawi. *Journal of Contemporary African Studies* 12: 127–150.

———. 1998. Politics of Language in Contemporary Malawi. In K. M. Phiri and K. R. Ross, eds., *Democratization in Malawi: A Stocktaking*. Blantyre: Christian Literature Association in Malawi (CLAIM).

———. 2000. Evolution of Political Terminology in Chichewa and the Changing Political Culture in Malawi. *Nordic Journal of African Studies* 9: 20–30.

———. 2001. Authority in Language: The Role of the Chichewa Board (1972–1995) in Prescription and Standardization of Chichewa. *Journal of Asian and African Studies* 62: 261–283.

Klein, Naomi. 2002. *Fences and Windows: Dispatches from the Front Lines of the Globalization Debate*. New York: Picador.

Kumar, Krishna, ed. 1993. *Rapid Appraisal Methods*. Washington DC: World Bank.

Kydd, Jonathan, and Robert E. Christiansen. 1982. Structural Change in Malawi since Independence: Consequences of a Development Strategy Based on Large-Scale Agriculture. *World Development* 10: 355–375.

Kymlicka, Will. 1995. *Multicultural Citizenship: A Liberal Theory of Minority Rights*. Oxford: Oxford University Press.

———. 2002. *Contemporary Political Philosophy*. Oxford: Oxford University Press.

La Fontaine, Jean S. 1998. *Speak of the Devil: Tales of Satanic Abuse in Contemporary England*. Cambridge: Cambridge University Press.

Laidlaw, James. 2002. For an Anthropology of Ethics and Freedom. *Journal of the Royal Anthropological Institute* 8: 311–332.

Last, Murray. 2000. Children and the Experience of Violence: Contrasting Cultures of Punishment in Northern Nigeria. *Africa* 70: 359–393.

Lazar, Sian. 2004. Education for Credit: Development as Citizenship Project in Bolivia. *Critique of Anthropology* 24: 301–319.

Lewis, David. 2002. Civil Society in African Contexts: Reflections on the Usefulness of a Concept. *Development and Change* 33: 569–586.

Lindholt, Lone. 2001. The African Charter: Contextual Universality. In K. Hastrup, ed., *Human Rights on Common Grounds: The Quest for Universality*. The Hague: Kluwer Law International.

Lwanda, John. 1996. *Promises, Power, Politics and Poverty: The Democratic Transition in Malawi 1961 to 1999*. Glasgow: Dudu Nsomba.

———. 2002. Tikutha: The Political Culture of the HIV/AIDS Epidemic in Malawi. In H. Englund, ed., *A Democracy of Chameleons: Politics and Culture in the New Malawi*. Uppsala: Nordic Africa Institute and Blantyre: Christian Literature Association in Malawi (CLAIM).

Malkki, Liisa. 1992. National Geographic: Rooting of Peoples and the Territorialization of National Identity among Scholars and Refugees. *Cultural Anthropology* 7: 24–44.

Malkki, Liisa, and Emily Martin. 2003. Children and the Gendered Politics of Globalization: In Remembrance of Sharon Stephens. *American Ethnologist* 30: 216–224.

Mamdani, Mahmood. 1996. *Citizen and Subject: Contemporary Africa and the Legacy of Late Colonialism*. Princeton, NJ: Princeton University Press.

Manda, Mtafu Almiton Zeleza. 2000. *The State and the Labour in Malawi*. Glasgow: Dudu Nsomba.

Mandala, Elias C. 1990. *Work and Control in a Peasant Economy: A History of the Lower Tchiri Valley in Malawi 1859–1960*. Madison: University of Wisconsin Press.

Mann, Michael. (1977) 1999. *An Outline of Icibemba Grammar*. Lusaka: Bookworld.

Mapanje, Jack. 2002. The Orality of Dictatorship: In Defence of My Country. In H. Englund, ed., *A Democracy of Chameleons: Politics and Culture in the New Malawi*. Uppsala: Nordic Africa Institute and Blantyre: Christian Literature Association in Malawi (CLAIM).

Marcus, George E. 1999. *Ethnography Through Thick and Thin*. Princeton, NJ: Princeton University Press.

Marshall, T. H. (1950) 1977. *Class, Citizenship, and Social Development*. Chicago: University of Chicago Press.

Maryns, Katrijn, and Jan Blommaert. 2002. Pretextuality and Pretextual Gaps: On Re-defining Linguistic Inequality. *Pragmatics* 12: 11–30.

Matiki, Alfred J. 2001. The Social Significance of English in Malawi. *World Englishes* 20: 201–218.

———. 2003. Linguistic Exclusion and the Opinions of Malawian Legislators. *Language Policy* 2: 153–178.

Mauss, Marcel. 1954. *The Gift: Forms and Functions of Exchange in Archaic Societies.* London: Cohen and West.

Mazrui, Ali A., and Alamin M. Mazrui. 1998. *The Power of Babel: Language in the African Experience.* Oxford: James Currey.

Mbembe, Achille. 2001. *On the Postcolony.* Berkeley: University of California Press.

McCracken, John. 1977. *Politics and Christianity in Malawi 1875–1940: The Impact of the Livingstonia Mission in the Northern Province.* Cambridge: Cambridge University Press.

———. 1988. Labour in Nyasaland: An Assessment of the 1960 Railway Workers' Strikes. *Journal of Southern African Studies* 14: 279–290.

Meyer, Birgit. 1999. *Translating the Devil: Religion and Modernity among the Ewe in Ghana.* Edinburgh: Edinburgh University Press for the International African Institute.

Mhone, Guy C. Z. 1992. The Political Economy of Malawi: An Overview. In G. C. Z. Mhone, ed., *Malawi at the Crossroads: The Post-Colonial Political Economy.* Harare: Southern African Political Economy Series (SAPES).

Migdal, Joel S. 2001. *State in Society: Studying How States and Societies Transform and Constitute One Another.* Cambridge: Cambridge University Press.

Mkandawire, Thandika. 2003. Threats to Democracy in Malawi. *The Lamp* 42: 16–17.

Moore, Henrietta L., and Todd Sanders. 2001. Introduction. In H. L. Moore and T. Sanders, eds., *Magical Interpretations, Material Realities: Modernity, Witchcraft and the Occult in Postcolonial Africa.* New York: Routledge.

Moto, Francis. 2001. Language and Societal Attitudes: A Study of Malawi's "New Language." *Nordic Journal of African Studies* 10: 320–343.

———. 2003. Elitists and the Preservation of Linguistic and Cultural Imperialism. In J. F. Pfaffe, ed., *Implementing Multilingual Education.* Zomba: Centre for Language Studies.

Mtenje, Alfred. 2002a. English Imperialism and Shifting Attitudes towards African Languages: The Case of Malawi. In K. Legère and S. Fitchat, eds., *Talking Freedom: Language and Democratisation in the SADC Region.* Windhoek: Gamsberg Macmillan.

———. 2002b. The Role of Language in National Development: A Case for Local Languages. Inaugural Lecture at the University of Malawi.

Mwale, Brian M. 2001. Orthographies of Cross-Border Languages. In J. F. Pfaffe, ed., *Cross-Border Languages within the Context of Mother Tongue Education.* Zomba: Centre for Language Studies.

National Statistical Office. 2002. *1998 Malawi Population and Housing Census: Analytical Report.* Zomba: National Statistical Office.

Navaro-Yashin, Yael. 2003. Legal/Illegal Counterpoints: Subjecthood and Subjectivity in an Unrecognized State. In R. A. Wilson and J. P. Mitchell, eds.,

Human Rights in Global Perspective: Anthropological Studies of Rights, Claims and Entitlements. London: Routledge.

Neocosmos, Michael. 2001. Towards Understanding New Forms of State Role in Africa in the Era of Globalization. *African Journal of Political Science* 6: 29–57.

Newell, Jonathan. 1995. "A Moment of Truth?" The Church and Political Change in Malawi, 1992. *Journal of Modern African Studies* 33: 243–262.

Niehaus, Isak. 2001. *Witchcraft, Power and Politics: Exploring the Occult in the South African Lowveld.* London: Pluto Press.

Nkrumah, Kwame. 1961. *I Speak of Freedom: A Statement of African Ideology.* London: Panaf.

Noys, Benjamin. 2003. The Provocations of Alain Badiou. *Theory, Culture & Society* 20: 123–132.

Nyamilandu, Steve E. 1999. Education for Democracy: Lessons from Ancient Greece. In M. Chimombo, ed., *Lessons in Hope: Education for Democracy in Malawi, Past, Present, Future.* Zomba: Chancellor College Publications.

Nyamnjoh, Francis B. 2002. "A Child is One Person's Only in the Womb": Domestication, Agency and Subjectivity in the Cameroonian Grassfields. In R. Werbner, ed., *Postcolonial Subjectivities in Africa.* London: Zed Books.

———. 2004. Reconciling the "Rhetoric of Rights" with Competing Notions of Personhood and Agency in Botswana. In H. Englund and F. B. Nyamnjoh, eds., *Rights and the Politics of Recognition in Africa.* London: Zed Books.

———. 2005. *Africa's Media, Democracy and the Politics of Belonging.* London: Zed Books.

Nyerere, Julius K. 1966. *Freedom and Unity.* Dar es Salaam: Oxford University Press.

———. 1968. *Freedom and Socialism.* Dar es Salaam: Oxford University Press.

O'Brien, Donald B. Cruise. 1996. A Lost Generation? Youth Identity and State Decay in West Africa. In R. Werbner and T. Ranger, eds., *Postcolonial Identities in Africa.* London: Zed Books.

Okafor, Obiora Chinedu. 2004. Modest Harvests: On the Significant (but Limited) Impact of Human Rights NGOs on Legislative and Executive Behaviour in Nigeria. *Journal of African Law* 48: 23–49.

Olukoshi, Adebayo O. 1998. The Elusive Prince of Denmark: Structural Adjustment and the Crisis of Government in Africa. *Nordic Africa Institute Research Report 104.*

Ott, Martin. 2000. The Role of the Christian Churches in Democratic Malawi (1994–1999). In M. Ott, K. M. Phiri, and N. Patel, eds., *Malawi's Second Democratic Elections: Process, Problems, and Prospects.* Blantyre: Christian Literature Association in Malawi (CLAIM).

Paley, Julia. 2004. Accountable Democracy: Citizens' Impact on Public Decision Making in Postdictatorship Chile. *American Ethnologist* 31: 497–513.

Pálsson, Gísli. 1995. *The Textual Life of Savants: Ethnography, Iceland, and the Linguistic Turn.* Chur: Harwood Academic Publishers.

Parekh, Bhikhu C. 2000. *Rethinking Multiculturalism: Cultural Diversity and Political Theory.* Basingstoke: Macmillan.

p'Bitek, Okot. (1967) 1984. *Song of Lawino & Song of Ocol.* Oxford: Heinemann.

———. 1971. *Two Songs.* Nairobi: East African Publishing House.

Philips, Susan. 1998. *Ideology in the Language of Judges: How Judges Practice Law, Politics and Courtroom Control.* Oxford: Oxford University Press.

Phiri, Kings M. 1998. Dr Banda's Cultural Legacy and Its Implications for a Democratic Malawi. In K. M. Phiri and K. R. Ross, eds., *Democratization in Malawi: A Stocktaking.* Blantyre: Christian Literature Association in Malawi (CLAIM).

Posner, Darrel N. 2003. The Colonial Origins of Ethnic Cleavages: The Case of Linguistic Divisions in Zambia. *Comparative Politics* 35: 127–146.

Povinelli, Elizabeth A. 2001. Radical Worlds: The Anthropology of Incommensurability and Inconceivability. *Annual Review of Anthropology* 30: 319–334.

———. 2003. *The Cunning of Recognition: Indigenous Alterities and the Making of Australian Multiculturalism.* Durham, NC: Duke University Press.

Pryor, Frederic L. 1990. *The Political Economy of Poverty, Equity and Growth: Malawi and Madagascar.* Oxford: Oxford University Press for the World Bank.

Quayson, Ato. 2001. Breaches in the Commonplace. *African Studies Review* 44: 151–165.

Ranger, Terence. 2004. Nationalist Historiography, Patriotic History and the History of the Nation: The Struggle over the Past in Zimbabwe. *Journal of Southern African Studies* 30: 215–234.

Raz, Joseph. 1986. *The Morality of Freedom.* Oxford: Clarendon Press.

Ribohn, Ulrika. 2002. "Human Rights and the Multiparty System Have Swallowed Our Traditions": Conceiving Women and Culture in the New Malawi. In H. Englund, ed., *A Democracy of Chameleons: Politics and Culture in the New Malawi.* Uppsala: Nordic Africa Institute and Blantyre: Christian Literature Association in Malawi (CLAIM).

Richards, Paul. 1996. *Fighting for the Rain Forest: War, Youth and Resources in Sierra Leone.* Oxford: James Currey for the International African Institute.

Riesman, Paul. 1977. *Freedom in Fulani Society: An Introspective Ethnography.* Chicago: University of Chicago Press.

———. 1986. The Person and the Life Cycle in African Social Life and Thought. *African Studies Review* 29: 71–137.

Riles, Annelise. 2001. *The Network Inside Out.* Ann Arbor: University of Michigan Press.

Robbins, Bruce. 1998. Comparative Cosmopolitanisms. In P. Cheah and B. Robbins, eds., *Cosmopolitics: Thinking and Feeling beyond the Nation.* Minneapolis: University of Minnesota Press.

Rose, Nikolas. 1999. *Powers of Freedom: Reframing Political Thought.* Cambridge: Cambridge University Press.

Ross, Kenneth R. 1998. Does Malawi (Still) Need a Truth Commission? In

K. M. Phiri and K. R. Ross, eds., *Democratization in Malawi: A Stocktaking.* Blantyre: Christian Literature Association in Malawi (CLAIM).

———. 2004. "Worrisome Trends": The Voice of the Churches in Malawi's Third Term Debate. *African Affairs* 103: 91–107.

Rotberg, Robert I. 1965. *The Rise of Nationalism in Central Africa: The Making of Malawi and Zambia, 1873–1964.* Cambridge, MA: Harvard University Press.

Samara, Tony Roshan. 2005. Youth, Crime and Urban Renewal in the Western Cape. *Journal of Southern African Studies* 31: 209–227.

Schatzberg, Michael. 2002. *Political Legitimacy in Middle Africa.* Bloomington: Indiana University Press.

Scheper-Hughes, Nancy, and Loïc Wacquant, eds. 2002. *Commodifying Bodies.* London: Sage.

Schoffeleers, Matthew. 1999. *In Search of Truth and Justice: Confrontations between Church and State in Malawi 1960–1994.* Blantyre: Christian Literature Association in Malawi (CLAIM).

Schumpeter, Joseph A. 1976. *Capitalism, Socialism and Democracy.* London: Allen & Unwin.

Scott, James C. 1998. *Seeing Like a State: How Certain Schemes to Improve the Human Condition Have Failed.* New Haven, CT: Yale University Press.

Sen, Amartya. 1981. *Poverty and Famines: An Essay in Entitlements and Deprivation.* Oxford: Oxford University Press.

———. 1999. *Development as Freedom.* Oxford: Oxford University Press.

Serpell, Robert. 1993. *The Significance of Schooling: Life Journeys in Africa.* Cambridge: Cambridge University Press.

Sharp, Lesley A. 2000. The Commodification of the Body and Its Parts. *Annual Review of Anthropology* 29: 287–328.

Shaw, Rosalind. 2002. *Memories of the Slave Trade: Ritual and the Historical Imagination in Sierra Leone.* Chicago: University of Chicago Press.

Shipton, Parker. 2003. Legalism and Loyalism: European, African, and Human "Rights." In B. Dean and J. M. Levi, eds., *At the Risk of Being Heard: Identity, Indigenous Rights, and Postcolonial Studies.* Ann Arbor: University of Michigan Press.

Shivji, Issa. 1989. *The Concept of Human Rights in Africa.* Dakar: Council for the Development of Social Science Research in Africa (CODESRIA).

Short, Philip. 1974. *Banda.* London: Routledge and Kegan Paul.

Simpson, Anthony. 2003. *"Half-London" in Zambia: Contested Identities in a Catholic Mission School.* Edinburgh: Edinburgh University Press for the International African Institute.

Sindima, Harvey J. 2002. *Malawi's First Republic: An Economic and Political Analysis.* Lanham, MD: University Press of America.

Skinner, Quentin. 1998. *Liberty before Liberalism.* Cambridge: Cambridge University Press.

Stambach, Amy. 2000. *Lessons from Mount Kilimanjaro: Schooling, Community and Gender in East Africa.* London: Routledge.

Stocking, George W. 1987. *Victorian Anthropology.* New York: Free Press.

Strathern, Marilyn. 2001. Global and Local Contexts. In L. Kalinoe and J. Leach, eds., *Rationales of Ownership: Ethnographic Studies of Transactions and Claims to Ownership in Contemporary Papua New Guinea.* New Delhi: UBS Publishers' Distributors.

———. 2004. Losing (out on) Intellectual Resources. In A. Pottage and M. Mundy, eds., *Law, Anthropology, and the Constitution of the Social: Making Persons and Things.* Cambridge: Cambridge University Press.

Talle, Aud. 1998. Sex for Leisure: Modernity among Female Bar Workers in Tanzania. In S. Abram and J. Waldren, eds., *Anthropological Perspectives on Local Development: Knowledge and Sentiment in Conflict.* New York: Routledge.

Taussig, Michael. 1996. *The Magic of the State.* New York: Routledge.

Tengatenga, James. 1998. Singing, Dancing and Believing: Civic Education in Malawian Idiom. In K. R. Ross, ed., *Faith at the Frontiers of Knowledge.* Blantyre: Christian Literature Association in Malawi (CLAIM).

Tenthani, Kizito. 2002. The NGOs of Malawi Act 2000: Reflections. *The Lamp* 37: 14.

———. 2003. Kodi tingadye maufulu achibadwidwe? *The Lamp* 41: 15.

Tsing, Anna Lowenhaupt. 2005. *Friction: An Ethnography of Global Connection.* Princeton, NJ: Princeton University Press.

Tully, James. 1995. *Strange Multiplicity: Constitutionalism in an Age of Diversity.* Cambridge: Cambridge University Press.

Turner, Victor W. 1957. *Schism and Continuity in an African Society: A Study of Ndembu Village Life.* Manchester: Manchester University Press.

Tvedt, Terje. 1998. *Angels of Mercy or Development Diplomats? NGOs and Foreign Aid.* Oxford: James Currey.

UNDP (United Nations Development Programme). 2001. *Malawi Human Development Report 2001.* Lilongwe: UNDP.

Vail, Leroy. 1983. The State and the Creation of Colonial Malawi's Agricultural Economy. In R. I. Rotberg, ed., *Imperialism, Colonialism, and Hunger: East and Central Africa.* Boston: Lexington Books.

Vail, Leroy, and Landeg White. 1989. Tribalism in the Political History of Malawi. In L. Vail, ed., *The Creation of Tribalism in Southern Africa.* Berkeley: University of California Press.

———. 1991. *Power and the Praise Poem: Southern African Voices in History.* London: James Currey.

van Donge, Jan Kees. 1995. Kamuzu's Legacy: The Democratization of Malawi. *African Affairs* 94: 227–257.

———. 1998. The Mwanza Trial as a Search for a Usable Malawian Political Past. *African Affairs* 97: 91–118.

———. 2002. Disordering the Market: The Liberalization of Burley Tobacco in Malawi in the 1990s. *Journal of Southern African Studies* 28: 89–115.

Vaughan, Megan. 1991. *Curing Their Ills: African Illness and Colonial Power.* Cambridge: Polity Press.

Venuti, Lawrence. 1998. *The Scandals of Translation: Towards an Ethics of Difference*. London: Routledge.

VonDoepp, Peter. 2002. Are Malawi's Local Clergy Civil Society Activists? The Limiting Impact of Creed, Context and Class. In H. Englund, ed., *A Democracy of Chameleons: Politics and Culture in the New Malawi*. Uppsala: Nordic Africa Institute and Blantyre: Christian Literature Association in Malawi (CLAIM).

Weate, Jeremy. 2003. Postcolonial Theory on the Brink: A Critique of Achille Mbembe's On the Postcolony. *African Identities* 1: 1–18.

Weber, Max. 1970. Politics as Vocation. In H. H. Gerth and C. W. Mills, eds., *From Max Weber*. London: Routledge & Kegan Paul.

Werbner, Richard, ed. 2002. *Postcolonial Subjectivities in Africa*. London: Zed Books.

——. 2004. *Reasonable Radicals and Citizenship in Botswana: The Public Anthropology of Kalanga Elites*. Bloomington: Indiana University Press.

White, Luise. 2000. *Speaking with Vampires: Rumor and History in Colonial Africa*. Berkeley: University of California Press.

Williams, David, and Tom Young. 1994. Governance, the World Bank, and Liberal Theory. *Political Studies* 42: 84–100.

Williams, T. David. 1978. *Malawi: The Politics of Despair*. Ithaca, NY: Cornell University Press.

Wilson, Richard A. 1997. Representing Human Rights Violations: Social Contexts and Subjectivities. In R. A. Wilson, ed., *Human Rights, Culture and Context: Anthropological Perspectives*. London: Pluto Press.

WLSA (Women and Law in Southern Africa Research Trust). 2000. *In Search of Justice: Women and the Administration of Justice in Malawi*. Blantyre: Dzuka.

World Bank. 1993. *Governance: The World Bank Experience*. Washington DC: World Bank.

Yengoyan, Aram A. 2003. Lyotard and Wittgenstein and the Question of Translation. In P. G. Rubel and A. Rosman, eds., *Translating Cultures: Perspectives on Translation and Anthropology*. Oxford: Berg.

Young, Tom. 1995. "A Project Yet To Be Realised": Global Liberalism and Contemporary Africa. *Millennium: Journal of International Studies* 24: 527–546.

Zeleza, Paul Tiyambe. 1997. Visions of Freedom and Democracy in Postcolonial African Literature. *Women's Studies Quarterly* 25: 10–35.

——. 2003. *Rethinking Africa's Globalization*. Vol. 1: *The Intellectual Challenges*. Trenton, NJ: Africa World Press.

Zingani, Willie T. 1984. *Njala Bwana*. Limbe: Popular Publications.

Index

Text:	10/13 Galliard
Display:	Galliard
Compositor:	BookMatters, Berkeley
Illustrator:	Bill Nelson
Printer and binder:	Maple-Vail Manufacturing Group